Modern man, surrounded by the material goods of his busy, mechanized culture, is very much alone. He may be alone because he is a member of a minority; or because he is too young—or too old; or because he is among the very talented, or because he is among the least talented; or he is a criminal or insane. Indeed, a depersonalized mass society, in which values are eroding and changing, makes relatedness to others and to oneself increasingly more difficult for almost everyone. These 27 provocative essays examine the many and varied kinds of estrangement that afflict our modern world.

NED E. HOOPES has taught at Hunter College High School, Evanston Township High School, Harvard, Yale and Pace College, and has served as host on the television program, READING ROOM.

THE LAUREL-LEAF LIBRARY brings together under a single imprint outstanding works of fiction and nonfiction particularly suitable for young adult readers, both in and out of the classroom. This series is under the editorship of M. Jerry Weiss, Distinguished Professor of Communications, Jersey City State College; in association with Ned E. Hoopes, and Charles F. Reasoner, Associate Professor, Elementary Education, New York University.

ALSO AVAILABLE IN THE LAUREL-LEAF LIBRARY

Edge of Awareness: 25 Contemporary Essays
edited by Ned E. Hoopes and Richard Peck

Great Essays: From the 16th Century to the Present
edited by John E. George and John A. Goodson

The Outsiders
by S. E. Hinton

The Outnumbered: Stories, Essays, and Poems About Minority Groups by America's Leading Writers
edited by Charlotte Brooks

Point of Departure: 19 Stories of Youth and Discovery
edited by Robert Gold

Flight to Freedom: The Story of the Underground Railroad
by Henrietta Buckmaster

Romeo and Juliet and *West Side Story*
edited by Norris Houghton

Man of La Mancha
by Dale Wasserman, Joe Darion and Mitch Leigh
Introduction by John Bettenbender

WHO AM I?

ESSAYS ON THE ALIENATED

EDITED BY

Ned E. Hoopes

Published by
DELL PUBLISHING CO., INC.
750 Third Avenue
New York, New York 10017

Copyright © 1969 by Ned E. Hoopes

All rights reserved. No part of this book may be
reproduced in any form or by any means without
the prior written permission of the Publisher,
excepting brief quotes used in connection with
reviews written specifically for inclusion in a
magazine or newspaper.

Laurel-Leaf Library ® TM 766734, Dell Publishing Co., Inc.
Manufactured in the United States of America
First Laurel Printing—August 1969

ACKNOWLEDGMENTS

"Who Am I?" by Marya Mannes: Reprinted by permission of Harold Ober Associates. Copyright © 1968 by Marya Mannes.

"On Alienated Concepts of Identity" by Ernest G. Schachtel: Reprinted by permission of *The American Journal of Psychoanalysis*, Vol. XXI, No. 2 (pp. 120-127) (1961) and the author.

"Imprisoned Ideas" by W. J. Brown, M.P.: © The Spectator Ltd., and used by permission.

"Images in the Lonely Crowd" by James A. Dyal: Reprinted by permission of James A. Dyal. In *Readings in Psychology: Understanding Human Behavior*, J. A. Dyal, Ed. (2nd Ed.), New York, McGraw-Hill, 1967. Originally published in Vital Speeches 1965, 31, 729-734.

"E. T. Hall and the Human Space Bubble" by William Kloman: Reprinted by permission of Curtis Brown, Ltd. Copyright © 1967 by William Kloman.

"The Role of the Undesirables" by Eric Hoffer: Copyright © 1952 by *Harper's* Magazine, Inc. Reprinted from the December 1952 issue of Harper's Magazine by permission of the author.

"Poverty Is a Tougher Problem Than Ever" by Robert Bendiner: © 1968 by The New York Times Company. Reprinted by permission of *The New York Times* and the author.

"A Negro Psychiatrist Explains the Negro Psyche" by Alvin F. Poussaint: © 1967 by The New York Times Company. Reprinted by permission of *The New York Times* and Alvin F. Poussaint, M.D., Assistant Professor of Psychiatry.

"The Negro as an American" by Robert C. Weaver: Center for the Study of Democratic Institutions, 1963. Used by permission.

"Dispatch from Wounded Knee" by Calvin Kentfield: © 1967 by The New York Times Company. Reprinted by permission of *The New York Times* and the author.

"The Last Holdouts" by Patricia Lynden: Copyright © 1967 by The Atlantic Monthly Company, Boston, Mass. Reprinted by permission of *The Atlantic Monthly* and the author.

"To Abolish Children" by Karl Shapiro: Reprinted by permission of *Esquire* Magazine. © 1968 by Esquire, Inc.

"The Early Resigned" by Paul Goodman: From *Growing Up Absurd* by Paul Goodman. Copyright © 1960 by Paul Goodman. Reprinted by permission of Random House, Inc.

"What's Happening, Baby?" by Paul C. Harper, Jr.: Reprinted by permission of Paul Harper, Chairman and Chief Executive Officer of Needham, Harper & Steers, Inc.

"These Are Three of the Alienated" by Steven Kelman: © 1967 by The New York Times Company. Reprinted by permission of *The New York Times* and the author.

"The Splendid Old" by Gabriel Fielding: Copyright © 1965 by Harper's Magazine, Inc. Reprinted from the February 1965 issue of *Harper's* Magazine by permission of the author.

"The Scholar and the 'Alienated Generation'" by A. Craig Baird: *Vital Speeches of the Day,* Vol. XXXIII, July 15, 1966. Copyright 1966 by A. Craig Baird and reprinted by his permission.

"Must Writers Hate the Universe?" by Joseph Wood Krutch: From *And Even If You Do,* Essay on Man, Manners & Machines by Joseph Wood Krutch. Reprinted by permission of William Morrow and Company, Inc. Copyright © 1967 by Joseph Wood Krutch.

"The Newsman: Society's Lonesome End" by Wes Gallagher: Reprinted by permission of the author.

"Breakthrough: The Saga of Jonas Salk" by Richard Carter: Copyright © 1965 by Richard Carter. From *Breakthrough* by Richard Carter. Reprinted by permission of Trident Press/ A Division of Simon & Schuster, Inc.

"My Own Private View of Myself" Marilyn Monroe as told to Richard Meryman: "Marilyn Lets Her Hair Down About Being Famous!" by Richard Meryman, *Life,* August 3, 1962. © Time Inc., 1962.

"Complex Query: What Makes a Good Spy?" by Arthur T. Hadley: © 1960 by The New York Times Company. Reprinted by permission of *The New York Times* and the author.

"A Young Psychiatrist Looks at His Profession" by Robert Coles: Copyright © 1961 by The Atlantic Monthly Company, Boston, Mass. Reprinted with permission of *The Atlantic Monthly* and the author.

"The Rejection of the Insane" by Greer Williams: Copyright © 1961 by The Atlantic Monthly Company, Boston, Mass. Reprinted with permission of *The Atlantic Monthly* and the author.

"Deposition: Testimony Concerning a Sickness" by William Burroughs: Copyright 1960 by Evergreen Review, Inc. Reprinted by permission of Harold Matson Company, Inc.

"The Criminal and the Community" by Gus Tyler: Reprinted by permission of Current History, Inc. from *Current History*, August 1967.

"Suicide in Denmark" by Herbert Hendin: Reprinted from The Columbia University *Forum*, Summer 1961, Vol. 4, No. 3. Copyright 1961 by the Trustees of Columbia University in the City of New York.

"Who in the world am I?
Oh, that's the great puzzle."

LEWIS CARROLL
Alice's Adventures in Wonderland II

CONTENTS

INTRODUCTION ... xi

THE DISAFFECTED
Alienated Modern Society

Who Am I? *by* MARYA MANNES ... 3
On Alienated Concepts of Identity
 by ERNEST G. SCHACHTEL ... 11
Imprisoned Ideas *by* W. J. BROWN, M.P. ... 22
Images in the Lonely Crowd *by* JAMES A. DYAL ... 27
E. T. Hall and the Human Space Bubble
 by WILLIAM KLOMAN ... 46

THE DISPARATE
Racial, Ethnic and Economic Minorities

The Role of the Undesirables *by* Eric Hoffer ... 61
Poverty Is a Tougher Problem Than Ever
 by ROBERT BENDINER ... 71
A Negro Psychiatrist Explains the Negro Psyche
 by ALVIN F. POUSSAINT ... 84
The Negro as an American *by* ROBERT C. WEAVER ... 95
Dispatch from Wounded Knee *by* CALVIN KENTFIELD ... 107
The Last Holdouts *by* PATRICIA LYNDEN ... 117

THE DIVIDED
Estranged Generations

To Abolish Children *by* KARL SHAPIRO ... 129
The Early Resigned *by* PAUL GOODMAN ... 139
What's Happening, Baby? *by* PAUL C. HARPER, JR. ... 155
These Are Three of the Alienated *by* STEVEN KELMAN ... 165
The Splendid Old *by* GABRIEL FIELDING ... 176

THE DISTINCTIVE
Individuals in a Mob

The Scholar and the "Alienated Generation" by A. CRAIG BAIRD	185
Must Writers Hate the Universe? by JOSEPH WOOD KRUTCH	193
The Newsman: Society's Lonesome End by WES GALLAGHER	204
Breakthrough: The Saga of Jonas Salk by RICHARD CARTER	211
My Own Private View of Myself by MARILYN MONROE *as Told to* RICHARD MERYMAN	218
Complex Query: What Makes a Good Spy? by ARTHUR T. HADLEY	228

THE DISTRESSED
Agitated Man

A Young Psychiatrist Looks at His Profession by ROBERT COLES	237
The Rejection of the Insane by GREER WILLIAMS	246
Deposition: Testimony Concerning a Sickness by WILLIAM BURROUGHS	256
The Criminal and the Community by GUS TYLER	264
Suicide in Denmark by HERBERT HENDIN	275

INTRODUCTION

"Alienation . . . is not a happening, man, it IS!" said the bearded boy with long hair and dirty fingernails, as he tried to define a term that is currently much in vogue—especially among the "under thirty" Americans. As he sat watching the clean-cut majority of students strolling along palm-lined sidewalks at a large Southern California university on their way to class, the young man grappled with a word that has been used to cover, not always comfortably, a multitude of twentieth-century social and personal maladies—none of which can easily be put into neat conceptual categories.

"Like, it's a slow, systematic, deliberate thing, you know? It's a changing of love into hate. I mean, alienation isn't always conscious, but it's there all the same—turning one man away from another." He might have been speaking as well for a whole group of individuals who have lost their sense of personal sameness and of historical continuity—a large and varied number of human beings who have either isolated themselves or been estranged from contemporary society.

Certain psychological or sociological concepts such as "complex" and "sublimation" have caught the public ear and have become household words (like the names of much advertised products or even of movie stars and singers). "Alienation"—like Coke or the Beatles—has become an essential part of the American's vocabulary. So much so, indeed, that it would be hard to imagine a typical campus or cocktail-party conversation, a play, a movie, a book in which the term wasn't mentioned at least once—sometimes inappropriately!

Who, then, are the alienated? Everyman and no man! Anyone and everyone who is drifting along in an age that seems to have lost its meaning, and in an environment that has depersonalized man.

The concept has become so common and the term has been applied so often to distinctive and different areas that the popular but ambiguous use of the word would probably baffle the social scientists who first introduced it. "The Alienated" has been applied, interchangeably, to social and political, economic and ethnic, racial and religious minorities, as well as to the young and the old, the distinguished citizens, and the maladjusted, truly sick people of the world.

"The Alienated" are those people who have been excluded or who have excluded themselves. They are the thousands of bored workers who find that what they are doing is monotonous or degrading or both. They are the young people who either commit "senseless acts of violence" or simply "don't care about anything" or who "care about everything, too much." They are the idle, lonely old who feel the world has left them behind; they are the rejectors of prevailing values of culture; they are the achievers—the "special ones" who strive so hard for recognition that they find everyone else somewhere off to the side of their own lives. They are the deeply maladjusted—the escapists, retreatists, nihilists, disparates and desperates, the dope addicts, the insane, the criminals and the self-destroyers.

Doubtless, the availability of the term "alienation" has served as a convenient way of filling the vast verbal vacuum left in popular culture by the erosion of terminology such as "good and evil," "right from wrong," "guilt or innocence." In short, "alienation" has become, today, an almost indispensible word for coping with the changing and expanding individual dimensions of a confusing universe.

In a disorganized society of conflicting opposites (annihilation *vs.* dreams of a better life) and of contradictions—between man's achievements and his problems and with his inability to deal with either, contemporary man is like a gangling, coltish creature learning how to walk.

This collection of modern, easy-to-read essays does not give solutions or even adequate explanations of such a complex concept, but it does describe "The Alienated" and examines the particular conditions which have led to their estrangement. Hopefully, it will give some idea about how to deal with the problems of anxiety, despair, depersonalization, apathy, rootlessness, loneliness, powerlessness, meaninglessness, isolation, pessimism, and a loss of purpose and beliefs. It should make the reader more aware and, therefore, more eager to do something about the problems for himself.

—NED E. HOOPES

THE DISAFFECTED
Alienated Modern Society

WHO AM I?

Marya Mannes

A social critic stresses the complications of the long, sometimes arduous, but necessary "journey into self."

Who are you? You singly, not you together. When did it start—that long day's journey into self? When do you really begin to know what you believe and where you're going? When do you know that you are unique—separate—alone?

The time of discovery is different for everybody. Some people find themselves in early childhood, some in middle-age, some—the tragic ones—never.

I suggest that the first recognition comes when others try to tell you what you are. And although what happened in my generation is supposed to have no relevance to what happens in yours, I know when it happened to me.

I may have been six years old when aunts and uncles and cousins used to say: "You look just like your mother!" or "You're the image of your brother!"

Now, for reasons that have nothing to do with duty or discipline in that distant day, I loved my family. I loved them because they were interesting, handsome, talented, and loving people. I was lucky. But in spite of that, I felt an immediate, instinctive resistance to any suggestion that I was like them or like anybody else. I didn't want to be like anybody else. I was Me, Myself. Separate. Alone.

This is probably as good a time as any to say that if I use the first-person pronoun—if I refer from time to time to my own long, arduous, bumbling journey into self—it is not because of narcissism, but because I have always believed that the particular is more illuminating than the general. Perhaps my dependence as a writer on direct observation rather than on scholarly research, on living example rather than on sociological method, is the natural result of illiteracy. I never went to college and therefore know much less than you people do. About books, I mean. Or the sciences.

But since the laboratory for the study of man is clearly life itself, then I have studied hard in the act of living, of looking, of feeling; involvement rather than detachment; doing as well as being.

We were talking of the first discoveries of uniqueness—of being oneself and no one else. Not your father, not your mother, not your sister, not your brother. I. Me.

It is then—when you begin not only to know it, but act it—that society moves in. Society says it wants people to be different but it doesn't really mean it. Parents like to believe their children are different from other children—smarter, of course, better-looking and so forth—but most parents are secretly disturbed when their children are *really* different—not like others at all. In fact, very early they start to pigeon-hole you in certain ways.

Take the difference of sex, for instance. Little girls are pink, little boys are blue. Little girls want dolls, little boys want trains.

For a long time, for instance, the word "tom-boy" to a girl held undertones of worry and disapproval. All it meant was that the girl liked to play ball, climb trees, and skin her knees instead of wearing frilly dresses and curtseying. The companion word for boys, of course, was "sissy"—meaning the kid liked music and poetry and hated fighting. These ignorant and damaging labels have now been discredited, thanks largely to you and the more enlightened members of our society. But there is still, alas, a large Squareland left where growing girls are told from the age of twelve onward not only by their mothers but by the mass media that marriage is the only valid female goal and that Career is a dirty word.

Even now—even when you here know how silly it is (at least, I hope you do), most parents hear wedding bells the minute a girl is born, most parents see an executive office when a boy is born, and the relentless conditioning starts on its merry way. Educate a girl for the marriage market, educate a boy for success. That you, as a human being, as a separate identity, may not want or fit in with either of these goals is considered not a sign of independence but of deviation—pointing to the couch or—in social terms—failure.

That is why these same parents—and they are still a majority—are bewildered, depressed, or plain horrified when their adolescents openly refuse to accept these goals or to share any common identity with any past. Who on earth, their parents moan, will marry this stringy girl with her false eyelashes and shuffling gait? Who will employ this bearded boy with his grunts and records, his pop and pot? On the other end, how gratified are parents when their cleancut athletic sons get high marks and their clean and pretty daughters marry the clean-cut boys who get good jobs?

You know, I pity you. I pity you for reasons you might not suspect. I pity you because your search for self has been made so self-conscious. You are overexposed in and by the mass media, which never for one instant night and day stop telling you what you are and who you are. With us, decades ago, there was no radio and no television. As adolescents we seldom read papers (they never reported on us) or magazines. The word "teenager," thank God, never existed. From twelve to seventeen we were painful to our parents and not very attractive to ourselves. Our skins and bodies did strange things and we felt strange things. The world paid no attention to us. It didn't interview us, quote us, and ask our advice. We didn't expect it to. We had twenty-five to fifty cents a week to spend for allowance (rich kids got a dollar), but who needed it? Books were in the house or you could borrow them, movies were a quarter, and if you were lucky your family took you to occasional plays or concerts. School was sometimes boring, but we expected it to be. Nobody told us learning ought to be fun. When it was—well, great!

Nothing much external happened, except for trips with the family and meetings with friends. There was a lot of unfilled, unstructured, unplanned free time—with no messages coming in from anywhere to distract us, no entertainment at arm's length, no guidance counselors or psychiatrists to tell us what was bugging us. We had a vast amount of inner space to fill by ourselves. In this inner space there was room and time for that very tender, very vulnerable thing called "I" to be born—and grow.

For there are really two births—the first physical, the second spiritual. Both share something in common: Premature expulsion, premature exposure, can damage both foetus and soul. The prenatal fluid that protects the foetus until it is ready for air has its counterpart in the secret world of the yet unborn identity.

Now I want to make it quite clear that this secret world of child and adolescent is not a matter of protection from reality. Just because a child may grow up in the relative security of home and school and neighborhood doesn't mean that the human comedy-tragedy is not a part of daily life. You are not cut off from experience because the world you live in is physically small. On the contrary, you can be put off from real experience because the world has become too large.

And that is precisely why I pity you. You stand naked and exposed in too large a world, and that prenatal sac of your soul has been so repeatedly punctured by external influences, persuasions, and pressures that it must take superhuman will to keep yourself intact. Many of you don't. Or at least you find the only answer to a fragmented self in a fragmented life—or a withdrawal from life.

How, in any case, are you ever going to know what you are or who you are when these hundreds of voices are doing the job *for* you? How do you know how much of what you think and do is what you *really* think and want to do, or how much is the feedback from what you hear about yourselves— daily, hourly? A lot of it, of course, is true.

You *are* the new power, if only in numbers. You *are* rich, if only in dollars. You *are* smarter than your parents, if only in acquired knowledge. A lot of you take drugs and pills or cop out in communal huddles, living on handouts. I question whether you are more interested in sex than we were, or even more active. The difference here is that it's now so easy to come by, in beds as well as in books, that it may mean less. Obstacles are great aphrodisiacs.

I would like to think that those of you who hate war are a majority. I would like to think that those of you who believe that sweeping changes must be made in our whole social, legal, political and economic life are a majority and an acting majority at that.

Whatever you are, you can't do anything about making a better society and a better world until you are a productive human being. And you can't be a productive human being, sorting the world out, until you sort yourself out.

Until you really attain an expansion of consciousness— not of another world, through hallucination, but of this world, through illumination. Not long ago Professor Lettwin, that dynamic, free-wheeling bear of M.I.T., told an audience of high-school students and undergraduates in Boston that in order to do what they wanted to do—to change the disastrous drift of society—they would have to keep their wits about them. You must be conscious, he exhorted, you must at all times keep your sense of judgment intact. Anything that blurs, that weakens your judgmental values will, in time, make you ineffective. Only your judgment, consciously arrived at, only the intellect and senses in the service of human compassion—will take you where you want to go—where this new society *must* go.

This I would also passionately advocate. As a long-time rebel, a seeker of new adventures, a destroyer of old myths, I have come to believe that this total awareness is the greatest single attribute of identity, and most preciously to be guarded. That it can be chemically achieved I would very much doubt. For moments, maybe. For the long haul, no. It is one thing—and who doesn't need it?—to seek escape from the pain of total awareness—in drink or pot. It is another to take the quick exit from reality with the distinct possibility that you may not make the reentry back. Or that if you do, you may never be yourself—your real, your useful, your creative self—again. Fly Now—Pay Later.

The price of conscious awareness is stiff—but not that stiff. The price is a very hard look at yourself—alone, and not bolstered by a crowd, a tribe—or even—a wife. And here is where I'm going to stick this already battered neck further out—on the institution of matrimony.

Your parents, I would imagine, consider your generation incomprehensible, sometimes frightening, and certainly unconventional. Everything you wear, grow on your face or head, think, believe, do, is way out of their norm.

Except marriage. In a world of undreamed-of scope and opportunity and choice, most of you do exactly what your parents did in a much more limited world. You rush to the altar to tie the legal tie from the age of eighteen onward to a girl no older. Here you are in the full flower of body and mind (and I speak of both sexes) and with the only pure freedom of action you will ever know again, and you tie yourself to one mate and one hearth before you know who you are.

If you're lucky, you will find yourselves *through* each

other—the ideal nature of love, the true—and rare—blessing of marriage.

If you're not lucky—and the evidence would call you a majority—you will be two half-persons, half-grown, prematurely bound, inhibiting each other's growth, choking up the road to your full development as a human being.

Many of our laws and institutions, as you well know, have not yet caught up with reality . . . the fact that men and women cannot be codified. So long as we do others no harm, how we choose to live is our own affair, and ours alone. How *you* choose to live is yours alone. And if you are able to bring about an intelligent society—I avoid the word "great"—one of the most important things you will have to do is remove the senseless stigmas that still prevail against single men or single women, and against whatever kind of love is the product of deep inner need.

One of your great influences already is that in your new sense of community—in part forced upon you by isolation from your elders—you have managed to blur already many of the lines of demarcation—between races, between sexes, between thought and feeling, between feeling and action—which have trapped the former generations in patterns of sterility. The best of you have not only discovered your conscience, but are living it.

But apart from the terrible issues of the day—to which the best of you address your conscience—war in Vietnam, the brutal war in the streets—how much are you living it as individuals, how much in group conformity?

How brave, how independent are you when you are alone? I ask this chiefly of my own sex, for I wonder whether girls now really know and want the chances and choices that are open to them, or whether they have been so conditioned by history and habit that they slip back into the old patterns of their mothers the minute they graduate. Oddly enough, this supposed choice between marriage and a career never bothered my generation as much as it seems to have bothered the postwar ones. And I lay the blame for it on a mass media—mainly television, advertising, and women's magazines—which maintain the fiction that the only valid goal for women is marriage and children and domesticity (with a little community work thrown in), and that women who demand and seek more than this from life are at best unfulfilled and at worst unfeminine. It is about time that we realized that many women make better teachers than mothers, better actresses than wives, better mistresses than housekeepers, better diplomats than cooks. Just as many men are better rakes than lawnmowers and better dreamers than providers. We have lost a great deal of talent and wasted a great many lives in the perpetuation of these myths that are called "the role of men" or "the role of women." And just as you have managed to dissipate some of them in your dress, I hope you will dissipate others in your lives. The only thing you need to aspire to, the only ultimate identity you must discover, is that of a human being. The sex, believe it or not, is secondary.

But in the search for this human identity, I urge you to remember one thing. I said before that our first recognition of it comes when we know we are not like anybody else, that we are unique. That is so.

But we did not spring into this world through galactic explosion—we did not even burst from the head of Zeus.

We came from somewhere. Not just the womb of our mothers and the seeds of our fathers but from a long, long procession of identities—whose genes we possess.

Whether we like it or not, we bear the past inside us. Good or bad, it cannot be excised, it cannot be rejected, . . . it should not be. Humanity is a continuous process, and without a past there is no future.

In your worship of Now, in your fierce insistence that only the present exists, that you are new on the face of the earth, owing nothing to history—you are cheating yourself. You are not only denying evolution but limiting your future.

You may say you have nothing in common with the preceding generation, you may lay the blame for the present entirely on their shoulders and on the mistakes of the past. But what of the others who came before? What of the great rebels, the great innovators, the great voices without which no light, no truth would ever have prevailed? Much of what poets and philosophers and artists and scientists said ten centuries ago is as valid now as it was then. Where would you be, where would we be, without them?

On a much humbler level, I remember the photograph albums so many families kept when I was a child. There, in our own, were these strange faces and strange clothes of the dead who preceded me: the tall, gaunt old baker in Poland, the opera singer in Germany, the immigrant furniture dealer in New York, the violinist in Breslau, the General near Kiel, the incredible web of cells and genes contained in my own self.

It took me more than twenty years to realize that they lived in me, that I was part of them, and that in spite of distance, time, and difference, I was part of them. I was not, in short, alone.

And neither are you. I suppose what I am asking for here is that, along with your pride of generation, you somehow maintain compassion for those who preceded you as well as for those who will come after you.

If you will, this is a community just as important as any living community of your own age and time, and if you deny your connection with it, you deny evolution, you deny the human race.

Don't play it too cool. The ultimate pattern of life is immense, there are other worlds in other galaxies that may have far transcended ours, and if you aren't turned on more by a shower of meteors than by an electric circus, you're half dead already.

You won't find yourself in a crowded room. You may find yourself under the crowded sky of night, where—if you attach yourself to a single star—you will discover that you are one of many millions, but still—One.

Listen to your own drum and march to it. You may fall on your face—but then, anybody who never does is—Nobody!

ON ALIENATED CONCEPTS OF IDENTITY

Ernest G. Schachtel

A psychiatrist suggests that people who fail to find their true selves often settle instead for pseudo-identities.

In daily life the question of identity arises when we want to claim something from the post office, or when we want to pay by check in a store where we are not known, or in crossing a border. On such occasions we are asked: "Who are you, so that I can know for sure it is you and nobody else?" And we establish our identity by showing a driver's license or a passport or some similar document which tells our name, our address, the date of our birth, and perhaps some physical characteristics. Together, these will tell us apart from anybody else and will also establish that we are the same person that was born on such and such a date. We have *papers* to establish our identity, and this paper-identity is something fixed and definite. This is also the meaning of the word "identity," as applied to people, for the average person.

Such paper-identity seems far removed, at first glance, from the current concern of psychoanalysts, philosophers, and other students of the contemporary scene, with man's search for and doubt in his identity. But actually it is quite central to it. It is a telling symbol of alienated identity. It is a kind of identity which is the product of bureaucratic needs of commerce or administration. Its most gruesome and tragic manifestations occurred in our time when men's identities were reduced to numbers in concentration and extermination camps, and when countless people fleeing from the terror of the totalitarian states were shunted from country to country because they did not have the right paper-identities.

In the case of paper-identities, the person who demands and examines one's papers is the one who, in his role as an official, is alienated from the other person as a human being. Similarly, the guards in the concentration camps were alienated from their victims. However, many of these victims, systematically robbed of any meaningful purpose and dignity in their lives, succumbed to their tormentors and lost their sense of identity long before they lost their lives.

In our own and many other societies the loss of identity takes place without the terror of the concentration camps, in more insidious ways. Many people in our time tend to think of their lives as though they were answering the kind of questionnaire that one has to fill out when, for example, applying for a passport. They tend to accept the paper-identity as their real identity. It is tempting to do so because it is something fixed and definite and does not require that the person be really in touch with himself. The paper-identity corresponds to the logical propositions concerning identity: $A = A$, and A is not non-A.

But man is not a logical proposition, and the paper-identity does not answer the question who this person, identified by some scrap of paper, is as a person. This question is not simple to answer. It has haunted many people increasingly in the last hundred years. They no longer feel certain who they are because in modern industrial society, as Hegel and Marx first showed, they are alienated from nature, alienated from their fellowmen, alienated from the work of their hands and minds, and alienated from themselves. I can only state here my belief that self-alienation, the doubt about and search for identity, always goes together with alienation from others and from the world around us.

The problem of identity and alienation from the self came to the attention of psychoanalysts in the last thirty years when they observed its role in an increasing number of patients. Karen Horney formulated it as the problem of the real self, as distinguished from the idealized self-image; Fromm as the problem of the original, real self as distinguished from the conventional or pseudo-self; Erikson, who has made the most detailed study in the development of the sense of identity, as the problem of ego-identity.

Many patients who come to us suffer in one form or another from the lack of a sense of identity. This may take the form of feeling like impostors—in their work, or in relation to their background, their past, or to some part of themselves that they repress or consciously want to hide because they feel ashamed or guilty. Or else they feel that they *ought* to *have* something they lack or imagine they lack, such as material possessions, prestige, or certain personal qualities or traits; or they feel that a different husband or wife, or friends different from those they have, would give them the status they want and thereby, miraculously, transform them into full-blown persons. When the lack of a sense of identity becomes conscious, it is often experienced —probably always—as a feeling that, compared with others, one is not fully a person.

Among adults one can observe two frequent reactions to the conscious or unconscious feeling of not being fully a person, of not having found an identity acceptable to oneself. One is an anxious retreat or depressive resignation, or a mixture of these. The other is a more or less conscious effort at disguise, at playing a role, at presenting an artificial façade to the world. These reactions are not mutually exclusive. They usually occur together, one of them being more emphasized or closer to consciousness than the other. The fear of exposure is present in both, but especially strong in people who rely on a façade. They tend to feel that they travel with a forged passport, under an assumed identity. When their disguise and the reasons for it have been analyzed, the sense of a lack of identity often comes to the fore as strongly as in those who, to begin with, have been aware of and suffered from the feeling of not really or fully being a person with a meaningful place in life. Both tend to feel that they do not really know who they are, what they want, or how they feel about other people.

When these people consult an analyst, they often expect, implicitly or explicitly, that he will tell them who they are or who they should be. Their wish and search is for a *definite, fixed identity*. They want to be a *personality*. Often these are people who suffer from overadaptation to whatever situation they are in, and to whomever they are dealing with at the moment. They have been described pointedly in several plays and stories by Pirandello. They long for a definite, fixed, circumscribed personality. "Having" such a personality, as one has a possession, they hope will solve their dilemma. Having such a personality, they feel, is good; not having it, bad. Their wish to "possess" a definite identity does not and cannot solve the problem of their alienation from themselves, because it actually is the continuation of alienation. They want to substitute a fixed, reified personality for the ongoing process of living, feeling, acting, and thinking in which alone they could find themselves. They search for a definite, stable shell called "personality" to which they want to cling. Their quest is self-defeating, because what they search for is an alienated concept of a thing, rather than a living, developing person. Their wish is a symptom, not a cure. In this symptom, however, both the malady of alienation and the longing for a more meaningful life find expression, even though in a way which perpetuates the ill from which they seek to escape. The self-conscious preoccupation with this wished-for magic object called "personality" interferes with the actual experience of living.

In calling the object of these people's search an alienated "concept" of identity, I do not mean a scientific or even an explicit concept. I am describing an implicit concept, which becomes apparent only in the analysis of the underlying, often not conscious, assumptions that direct this kind of search. This applies equally to the following examples of alienated concepts of identity.

There is one psychoanalytic term that has gained wide popularity and in popular use has changed its meaning. Such popular use always indicates a significant fact about a society and therefore deserves our attention. I refer to the term "ego." People say that something is good or bad for their "ego." They mean by this that their self-feeling—in the sense of the status which they accord to themselves—rises when something is good and falls when something is bad for their ego. In this usage ego is only part of the person. My "ego" is not identical with "I" or "self." It is not identical with the I who is well or ill, who sees and hears and touches and tastes and smells, who acts, walks, sits, stands, lies, who is moved by others, by what is seen and experienced. Moreover, what is "good" or "bad" for my ego is not at all necessarily good or bad for me, although I may be inclined to think so. The popular "ego" gains from success, winning in competition, status, being admired, flattered, loved; it does not gain from facing the truth, from loving somebody else, from humility. It behaves like a stock or a piece of merchandise endowed with self-awareness: if it is much in demand it rises, is blown up, feels important; if not, it falls, shrinks, feels it is nothing. Thus, it is an *alienated* part of the self.

But while it is only part of the self, it has the tendency to become the *focal point* of the feeling of identity and to dominate the whole life of the people who are involved with their "ego" to a significant degree. Their mood fluctuates with their "ego." They are haunted by their "ego" and preoccupied with its enhancement or its downfall. They no longer seem to feel that they have a life apart from their "ego," but they stand or fall with it. The "ego" has become their identity and at the same time the main object of their worry, ambition, and preoccupation, crowding out any real concern with themselves and with others. The popular ego can serve as the most important model of an alienated concept of identity, even though it may be surpassed in rigidity and fixedness by some other examples of such concepts, to which I shall turn now.

In her thoughtful book, *On Shame and the Search for Identity,* Helen Lynd quotes Dostoyevsky's Mitya Karamazov, who, on trial for the murder of his father, suffers his worst misery when the prosecutor asks him to take off his socks. "They were very dirty . . . and now everyone could see it. All his life he had thought both his big toes hideous. He particularly loathed the coarse, flat, crooked nail on the right one and now they would all see it. Feeling intolerably ashamed. . . ." The accidental, unchangeable appearance of his feet, of the nail of his right big toe, here becomes the focal point of his identity. It is on this that he feels the peasants who stand around him and look at him will judge him and that he judges himself. Very often real or imagined physical attributes, parts of the body image or the entire body image, become focal points of identity. Many people build around such a negative identity the feeling that this particular feature unalterably determines the course of their lives, and that they are thereby doomed to unhappiness. Usually, in these cases, qualities such as attractiveness and beauty are no longer felt to be based on the alive expression and flux of human feelings, but have become fixed and dead features, or a series of poses, as in so many Hollywood stars or fashion models. These features are cut off from the center of the person and worn like a mask. Unattractiveness is experienced as not possessing this mask.

In the same way, other real or imagined attributes, or the lack of them, become focal points for a reified, alienated, negative identity. For example: feeling not sufficiently masculine or feminine, being born on the wrong side of the tracks, being a member of a minority group against which racial or religious prejudices are directed, and, in the most general form, feeling intrinsically inadequate or "bad." I do not imply, of course, that in our society the accidental circumstance of being born as the member of one social, national, or religious group or class rather than another does not result in very real, objective difficulties, disadvantages or privileges. I am concerned here only with the *attitude* which the person takes toward such handicaps or advantages, which is important for his ability to deal with them. In this attitude the structure of the sense of identity and the way in which such factors as the social background and innate advantages or handicaps are incorporated in the sense of identity play a decisive role.

What are the dynamics of such alienated concepts of identity? Sometimes they crystallize around repeated parental remarks which, rather than referring to a particular act of the child, say or imply that the child *is* or *lacks,* by its very nature, such and such; that Tom is a lazy good-for-nothing or that he is "just like Uncle Harry," who happens to be the black sheep in the family. Frequently they develop from an ego-ideal that is alien to the child's own personality, but about which he has come to feel that, unless he is such and such, he is nothing. Whatever their genetic origin, I shall consider here mainly the phenomenological structure of alienated identity concepts and the dynamics of this structure which tends to perpetuate self-alienation.

By making some quality or circumstance, real or exaggerated or imagined, the focal point of a reified identity, I look upon myself as though I were a thing (*res*) and the quality or circumstance were a fixed attribute of this thing or object. But the "I" that feels that I am this or that, in doing so, distances itself from the very same reified object attribute which it experiences as determining its identity and very often as a bane on its life. In feeling that I am such and such, I distinguish between the unfortunate I and the presumably unalterable quality or lack which, for all time, condemns me to have this negative identity. I do not feel that *I* am *doing* this or that or failing to do it, but that there *is* a something in me or about me, or that I lack something and that this, once and for all, *makes* me this or that, fixes my identity.

The person who has this attitude toward himself usually is unaware of its being a particular attitude with concrete and far-reaching implications. He takes his attitude for granted as a natural, inevitable one and is aware only of the painful self-consciousness and self-preoccupation it involves. He cannot imagine how anyone with his "fate" could have any other attitude.

The two most significant implications of this attitude to oneself are (1) the severance from the living I of the reified attribute which is experienced as a fixed, unchangeable quality, and (2) the severance of this reified attribute from its dynamic and structural connection with other qualities, needs, acts, and experiences of the person. In other words, the reified attribute is cut off from the living, developing, fluctuating I in *time*, since it is experienced as immutable. But it is also cut off from being experienced as an *integral* part of the living personality, connected with the totality of the person's strivings, attitudes, perceptions, feelings, with his acting and failing to act.

In reality, of course, we can observe that certain actions, moods, and experiences cause changes in the role of the negative identity in the conscious feelings and thoughts of the person. However, he usually does not experience the reified attribute which forms the core of his negative self-feeling as something connected with, and due to, his own actions and attitudes, but as something fixed on which he has no influence. Furthermore, just as the person's feeling about himself may fluctuate with the ups and downs of his "ego," so it also varies with the intensity of the negative self-feeling based on some reified attribute which, at times, may disappear altogether from the conscious thoughts of the person. However, when it reappears it is "recognized" as the same unfortunate quality that throughout the past has tainted—and will forever taint—the person's life. Thus, in spite of such fluctuations, the alienated attribute is experienced as a "something" that basically does not and cannot change.

To be saddled with a reified, negative identity seems, on the face of it, nothing but a painful burden. Yet one often can see people cling to such negative self-images with a great deal of stubbornness and in the face of contradictory evidence. In psychoanalytic therapy, it is often seen that the patient who comes for help tries to convince the therapist that nothing can be done for him, since he is born with such and such a handicap or without such and such an advantage. On closer scrutiny, one may find that such insistence by the patient on the hopelessness of the situation has a way of occurring at a point when the patient is afraid to face an issue, or when he wants to be pitied rather than helped. Thus, the reified identity concept often provides a protection against an anxiety-arousing challenge, a way out of a feared situation, and thereby a certain relief.

This relief is dynamically similar to the relief observable in certain hypochondriacal and paranoid patients. It sounds paradoxical to speak of relief in the case of patients who are so obviously beset by worry, suffering, and fear as the hypochondriac and the paranoid. However, as Sullivan has pointed out, the hypochondriacal patient who is preoccupied with imagined, anticipated, or real ailments sees himself as the "customarily handicapped" one and thereby avoids the anxiety-provoking prospect of facing and dealing with his real problems. His hypochondriacal preoccupation gets the patient, in Sullivan's words, "off the spot with himself"— namely, off the spot where he would have to deal with his realistic personality problems.

The person living with an alienated and reified, negative identity concept of himself closely resembles the hypochondriacal patient, except that his unhappy preoccupation concerns not a physical ailment but a reified physical or psychic quality that has become the focal point of his self-image. The relief he gains from his burdensome preoccupation is due to the fact that the reified "bad" quality no longer is viewed as part of the ongoing process of living and of goal-directed thought and action. It has been severed from the "I" that acts with foresight and responsiblity and is looked upon as an inherent, unalterable, unfortunate something, an ossified part of oneself that no longer participates in the flux, growth, and development of life. It is experienced as an unchangeable fate whose bearer is doomed to live and die with it. The relief this brings is that the person no longer feels *responsible* for the supposed consequences of this fixed attribute; he is not *doing* anything for which he can be blamed, even though he may feel ashamed and unacceptable for *being* such and such. The preoccupation with the reified identity directs attention away from what he *does* to what he supposedly *is*. Furthermore, he now no longer has to do anything about it because, obviously, he can't do anything about it. Thus, the anxiety, fear, and effort that would be connected with facing and acting upon the real problem is avoided by putting up with the negative, fixed identity which, in addition, may be used to indulge self-pity and to enlist the sympathy of others.

The similarity in the dynamics of hypochondria and paranoia, on the one hand, and the alienated, reified self-concept, on the other, lies in this *shift of responsibility and of focus* from my own actions and conduct of life to something else over which I have no control. In the alienated self-concept this something else is a reified quality, or the lack of such a quality; in hypochondria an ailment, real or imagined; in paranoia the delusional persecutors. The difference between paranoia and the alienated self-concept lies in the fact that in paranoia the shift in responsibility is brought about by delusions distorting reality, while in the alienated, negative identity concept it is brought about by an attitude which excludes part of oneself from the process of living and freezes it into a cancer-like, uncontrollable, and unalterable thing. This "thing" very often also becomes the focus, in the paranoid neuroses, of the imagined judgments, observation, and talk of other people about the patient. He believes that, just as his own thoughts tend to revolve around some reified and alienated quality, other people will be similarly preoccupied with this quality in him.

So far I have discussed mainly negative self-images. However, alienated identity concepts may be positive as well as negative. Alienated identity of the positive variety occurs in vanity, conceit and—in its more pathological form—in delusions of grandeur, just as in its negative counterpart the "I" of the vain person is severed from a fixed attribute on which the vanity is based. The person feels that he *possesses* this quality. It becomes the focal point of his identity and serves as its prop. Beauty, masculinity or feminity, being born on the right side of the tracks, success, money, prestige, or "being good" may serve as such a prop. While in the negative identity feeling a reified attribute haunts the person, such an attribute serves the positive self-image as a support. Yet it is equally alienated from the living person. This is expressed nicely in the phrase "a stuffed shirt." It is not the person in the shirt but some dead matter, some stuffing that is used to bolster and aggrandize the self-feeling. It often becomes apparent in the behavior of the person that he *leans* on this real or imagined attribute, just as it often is apparent that a person feels pulled down by the weight of some alienated negative attribute.

The reliance on an identity, on a self-image based on the prop of some reified attribute remains precarious even where it seems to work, after a fashion, as it does in the self-satisfaction of the vain. This precariousness is inevitable, since the positive self-evaluation of such a person does not rest on a feeling of wholeness and meaningfulness in life, in thought, feeling, and deed. He is always threatened with the danger of losing this "thing," this possession, on which his self-esteem is based. This is the theme of Oscar Wilde's novel, *The Picture of Dorian Gray*. Dorian Gray exchanges his identity with the portrait of his youthful charm. He becomes the picture of himself as the beautiful youth, alienated from his actual life, which affects the portrait he has hidden in the attic, marking it over the years with his cruelty, selfishness, and greed, and with his advancing age. The portrait is the skeleton in the closet, the secret threat that hangs over the unchanging mask. Today, especially in this country where youth has become a public fetish, many thousands try to preserve its alienated mask while terrified by the prospect of suddenly growing old, when the mask can no longer be worn or will become grotesque.

I believe that in every case of alienated identity concepts there is a secret counterimage. In Dorian Gray, this is the actual, living person, transplanted to the portrait. Very often such a hidden self announces itself merely in a vague background feeling that the person would be lost, would be nothing if it were not for the alienated, reified quality on which the feeling of being something, somebody, or the feeling of vanity, is based. In this feeling both a truth and an irrational anxiety find expression. The truth is that no man who looks upon himself as a thing and bases his existence on the support of some reified attribute of this thing has found himself and his place in life. The irrational anxiety is the feeling that without the prop of such an attribute he could not live.

Similarly, in the negative alienated identity concepts there usually is a positive counterimage. It may take a generalized, vague form: If it were not for such and such (the reified attribute forming the focus of the negative identity), I would be all right, successful, wonderful, etc. Or it may take the more concrete form of some grandiose, exaggerated fantasy about one's positive qualities. These positive counterimages, too, express both an irrational hope and a truth. The irrational hope is that one may have some magical quality which will transport him into a state of security, or even superiority, because then he will possess that attribute which, instead of haunting him, will save him. But actually it is nothing but the equally reified counterpart of what at present drags him down. The truth is that man has potentialities for overcoming his alienation from himself and for living without the burden and the artificial props of alienated, reified identity concepts.

Goethe, in an interpretation of the Delphic word, "Know thyself," distinguishes between helpful self-awareness and futile and self-tormenting rumination. He opposes the "ascetic" interpretation he finds among "our modern hypochondrists" and those who turn their vengeance against themselves. Instead, he sees the real meaning of self-knowledge in taking notice of oneself and becoming aware of one's relation to other people and to the world. The pseudo-self-knowledge against which he speaks foreshadows the widespread present-day self-preoccupation which is concerned, fruitlessly, with an alienated, negative sense of identity. In contrast to this, Goethe counsels a productive self-knowledge: to pay attention to what one is actually doing in his relation to others, to the world and—we might add—to himself.

IMPRISONED IDEAS

W. J. Brown, M.P.

A member of the British Parliament outlines the dangers of becoming a slave of institutions or organizations.

There are many classifications into which men and women may be divided—as upper, middle or lower class; rich, well-to-do and poor; religious, sceptical and atheist; Conservative, Liberal, Labour; Catholic, Protestant; master and man; and so forth and so on, *ad infinitum*. But, as I think, the only categorization which really matters is that which divides men as between the Servants of the Spirit and the Prisoners of the Organization. That classification, which cuts right across all the other classifications, is indeed the fundamental one. The idea, the inspiration, originates in the internal world, the world of the spirit. But, just as the human spirit must incarnate in a body, so must the idea incarnate in an organization. Whether the organization be political, religious or social is immaterial to my present argument. The point is that, the idea having embodied itself in organization, the organization then proceeds gradually to slay the idea which gave it birth.

We may see this process at work in many fields. Let us take one or two by way of illustration. In the field of religion, a prophet, an inspired man, will see a vision of truth. He expresses that vision as best he may in words. He will not say all he saw. For every expression of truth is a limitation of it. But he will, so to speak, express the sense of his vision. What he says is only partly understood by those who hear him; and when they repeat what they understand him to have meant, there will already be a considerable departure from the original vision of the prophet. Upon what his disciples understand of the prophet's message, an organization, a church, will be built. The half-understood message will crystallize into a creed. Before long, the principal concern of the church will be to sustain itself as an organization. To this end, any departure from the creed must be controverted and, if necessary, suppressed as heresy. In a few score or few hundred years what was conceived as a vehicle of a new and higher truth has become a prison for the souls of men. And men are murdering each other for the love of God. The thing has become its opposite.

In the field of politics, the dispossessed dream of a social order which shall be based on righteousness, a system in which men shall not exploit their fellowmen, in which each shall contribute according to his capacity and each shall receive according to his need. Upon this conception a political party is built. It gives battle, over the years, to the existing order of things. As with the church, it is not long before the primary concern of the party is to sustain itself. Here, again, any departure from the political creed must be repressed. The "party line" must be kept straight and dissent kept under. In the course of time the party achieves power. By this time it is led no longer by starry-eyed idealists, but by extremely tough guys—who then proceed to use their newly acquired power to establish a stronger despotism than the one they overthrew, and to sew up all the holes in it that they themselves discovered in the old. What emerges is not freedom and social justice, but a more comprehensive and totalitarian control, used to maintain a new privileged class, which, because of the earlier experience of its members, is still more ruthless then the old.

Similar illustrations could be drawn from all fields of life. But these two will suffice to demonstrate the truth with which I am here concerned. It is that, the idea having given birth to the organization, the organization develops a self-interest which has no connection with, and becomes inimical to, the idea with which it began. Now, the thing which permits this process of diversion to take place, so that the organization comes to stand for the opposite of the idea which originally inspired it, is the tendency in men and women to become Prisoners of the Organization, instead of being Servants of the Spirit. In this tendency there are many elements. There is a sense in which you cannot run an organization without becoming its prisoner. Organization has its own necessities, in the interests of which the original idea has to be somewhat qualified. As soon as the idea passes from the unmanifested and embodies itself in the actual, it begins to be invaded by what the poet called "the world's slow stain." In this there need be no conscious infidelity on the part of the leaders. Better, they may well argue, that the great idea should be only partly manifested than that it should remain merely an idea *in vacuo*. Better half the ideal loaf than no bread at all.

Next, the wider the area to which the idea is introduced, the larger the circle of men and women to whom it is propagated through the organization, the more it must be "stepped down" for propaganda purposes. The idea which gives birth to a party which wants to establish the cooperative commonwealth must be translated into practical proposals, such as the eight-hour day, the five-day week and what not, if it is to attract a mass backing. And so the organization becomes less the vehicle of the idea than a channel through which particular interests must be served. The service of such particular interests attracts the backing of other organized bodies more interested in the limited objectives which the organization has now adopted than in the great idea itself. And the pressure of such bodies is felt by the organization, with the result that the idea tends to retreat into the background in favor of less ambitious objectives. In this world the Devil walks, and it is necessary sometimes to hold a candle to the Devil.

Another element is this. Prophets always stand a good chance of being bumped off. This chance is increased if they come down from the hills into the marketplace, and still further increased if they come down unarmed. Prophets should only go unarmed into the marketplace if they think that their work is done, and are prepared to depart hence. Some prophets take to arms. Even where the original prophet does not, his disciples may do so. The organization which they build will almost certainly do so. The Devil must be fought with the Devil's weapons. This is argumentatively sound but practically disastrous. For it means that the servants of God, the disciples of the idea, tend to descend to the Devil's level. As the organization grows, it deteriorates. Its leaders are not the men they were.

Among the rank and file many things combine to keep them in the organization, even when they become uneasily conscious that there is a dawning, and even a yawning, gap between organization and idea. First there is the force of inertia. It is easier not to resign than to resign. Drift is easier than decision. Next there is the factor of personal humility, the tendency to assume that, difficult as the thing seems, the leaders, after all, probably know best. Next there is the factor of sentiment. All of us tend to project onto the organization of which we are members the virtues we would like it to have, and to be blind to its defects. And, finally, men are gregarious creatures and dislike falling out of the ranks away from the comrades of years. Gradually the organization changes. As it changes it attracts new elements which approve the change. Not because of conscious calculation, which comes much later, when the idea has been deserted, but because organization develops its own logic, its own *raison d'être*, and because men tend to become the prisoners of the organization, the organization can finish up by standing for the precise opposite of the idea which called it into being.

What is the moral to be drawn from all this? One moral, it would not be wholly facetious to suggest, might be that the first rule for any organization should be a rule providing for its dissolution within a limited period of time. "This organization shall be dissolved not later than . . . ." But the deeper moral is concerned with our attitude to organization as such. The moral is that, even when we are members of an organization, our attitude to it should be one of partial detachment. We must be above it even while we are in it. We should join it in the knowledge that there we may have no abiding place. We should be weekly tenants; not long-lease-holders. We should accept no such commitments as would prevent our leaving it when circumstances make this necessary. We should reckon on being in almost perpetual rebellion within it. Above all, we should regard all loyalties to organization as tentative and provisional. The whole concept of "my party, right or wrong," "my union, right or wrong," "my church, right or wrong" should be utterly alien to our thinking.

We must be Servants of the Spirit, not Prisoners of the Organization. We must keep in touch with the sources of life, not lose ourselves in its temporary vehicles. And whenever the demand of the spirit, the categorical imperatives of the soul, conflict with the demands of the organization, it is all contained in one of the legendary sayings of Jesus, which bears all the marks of authenticity:

> This world is a bridge. Ye shall pass over it. But ye shall build no houses upon it.

Bivouacs. Yes! Tents. Maybe! Houses. No!

IMAGES IN THE LONELY CROWD

James A. Dyal

A psychology professor punctures the illusions of the person who seeks group approval so completely that he loses sight of his identity.

THERAPIST: Perhaps we can begin by your telling me why you are here.

PATIENT: I really don't know why I'm here. I'm not having a nervous breakdown or anything—I doubt if there is anything wrong, I feel normal enough most of the time. I'm a regular guy—just like anyone else, but sometimes I'm not sure what is wrong, but I just don't seem to be getting as much out of life as I should—sometimes I just go into a slump and can't do anything—you see, I'm an artist, and sometimes I just freeze up and can't do anything for weeks —and when I feel myself not being able to do anything creative, I tighten up even further and get more anxious—and that's the phase I'm in now.—I was hoping that you could give me a tranquilizer or something, and make me feel better. I'm sure you've seen problems like this before, and maybe you can tell me what I'm doing wrong—if you'll just tell me what I'm doing wrong, I'll certainly try to change.

THERAPIST: As you see it, you're not sure there is a problem at all, but you do find yourself being anxious and unable to paint, and you'd like me to take away your anxiety and show what you're doing wrong.

PATIENT: Yes, I guess that's it. You know, another thing that bothers me is that sometimes I just don't care about my work. It's funny, I'm anxious, but I just don't care, too—this was especially true when I worked for that department store as a commercial artist. The head of the department was a businessman type instead of an artist—his only concern was whether or not it would sell. He always used to say, "I don't care if it's good art, I want it to grab people's attention and sell merchandise." He was a real bastard—wouldn't let you think for yourself—it had to be his way. You know, I really tried at that job at first, but finally I just got the "I don't give a damn" attitude. It was about this time that I started drinking quite a bit. I got to the point where I just didn't have much control over it—well, in fact, I had no control—but I'm a little better, I joined A.A., and that has helped. I feel a part of this group and I think they are really concerned about me and I've learned to help other people. But I'm not over the hump yet, I still don't trust my control. Another thing that bothers me—before I went to college I was a pretty introverted person, I used to really enjoy just spending time by myself—you know, like a solitude of a long walk in the woods, just listening to the sounds, the birds, rustling leaves, just feeling the cool earth—just thinking and feeling. I really missed that in college, there it was so frantic. But not at first, at first I was pretty much to myself, then I got on this kick of trying to get other people to like me. I got into so many activities—they were all worthwhile, I guess, but I felt so frantic and fragmented at times. But I'll have to admit that I became pretty smooth socially, I'm usually the life of the party. Yet, sometimes I feel that I'm such a phoney—like I'm putting on a mask for other people to see—you know, sometimes I find myself arguing against things that I really believe, just because I am sensitive to what other people expect of me—. I just don't stand up for my own convictions until I'm not sure I have any feelings or thoughts that are my own—I seem to be constantly criticizing myself—and yet, I don't know my real self at all—

You know, I had a dream the other night. I was at this cocktail party—it was at this really sumptuous home, everything was elegant, and I was very smooth and agreeable— just like everyone else—we were all very sociable—and suddenly, the scene changed—the sounds of the party faded into the sounds of a stream near my special place when I was a boy—and then the scene shifted back to the party, and the walls had turned to mirrors, and looking in the mirror we saw ourselves, and there was nothing there—we were transparent, there was no substance in us—our faces were all alike—we were interchangeable—and I had this terrible feeling of loneliness and foreignness, I reached out for my friends, and they for me, but we couldn't touch—we were strangers to each other—we tried to escape but there was no way out.—I woke up in a cold sweat, sick to my stomach and with a terrible feeling of having lost something very important—and the sickening fear that I would never find it again—it was a terribly frightening dream—but it did have one good effect—as soon as I woke up I went to my sketch pad and tried to draw that last scene—I'm going to develop that sketch into something really good and I already have a name for it. I'll call it "Images in the Lonely Crowd."

You have just heard portions of psychodiagnostic interview with Mr. West Mann. Many of the important symptoms of his sickness are clear: he is anxious, he is apathetic, he longs for a time when he was more at one with himself, when he was less conflicted and fragmented. He has a feeling of a loss of control over his own life. His feelings and thoughts seem to be isolated from each other; he is split and caught; he wants a way out, but finds no exit.

Although the symptoms are clear, the diagnosis and treatment are obscure. His is a difficult case, and we shall need to consult with many specialists in order to make sense of his sickness.

Since the causes are many and diverse, no one could hope to be very knowledgeable in more than a few of the areas. I consider it my task to point to some of the directions; to ask some of the right questions, to raise some of the important issues, but certainly not to provide any answers. I'm going to begin with chemical and biological forces which serve to limit us or to free us.

The biochemists have begun to build compounds whose ultimate effect on mankind may be far greater than the product of the nuclear physicists. As a result of their efforts, we have already provided the psychiatrists with a vast arsenal of drugs for the control of human behavior. We have the major tranquilizers such as Chlorpromazine and other phenothiazine derivatives, which are effective in controlling the symptoms of schizophrenia and other psychoses. We have minor tranquilizers, including such meprobamate compounds as Equanil and Miltown, which are effective in relieving anxiety.

We have stimulant drugs such as amphetamine, which make you feel good, like everything is going well, reduce your fatigue and, thus, help to overcome tiredness and apathy, help you to be someone else. We have monoamine oxidase inhibitors, which have long-term antidepressant effects. We have drugs which mimic psychotic reactions such as LSD-25 and Ditran—or perhaps you would like to have a religious experience—you can get Christ in a capsule in the form of psilocybin. Psychiatrists are using these drugs to control the mind *now*.

> Most of the available evidence concerning the ability of drugs to control the mind or to control behavior comes from exactly this clinical use. The physician usually does not worry too much about the social goodness or badness of controlling behavior, since many patients come to him asking that their behavior, feelings, or thoughts be controlled. Other patients, of course, are brought to him by relatives or by society because their behavior is such that others feel it needs control.

Drugs can be used to establish "good" behavior and abolish "bad" behavior. The scientist tends to feel that it is not his place to say how laboratory knowledge will be used—and since the physician is too busy treating patients and fighting Medicare to worry about the social consequences of his treatments, who is to decide what is good or bad behavior? What government agency will decide what are good or bad thoughts? If we begin to look for biological determinants of Mann's behavior, we need to start at the beginning—at conception—and here again the biochemists and geneticists are showing us how our structure is so completely dependent on the unique messages for development that are coded in DNA molecules—the specific patterns of structure are unique—the specific person is unique from conception—yet he is already molded by the code of DNA with the aid of chemical messengers of RNA. I, for one, am thankful for this molding and complete determination of our structure. Who wants seven fingers on one hand and three on the other? I prefer to have reasonably stereotyped ears!

To look a step further, structure is intimately tied to function, and it appears that a case can be made for even complex behavior such as intellectual functioning and general temperament to be determined in part by genetics. It is not an extravagant generalization to say that *we are to a large extent what our genes make us.*

Furthermore, it appears that we have a long tradition behind us which controls us in most subtle ways. As he appears at birth, before the cultural conditioning gets underway, the human child is a wild animal, the product of millions of years of evolution. Is this product basically a creator or a destroyer? On the basis of anthropological researches of Professor Raymond Dart, Robert Ardrey argues in *African Genesis* that man is descended from Cain; "Man is a predator whose natural instinct is to kill with a weapon." It is a cosmic irony that an instinct for safeguarding the survival of the species has "become in *Homo sapiens* a prime mover towards destruction." Is the exquisite complexity of the DNA helix to end in a hydrogen thermonuclear reaction? Or, perhaps the biochemists will save us after all, by learning to rearrange our molecules so that hostility and self-destruction are no longer a potential in the genetic package. It may not occur in 1984, and it may occur too late—or it may occur too soon.

I should also mention that biochemists, biologists, and psychopharmacologists are beginning to pin down much more precisely the ways in which motivation, emotion, and learning depend on stimulation of neural centers in the hypothalamus, or in the septal area of the brain. How immediate situational aggression or long-term chronic aggression may depend on the proportion of adrenalin or noradrenalin secreted by the adrenal medulla. High adrenalin produces fear and anxiety and a tendency to withdraw or flee; high noradrenalin produces anger and attack. Furthermore, the importance of *genetic* factors here is tentatively suggested by the fact that analysis of the adrenals of lions shows a predominance of noradrenalin while that of rabbits shows a predominance of adrenalin. *It is not too much to say that we are in large part what our glands make us.*

Having considered at least some highpoints of biological and biochemical determination I want now to move to an examination of the multiplicity of forces outside the individual which push or pull him in one direction or another. Here, of course, we have the whole set of sociocultural processes. I certainly avow the potential dehumanizing effects of mass society, in education, in communications, in politics, and in economics. Yet, I must confess from the outset that I have been concerned with the degree to which such considerations have become so commonplace to you as to now be a matter of clichés. And thus you are no longer sensitive to the commonplace.

The dilemma of man in the mid-twentieth century is seldom whether to fight an obvious tyranny or to succumb; it is rather to be able to identify the tyranny or to know when we have succumbed. The basic question is not now and never has been "to conform or not to conform," the question is to what do we conform and to what end? The symptoms of conformity which are often pointed to—such as mass housing, mass production, mass marketing, as a common taste in things which permeates all of Western communities—do not really concern me. I'm not really disturbed by the fact that a couple of years ago every American female from six to sixty had exactly the same hairdo, and that this was determined by the hairdressers of Jacqueline Kennedy, or that all of our men wear Ivy League suits—here I believe like the ancient Stoics, who felt that one should conform to custom where nothing important was at stake merely on the basis of the least effort. Conformity to mass culture is in many ways less disconcerting than conformity in our small face-to-face groups. The myth of the mass man to which we should conform is important only to the extent that we permit it to restrict our freedom or to set our goals in our everyday relations. Having said this, the problem is to know when it is doing so. The subtlety of the discriminations which we must make and their cultural importance is discussed by William Whyte in *The Organization Man* when he says:

> There are only a few times in organization life when [man] can wrench his destiny into his own hands—and if he does not fight then, he will make a surrender that will later mock him. But when is that time? Will he know the time when he sees it? By what standards is he to judge? He does feel an obligation to the group; he does sense moral restraints on his free will. If he goes against the group, is he being courageous or stubborn? Helpful or selfish? Is he, as he so often wonders, right after all? If he suppresses his own ideas, if he doesn't respond and a controversial point doesn't get debated,

were these acts of group cooperation or individual surrender? Too often, even the ability to ask such questions is surrendered, yet, it is in the resolution of a multitude of such dilemmas . . . that the real issue of individualism lies today.

In *The Organization Man* we see three themes which are an integral part of what Mr. Whyte calls the "Twentieth-Century Social Ethic" which has superceded the Protestant ethic. The first of those is scientism, which is the implicit assumption that eventually all human problems will give way to scientific solutions. That the procedure and assumptions which have worked well for physics will eventually yield an exact science of man—and that much scientific knowledge is already available and is to be applied by social engineers whose good will is overpowering and without question. The Machiavellian hell of the twenty-first century is not likely to be engineered by "Big Brother's bad henchmen"; but by a mild-looking group of therapists who, like the Grand Inquisitor, would be doing what they did to help you. Specifically, they will engineer a society in which you can belong. In which you can savor the security of total integration into the Group (with a big G). Of course, in order to belong you must *adjust* yourself to the group rather than vice versa. "The rock of salvation is the group and maladjustment is disagreement with it."

The Good Society will "be a society unified and purged of conflict." Although I do not encourage conflict for the sake of conflict, it is to my way of thinking a powerful stimulus to creative action, and I am reluctant to see conflict discouraged. The present period of racial conflict and civil disobedience is much to be preferred to a status quo of injustice and limitation of freedom. The Negro finally insists on economic, political, and educational freedom now—on the other hand, psychological freedom cannot be won in a picket line or a fifty-mile march.

The themes of scientism and belongingness merge into the theme of togetherness, in which the false underlying assumption is that the group is superior to the individual. Witness the recent emphasis on brainstorming as the key to creative thinking. Furthermore, the ultimate aim of the group-dynamics people is to achieve agreement, the particular solution is less important than the fact that everybody feels good about it. This unreasonable exalting of the "we" feeling makes it more difficult to achieve an "I" feeling. The antagonism to the individual personality which is inherent in the social ethic is nicely illustrated by the device developed by the Harwald Company, called a Group Thinkometer. "The Group Thinkometer is an electric meter the dial of which is graduated in degrees of interest. Feeding into it are ten remote-control switches which can be distributed around," or preferably under a conference table. By pressing the switch, each person can indicate disapproval of an idea which is being proposed by someone else, thus one can veto a colleague's idea without his knowing who did it. The Harwald Company proudly suggests that their device has eliminated the personality factor almost entirely. Although it is probably true that most group-relations people would shun this device, it does seem to be a symbolic fruit of the social-ethic.

Clark Kerr, former Chancellor of the University of California at Berkeley, feels that there is so much danger in groupism that we should enter into group allegiances only tentatively. He says:

> The danger is not that loyalties are divided today but that they may be undivided tomorrow.... I would urge each individual to avoid total involvement in any organization; to seek to whatever extent lies within his power to limit each group to the minimum control necessary for performance of essential functions to struggle against the effort to absorb; to lend his energies to many organizations and give himself completely to none; to teach children, in the home and in the school, "to be laws to themselves and to depend on themselves," as Walt Whitman urged us many years ago— for that is the well source of the independent spirit.

In order to be a successful follower of the social ethic, Western man must be able to be sensitive to the expectations of others, not because he is interested in others, but because he must use them to tell him what to say, what to think and feel; who to be. David Reisman in *The Lonely Crowd* describes the typical American man as other-directed—

> a sort of "radar man" who lives as though he wore a receiving set on his head in order to get signals from

everyone else as to what he should believe and how he should behave. He is sensitive to social situations in the sense of wanting to do what is expected, to conform, to avoid ideas or behaviors that might be disapproved. He is dependent on society in much the same way that a child is dependent on his parents.

A similar view appears in Erich Fromm's discussion of the marketing orientation as typical of Western man. All transactions with other people or things are viewed in the mode of the fundamental relation between buyer and seller. Even in his closest relationships, such as in love relations, the other person is valued in terms of desirability on the appearance and personality markets; and each person enters into the marriage contract with an exchange of personality packages with a hope for a fair bargain.

I view Fromm's concept of marketing orientation as a subspecies of a more general discription of Western culture which is in great contrast with Eastern culture; namely our tendency to be *product*-oriented rather than *process*-oriented. We exalt the end of our efforts and value little the process whereby we attain the goals—and the goals themselves are relatively static, being enmeshed so completely in the definition of a good man as an economically successful man who is able to acquire things.

This product orientation pervades every facet of our culture, it manifests itself in education as an emphasis on the practical; for example, the most popular stereotype of the scientist really describes the technician or inventor, who is the applier of science. Even among our liberal-arts undergraduates it is subtly represented in the disparagement of pure research, which has no immediately obvious consequences. It is my feeling that one of the major causes of a lack of involvement of many liberal-arts majors in their studies is an unrecognized guilt feeling about not doing something that has an obvious payoff in the marketplace. An attitude which is all too often reinforced by parents who are also victims of the marketing orientation. Knowing for the sake of knowing—the richness, excitation, frustration, exaltation of the knowing process is sacrificed to the flatness of the educational product—a grade and a degree. The American theme is knowing for the sake of doing, and doing for the sake of acquiring, and acquiring because our possessions provide tangible testimony to others and especially to ourselves of our success in the marketplace—they reassure us that we are good people. *The New York Times* once printed a news item under the heading "B.Sc. & Ph.D.—$40,000," pointing to the additional income which a Ph.D. degree in industry would attain over his lifetime. This interesting socio-economic datum says that knowledge is a good product to possess because it pays off in the marketplace.

Fromm points out "how drastically commercial categories have entered even religious thinking" by quoting the following passage from an article by Bishop Sheen on the birth of Christ. Sheen says:

> Our reason tells us that if anyone of the claimants for the role of God's son came from God, the least that God could do to support His Representative's claim would be to preannounce His coming. [After all, even] automobile manufacturers tell us when to expect a new model.

Or a more extreme statement by Billy Graham, "I am selling the greatest product in the world; why shouldn't it be promoted as well as soap?" Or another rather exceptional example comes from the advice given by the Protestant Council of New York City to speakers on radio and televison programs. I quote:

> Subject matter should project love, joy, courage, hope, faith, trust in God, and good will. Generally avoid condemnation, criticism, controversy. In a very real sense we are "selling" religion, the good news of the Gospel. Therefore, admonitions and training of Christians on cross-bearing, forsaking all else, sacrifices, and service usually cause the average listener to turn the dial. . . . As apostles, can we not extend an invitation, in effect: "Come and enjoy our privileges, meet good friends, see what God can do for you."

In economics the competition inherent in capitalism has provided us with an affluent society which may provide individuals with increased personal freedom—it is as difficult to fault the abolition of poverty as it is to object to striking the chains from slaves. Yet, for the vast middle class of

America, economic affluence may provide the very chains that bind them in continual slavery to things and the immediate satisfaction of all desires. The hucksters of television ask us to be a part of the smoothly functioning affluent group—join the *sociables* and drink Pepsi—and, of course, we all know that Spring is the most *desirable* cigarette that we can smoke. The Tube projects before us a true-to-life version of Huxley's *Brave New World* in which the dominant ethic is to have fun. "Never put off till tomorrow the fun you can have today." Having fun consists in the satisfaction of "taking in" commodities. ". . . sights, food, drinks, cigarettes, people, lectures, movies, books—all are consumed, swallowed." As Fromm puts it,

> The world is one great object for our appetite, a big apple, a big bottle, a big breast; we are the sucklers, the eternally expectant ones, the hopeful ones—and the eternally disappointed ones. Our character is geared to exchange and to receive, to barter and to consume; everything, spiritual as well as material objects, become an object of exchange and of consumption.

As you have seen, the sociocultural character analysis which I have pieced together reflects primarily the views of William Whyte, David Reisman, and Erich Fromm, and it is their diagnosis of Western man in the 1950s. To what extent is it still a valid description for the 1960s? Have these conformity rebels had sufficient influence in our society, so as to initiate a counterrevolution? No doubt, they have had some effect, but hasn't their influence been blunted and encapsulated by intellectualism about the diagnosis itself? Have we protected ourselves from the caustic commentaries of the 1950s by turning them into the clichés of the 1960s?

As much as I would like to continue to center on modern man from a sociocultural perspective, I must leave time for the diagnostic evaluations of the psychologist, the theologian, and the philosopher.

The psychologist occupies the broad domain from psychopharmacology and psychobiology, on the one hand, to social psychology, on the other. He is sensitive to the multiplicity of genetic, biological, and sociocultural factors which restrict man's freedom and determine his behavior. Most psychological images of man accept and contribute heavily to the conception of man as essentially unfree. Freudian psychology, for example, tells us how we are controlled by early experience and unconscious inner impulses over which we have no control. Another alienating force within psychology has been the cult of adjustment. The force of this view has been for the psychologist to capitulate to sociocultural norms in his definition of normality. It is the task of the parents to facilitate the child's adjustment to society, with little mention of the possibility of changing society. Such a passive model of man has to be stretched beyond credibility in order to understand a man like the late Martin Luther King. The bulk of our psychological images of man view him as determined

> by his heredity, his intelligence, his personality type, perhaps even his tendency toward mental aberration. He is above all the product of his conditioning—the inevitable result of the fortuitous events which have shaped his behavior. Many of our most astute behavioral scientists agree that this process of conditioning, of shaping up the individual's behavior, will not much longer be left to chance, but will be planned. Certainly the behavioral sciences are developing a technology which will enable us to control the individual's behavior to a degree which at the present moment would seem fantastic.

Thus, the two major contemporary themes in psychology—behaviorism and Freudianism—have contributed to the dehumanization and loss of identity of man. Yet, in spite of these overwhelming forces which seek to stamp out freedom, the need for identity is strong. In fact, everyone succeeds in forming some unique emotional and rational interpretation of himself in relation to the world and thus establishes some sort of an identity. The identity crisis is especially crucial during the periods of adolescence and early adulthood—yet, for the truly *healthy* person, the definition of self continues throughout his life. The neurotic, on the other hand, tends to accept a premature solution to his identity crisis. This results in an immature safety-oriented person who cannot tolerate feelings of normal anxiety and motivational or cultural conflicts. The safety-oriented person identifies himself with those sources of strength and power around him. He can feel secure by acquiring *things;* and he identifies himself with what he possesses. He can also avoid further explorations of himself by identifying himself with the group. Through group status and role identifications a certain sense of identity is attained. Nation, religion, or occupation serve as thought quenchers and we accept a cliché as ourselves. "I am an American," "I am a Protestant," "I am a college professor," "I am a husband," "I am a father," and on and on—but there is a lot more to me than any of my roles in singularity or in summation. The person who refuses to recognize this stops short of identifying himself with his highest potential.

The neurotic—and I should say that what I mean by neurotic behavior is self-defeating behavior—and thus, you should translate the phrase "the neurotic" to mean "each of us to the extent that we are neurotic"— the neurotic is most characterized by highly defensive behavior. He feels that he must defend himself against his inner impulses. He does so by denial and distortion of these impulses. He denies or distorts his hostile impulses. He refuses to accept himself in his creatureliness. He may project his unacceptable impulses out onto others and perceive the world as a frightening place which is out to get him. Of course, his perception of the world as hostile makes him even more threatened and defensive and a vicious circle, self-fulfilling prophecy is generated. In our neurosis we are threatened by others who are seen as more powerful, more intelligent, more loving, or more adept at interpersonal relations than we are. We often tend to reduce our anxiety about our relations to others by sacrificing ourselves to the other person or to the group— by complete submission to the group requirements—by making our thoughts and desires fit only those which are approved by our group, we reduce our fear of being rejected by the group. Our motto here seems to be—*You won't hurt me if you see how much I need you.* Or we may resolve our conflict with the group by trying to make ourselves independent of the group. We may define ourselves outside of the group and avoid dependence on the group by amassing political or economic power. Success in the marketplace not only reassures us that we are basically worthy but also permits us to be less manipulated by other people. Regardless of the particular form the behavior may take, the underlying psychodynamic motto seems to be: *You can't hurt me because I don't need you.*

In our caughtness—in our neurosis—we also fear to recognize our limitations. We prefer to rationalize, blame others and explain away our short comings. Too often we set for ourselves impossible goals and continue to castigate ourselves for falling short of them. In fact, Karen Horney, an eminent psychoanalyst, maintains that a conflict between a neurotically overidealized self-concept and the individual's actual self is the basis of all neurosis. Man *cannot* actualize his desire for omnipotence; thus, from the point of view of psychology, the influence of Christianity in setting Christ as a model for human behavior can have consequences which are tyrannical and self-destructive. This dilemma is a topic of concern for the theologian, David Roberts, in his book *Psychotherapy and a Christian View of Man*. If divine love, completely unconditional love,

> is taken as the norm for human life, then insofar as man falls short of it he is sinful. . . . Yet because Christ is regarded as the only man who ever has or even could fulfill this ideal, it seems unreasonable that man should be condemned for not fulfilling Christ in themselves. . . . The central question which thus emerges has to do with the effectiveness of ideal standards. . . . The *static* view assumes that ethical and religious progress is most effectively promoted by holding before the eyes of men a vision of perfection which will keep them perpetually ashamed of themselves. . . . This doctrine scolds them for being replicas of Christ and then scolds them if they believe that they could be.

Such a view is called "static" because it emphasizes the activity of God in granting grace, and deemphasizes man's *continuing* necessity to act to save himself. It tends to foster a view of the relationships between man and God as unchanging and to promote a tendency for the individual to regard *himself* as an unchanging being.

The psychological consequences of this static view of salvation are many: One of them is *hypocrisy;* the condition of gross disparity between the individual's professional beliefs and his behavior.

> His action and inward attitudes say more eloquently than words ever can that there is no mutually enriched

interplay between the norm he assents to and policies he lives by. Insofar as a man is aware of such hypocrisy, either he may be deeply troubled by his failure or he may find ways of remaining fairly jaunty about it. But in both instances the situation perpetuates conflict.

In the first instance he remains caught in an unresolved despair, a despair which cuts away his vitality and generates a chronic anxiety against which he must spend most of his life defending. In the second instance he may react in two opposite ways to try to resolve the conflict. He may repudiate himself and put his wicked self aside. Such an affirmation often results in the expression of self-hatred and hatred for mankind under the guise of Christian piety. The opposite extreme resolution of the conflict is to reject the ideal and initiate a defiant attack upon Christianity such as represented by Nietzsche.

In my opinion, these extreme attempts to resolve the conflict by either repudiating man or repudiating God do not resolve the conflict but merely perpetuate the despair. More and more I see that there is a close parallel between the psychological concept of neurosis and the theological concept of sin. We should remember that the notion of divine judgment may very well refer to "those conditions in man's soul and his society which keep him estranged from love; and as we look at the world we may feel that this is punishment enough." "Hell is still very much with us in those states of being which we call neurosis and psychosis." It may be as one psychiatrist maintains:

> The notion of mental illness has outlived whatever usefulness it might have had and now functions merely as a convenient myth . . . whose function is to disguise and thus render more palatable the bitter pill of moral conflicts in human relations.

We can describe the neurotic-sinful person as one who is bound by infantile emotions, whose perceptions of present situations are distorted by carryovers from previous human relationships which have failed to provide the needed warmth and assurance of love. By describing him as bound to the past we imply that his freedom of choice is considerably constricted; that his behavior is heavily determined by unconscious factors beyond his control.

The conception of psychological and theological issues which I have been proposing is quite consonant with many facets of the philosophy of Existentialism. It seems appropriate to conclude my ruminations with the philosophical since it has been the time-honored prerogative of the Philosopher to have the last word.

The Existentialist sees Western man as estranged in a fourfold manner. He is alienated from nature, from himself, from others, and from God. This term "alienation" has become so common a description that I felt that I needed to go back to Webster so that we might have some common foundation. I found it to have these synonyms: foreign, distant, unsympathetic, remote, and irrelevant. With man's increased urbanization the rhythmic pulse of nature becomes foreign and irrelevant. Man seldom has an extended opportunity to find himself in awe of nature and to place himself in relation to the universe—past, present, and future. He cannot affirm the words of Pascal:

> When I consider the brief span of life, swallowed up in an eternity past and to come, the little space which I occupy, lost in the immensity of space of which I know nothing and which knows nothing of me, I am terrified and I am astonished that I am here rather than there.

We are alienated from ourselves because we abstract ourselves from our feelings. We force our conceptions of ourselves into relatively static, unchanging molds rather than seeing ourselves as a process of becoming. Existentialism thus doesn't make much sense to people who have settled back into a rigid, complacent and unyielding view of themselves and other people. It does appeal "to people who are beginning to wonder about themselves, and to see existence as full of questions."

It is this search for meaning in oneself which is the basic characteristic and goal of an existential theory of man. Soren Kierkegaard, who may be considered to be the modern founder of the existentialist movement, had as his primary aim in life to tear people away from their commonplace lives and to force them to be really conscious of self—to

continually probe and search for an answer to the question—
"What sort of being am I?" All other questions are subordinate—all other questions are merely instrumental in answering this big question. Even the questions and procedures of science are useful only to the extent that they help people to answer this question. In fact, it is the view of existentialism that science and the scientific attitude is often one of the very things which keep man from understanding himself. That is, science defines man and the universe in terms of generalizations, abstractions, or essences and places little emphasis on the process of experiencing in the unique individual. Even psychology has, for the most part, patterned itself after the God-science, physics, that is, its emphasis is on laws which hold for groups of people but which tell us very little about a specific, existing individual. Science tends to deaden its subject matter to make it static so that it is easier to conceptualize or think about and this very fact forces it to have little to say about what it means to exist or to be.

Man is alienated from himself to the degree that he refuses to choose to recognize his own limitations, his primary limitation being his own contingency—the realization that there is nothing necessary about one's existence—that man may cease to exist at anytime. However, the real force of man's predicament becomes existentially meaningful to a person when that person avoids thinking of death in general terms and refers it to himself—that is, the important thing is not the abstraction that all men are mortal, but the fact that I am mortal—that I will die—that there is a specific moment in the future when I will cease to exist.

Thus, as Kierkegaard has put it, the individual "achieves full recognition of himself through being saddled with a tragic sense of life and death." But it is too often the case that this tragedy is too hard for a person to bear and he thus, time after time, chooses to forget or avoid his contingency. Because the average person is afraid to realize that he is *unique and alone,* he learns many ways to avoid confronting himself by the use of all the mechanisms of adjustment and defense which the psychologists have discovered. We may narcoticize or deaden ourselves either literally through alcohol, heroin, or Equanil, or psychologically by repressing and distorting our feelings or engaging in a flurry of activity, or in choosing to be trivial. Instead of choosing to be ourselves, we often choose to be someone other than ourselves. One way that we do this is by identifying ourselves completely with our social roles and with our façades or false fronts.

Another prevalent way of behaving nonexistentially is to choose not to be ourselves through conformity—to let one's self become swallowed up in the generalized man of common responses and attitudes. The person comes to feel that it is dangerous to be different and, although he temporarily escapes the anxiety of nonbeing in this way, he pays the awful price of loss of his own awareness, his potentialities and whatever characterizes him as a unique and original being. In striving to conform man loses himself, and thus paradoxically feels alienated from others. The existentialist, in pointing to man's alienation from others, will applaud Erich Fromm when he says,

> Human relations are essentially those of alienated automatons, each basing his security on staying close to the herd, and not being different in thought, feeling, or action. While everybody tries to be as close as possible to the rest, everybody remains utterly alone, pervaded by the deep sense of insecurity, anxiety and guilt which always result when human separateness cannot be overcome. Our civilization offers many palliatives which help people to be consciously unaware of their most fundamental human desires, of the longing for transcendence and unity. Inasmuch as the routine alone does not succeed in this, man overcomes his unconscious despair by the routine of amusement, the passive consumption of sounds and sights offered by the amusement industry; furthermore, by the satisfaction of buying ever new things, and soon exchanging them for others. Modern man is actually close to the picture Huxley describes in his *Brave New World:* well fed, well clad, satisfied sexually, yet without self, without any except the most superficial contact with his fellowmen.

Mr. West Mann is alienated from God because he treats people as things, and worships things as idols. In Old Testament usage the term "alienation" was synonymous with idolatry. In idolatry man worships a partial quality of himself, whereas in monotheostic religions God as a wholeness is unrecognizable, undefinable, and ineffable. God is not a "thing" but Christians regress to idolatry by their "grand old man in the sky" theology.

> Man projects his power of love and of reason unto God: he does not feel them any more as his own powers, and then he prays to God to give him back some of what . . . he has projected onto God.

Any religious view which places responsibility for man's freedom and salvation exclusively on the Grace of God where man has no responsibility is from this existentialist view idolatrous. Man's responsibility for himself is emphasized both by Kierkegaard, a Christian existentialist, and by Sartre, an atheist.

Kierkegaard puts it this way—

> One cannot know what it is to be a Christian until he knows what it is to exist. . . . The Christian heroism is to venture wholly to be oneself as an individual, this definite man, alone before the face of God, alone in this tremendous exertion and this tremendous responsibility.

Sartre, on the other hand, cannot stomach any appeal to an authority beyond the individual's own authority. He is disgusted to the point of nausea by the reliance which people place on values set up by others, including religion, and for which the individual takes no personal responsibility.

Thus, whether we are dealing with the Christian or the atheistic brands of Existentialism, the first goal and the primary result of an existential approach to life is to make a person aware of what he is and to make the full responsibility of his existence dependent on him. To the extent that he is not willing to confront himself as he really is, in all of his anxiety, hostility, love, and fear, then he progressively loses himself and psychologically becomes more and more rigid, less and less free to control his own destiny.

E. T. HALL AND THE HUMAN SPACE BUBBLE

William Kloman

An anthropologist probes the stresses caused by urban crowding in an effort to make cities fit for human habitation.

"New York City may already be dead. We may not be able to bring it back. And if we lose New York, it could be the death of the nation."

The speaker was an anthropologist named Edward T. Hall; his audience, a select gathering of scientists, city planners, architects, and environmental experts at the Smithsonian Institution. A man who has made a career of probing the communications blocks that exist between cultures, Hall has developed ideas about men's varying needs for space that could have important implications for the future of our urban centers. Appointed to a professorship in the study of intersocietal communications at Northwestern University, he is one of a growing number of scientists seeking ways of making our cities fit for human habitation.

Hall is not a man who indulges in sensationalism for its own sake. His comments on New York are based on an organic analogy. As he explains it: "Death occurs when the body stops replacing itself. Any living organism must have the power to regenerate itself automatically. When the city loses its middle class, it can no longer raise enough money to support itself. The city also has to be a safe place to live. When the various segments start destroying each other, you have a disorder analogous to cancer in the body."

The crisis is especially dangerous if, as the noted Greek city planner Constantine Doxiadis suspects, we are rapidly moving toward a time when existing cities will merge into "a continuous system which will cover our countries from one end to the other and over national boundaries to form a universal city." But if we do not soon learn to house and transport populations in a less stressful way and to dispose of waste products without fouling the environment, Hall contends, we may end up with a situation similar to that of a neglected aquarium, which, in a matter of hours, can turn into a stinking mass of lethal sewage. What is imperative is a way of conveying the urgency of the situation to the people responsible for making decisions.

Now fifty-two, Hall has spent much of his life bridging the chasm that too often separates academic anthropologists from practical problems. His concern for the plight of our cities has come as a gradual, if altogether natural, outgrowth of his studies of cultural frictions. It is an involvement that began in the early days of the New Deal when the government sent him to manage a Navajo work camp in Arizona. His predecessor had been unable to interest the Indians in working on the irrigation dams that the government was paying them to build, even though he had carefully explained the benefits to be had from making their land arable. Hall gradually understood that the difference was one of an entire sense of life. Because Navajos had no concept of future time, all the talk about future benefits from irrigation had made no sense to them. What they *did* understand, however, was a bargain. Once Hall put the project in terms the Navajos could grasp—so many hours' work for so much money—the work began.

After World War II, Hall was made responsible for training technicians and Foreign Service officers assigned to overseas posts with the Point Four program. He taught them, for instance, that Arabs consider it a friendly gesture to "bathe you in their breath" while they talk. Americans, answering *their* culturally learned response to avoid olfactory involvement, would often insult well-meaning Arabs by backing away.

To explore such problems, Hall has had to create a new scientific discipline, which, because it emphasizes culture-based variations in the handling of space, he calls "proxemics." In the 1930s, the linguistic scholar Benjamin Lee Whorf suggested that language, in addition to being a medium for expressing thought, was also a primary instrument in the formation of thought. Thus people who speak different languages will think—and react—in different ways.

Hall agrees, but adds that "the principles laid down by Whorf, in relation to language, apply to the rest of human behavior as well—in fact, to all culture." He rejects the assumption that "when two human beings are subject to the same 'experience,' virtually the same data are being fed to the two central nervous systems and that the two brains record similarly." He cites the example of Americans and Spaniards at a bullfight. "The American experiences the fear that he would have if he were in the ring; the Spaniard, vicariously, the joy in the control the matador exercises over the bull." The difference is cultural. "People of different cultures," he maintains, *"inhabit different sensory worlds."*

In *The Silent Language,* published in 1959, Hall lays the foundation for his contention that the most crucial differences among cultures occur outside normal awareness. The "silent language" of behavior—culturally learned—has a vocabulary, but we are only beginning to understand it. People of various cultures experience such fundamental things as time, space, and hierarchies in different ways. How long do you wait past the appointed hour for a pre-arranged interview? In a Latin country forty-five minutes might not be thought unusual, but an American businessman will begin to feel restive, insulted, and put-upon after twenty minutes.

Communication breakdowns occur even among people speaking the same language. For example, Hall was asked by the Job Corps in Chicago to find out why well-qualified Negro applicants often did so badly when they went for employment interviews. By filming a series of interviews and examining the results with the help of Negro observers, he concluded that a major difficulty arose because whites and Negroes have different ways of communicating the attitude of "paying attention." Middle-class whites customarily punctuate their exchanges with nods of the head and short verbal cues, such as "yes" and "uh-huh." White interviewers, receiving only a fixed stare from Negro interviewees, assumed that the Negroes were either stupid or not paying attention.

By the time he published *The Hidden Dimension* in 1966, Hall had become preoccupied with a specific area of cultural difference—that of the perception of space. It was inevitable that he should become involved with the city, where the problems of crowding and the allocation of space are most pressing. Many of his ideas revolve around the concept of territoriality, which the English ornithologist H. E. Howard first described in 1920. The mechanisms by which organisms lay claim to an area and defend it against members of their own species were further illuminated by Heini P. Hediger, the Zurich zoologist, whose studies of wild animals in the captive state appeared in the 1950s. Drawing on the work of such men, Hall began to apply territoriality to the human species, and in doing so, his central thesis emerged. "One of the most important functions of territoriality," Hall writes, "is proper spacing, which protects against overexploitation of that part of the environment on which a species depends for its living."

Besides food, water, and shelter, Hall says, we need a certain amount of space in which to conduct our daily lives. Each organism, he has written, "no matter how simple or complex, has around it a sacred bubble of space, a bit of mobile territoriality which only a few other organisms are allowed to penetrate and then only for short periods of time." The bubble varies in size, depending on such factors as the emotional state, immediate activity, position in a social hierarchy, and cultural background of the individual. What may be a comfortable living space of a Latin American, who requires a certain amount of physical contact with his fellows, may be unbearably crowded to an Englishman, who requires a somewhat larger bubble of space around him to feel at ease. Similarly, other unspoken needs—for variety, visual beauty, and quiet—differ from one culture to another.

What happens when the bubbles overlap? It is this question that has led Hall to concentrate increasingly on the urban predicament. Tensions caused by lapses of understanding between cultures are heightened by the stressful conditions of the city. But more important, "changes in the bubble caused by outside influences"—the design of a public housing project, for instance—"may force on the occupant the feeling that he has been thrown into aggressive relationships with strangers or has been sealed off and removed from people. If man's bubble is crushed, or dented, or pushed out of shape, he suffers virtually as much damage as though his body were crushed or dented or pushed out of shape. The only difference is that the effects take longer to make themselves evident."

The most ominous aspect of urban crowding is pointed up

by recent discoveries that suggest a physiological density-control factor in certain mammals. The yearly mass suicide of Scandinavian lemmings, the weird death dance of the March hare, and similar self-destructive behavior among a species of rat on some Pacific islands have recently been interpreted as direct results of stress caused by overcrowding. Man may not be immune to this control factor. Even if technology permits us to produce unlimited quantities of food—putting to rest the Malthusian apprehension that population eventually outstrips food supply—there remains the certainty that the supply of terrestrial space, which may be just as vital a factor in the maintenance of life, is a fixed quantity on this globe.

In *The Hidden Dimension* Hall recounts the experiments of an ethologist, John Christian, with Sika deer on James Island in the Chesapeake Bay. Several of the deer had been released on the otherwise unpopulated island in 1916. By 1955 the herd numbered about three hundred, or one deer per acre. Since Sika deer were presumed to require about this much space, Christian began to watch the development of the herd.

In the first three months of 1958 more than half the deer died. The following year the population dropped to about eighty. Examination of the dead animals, most of which were does and young deer, indicated that the cause of death was shock, following severe metabolic disturbance caused by prolonged hyperactivity of the adrenal glands. Since food was in good supply on the island, and since, except for the adrenal disturbance, the animals were in good health, Christian concluded that the massive mortality among the deer was caused simply by the stress of crowding beyond density levels that the deer were able to tolerate.

The stages prior to population collapse have been described by John Calhoun, an ethologist who experimented with domesticated Norway rats. Earlier experiments had indicated the spatial requirements of the rats in the wild state. Between 1958 and 1961 Calhoun permitted the density of a laboratory rat population to reach approximately twice that of the estimated normal healthy maximum. Since he was primarily interested in the long-term effects of stress on the social habits of his subjects, he removed excess infants to prevent total population collapse.

What developed is known as a "behavioral sink." The

normal structure of rat society suffered a severe breakdown. Traditional family groupings were abandoned, and many males lost all sense of sexual discrimination, mounting aged and infant rats or other males. Sadism, in the form of tail-biting, became prevalent. Other rats, unable to compete with hyperactive satyr-rats, lost interest in sex altogether. Courtship and mating customs—a rather rigid routine among Norway rats—were abandoned in favor of promiscuous affairs. Females stopped taking care of their young and let their nests become cluttered. Some animals went abroad only at night, while the others slept.

Certain aggressive aristocrats were able to protect their territories within the pen, and continued to observe the rules of rat society, but the mass of the population, under the stress of crowding, became unruly and neurotic. The constant turmoil of the "sink" resulted in a sharp increase in the death rate, especially among females and the young. Infant mortality rose to 75 percent. Kidneys, livers, and adrenals of dead animals showed signs of adrenal hyperactivity usually associated with extreme stress. Such experiments indicate, Hall says, that "animals regulate their own density as a function of self-preservation."

What all this has to do with human population, crammed into subway cars or stacked up in high-density vertical slums, has not been scientifically demonstrated. Hall would like to see the results of systematic autopsies on humans who have spent their lives in the stressful conditions of the urban crush. Constant invasion of the "space bubbles," he suggests, probably leads to overactive adrenals and increases the likelihood of physiological breakdown due to adrenal shock.

The behavior of the Norway rats raises fascinating speculations. Crimes of violence, sexual deviation, breakdown of family ties, lapse of habits of cleanliness, and many other symptoms of social disorganization in our cities might be traceable to the effects of crowding. We seem far from the mass-death condition of lemmings, but this, by implication, is a possibility if nothing is done to alleviate the stress of urban life, especially among the poor. Hall feels that the vital question raised by these studies is whether man can "learn enough about the relationship between space and human behavior and put his knowledge to work with sufficient speed to save himself from disaster."

Part of our difficulty in easing stress in the cities, Hall

believes, is the natural ambivalence of Americans toward government planning. Europeans, who have lived with the problem of crowding longer than we have, and who have never had the opportunity to waste resources on the scale that Americans are willing to tolerate, tend to accept government control of the use of resources—including space—as natural. Hall cites the London County Council as an example of a planning body with experience, scope, and staff adequate to do the job we often relegate to impotent committees of inadequately trained appointees.

"People think when we're talking about planning we're just dealing with aesthetics," he says. "And most of our people think aesthetics deals with nonessentials. With frills. The fact is that even if our urban problems were only aesthetic problems, they would still be important. Nobody knows what a poem or a painting does, but we know poets and artists are important parts of society. If we were to eliminate all artistic beauty from the environment, we have no idea what the effect would be."

The development of the city can no longer be left to the interplay of chance, personal desire for profit, and political expediency. We live in a world increasingly dominated by our "extensions"—of which the automobile is a perfect example. But Hall warns that man has given little thought to the frightening possibility that, in molding the total world in which he lives—his "biotope"—he "is actually determining *what kind of an organism* he will be." For the moment, we are faced by a question of the quality of life. Eventually, it could be a question of life itself.

Hall feels that "if we had a mechanical model of a city—something that showed how all the different parts work together—we'd be on much firmer ground in dealing with urban problems." A working model of a city could, for instance, let us demonstrate the long-term effects of air pollution in a way far more striking than that of all the outraged newspaper editorials ever written on the subject.

The city, he maintains, is a kind of gigantic teaching machine. The high concentration of information available in the city and the variety of persons attracted to it force the city dweller to learn a great deal about life. "The best way to learn about the city is to go out and look at it," Hall said when I visited him in Chicago recently. "Look at it carefully and ask the right questions." And so we went out to use Chicago as a teaching machine.

A few blocks from Hall's home—a comfortable town house with high ceilings and plenty of space, just west of the lakeside "Gold Coast"—we came upon Carl Sandburg Village. This massive complex of high-rise apartment buildings is a privately owned project underwritten by government funds. It was originally intended for former slum dwellers, but somehow Carl Sandburg Village turned into middle-class "luxury" housing. The project was now about to spread across North Clark Street, requiring the demolition of several old and solid businesses.

We visited one of the places, a hardware store, whose owners, Mr. and Mrs. Fred Ruhling, complained that they were being reimbursed for but a fraction of their store's worth. They hadn't wanted to sell, but the city had exercised its power of eminent domain. Hall explained that the worth of a concern such as the Ruhlings' store could not be measured in terms of money alone. An old family business does more than sell products. People like the Ruhlings can tell you where to find a reliable babysitter or how to contact a physician or what to do if your car breaks down. In the confusing urban milieu a certain number of such "high context" centers must be maintained.

Driving west, past a no man's land of drab storefronts and tangled traffic, we came upon the first of the public, low-income housing projects we were to see. The bustling, self-conscious sophistication of Michigan Avenue, the sin-tinged cow town familiar to tipsy conventioneers, the lush green suburbs of the north—these are only the public aspects of Chicago. To the west and the south an endless chain of depressing, characterless high-rises, plunked down on grassless, treeless plots, sheltered the bulk of the city's population.

On West Division Street the Mother Cabrini–William Greene development houses nearly eighteen thousand people, most of them in buildings of ten to nineteen stories. Although the concentration of humanity in the project's seventy-eight buildings is extremely high—averaging more than two hundred people per each apartment house—their most striking feature is the almost total lack of activity around them. Small, fenced-in rectangles, designated in the inscrutable vocabulary of the housing authorities as "tot lots," stand deserted. It seems that mothers, separated from the playgrounds by sixteen floors and unreliable elevators, are reluctant to send their children out to play.

"The people who have to live in these places don't want trees around," Hall explained, "because they give muggers a place to hide." Public lavatories on the ground floors are ruled out for the same reason. Small children, when unattended, use the elevators as toilets.

The previous day a taxi driver had pointed out the Cabrini project to me. "We build those people nice places like this out of tax money, and they don't take any pride in them." To that extent he was right. Cinderblock walls remain undecorated; concrete floors, uncarpeted. When old tenants move out, the cells are washed down with a garden hose. "It wouldn't take much imagination to fix one of those places up real nice," the driver had said. "The only thing I can figure is that colored people and hillbillies are just different from us. They don't care about nice things."

The housing projects are unappreciated mainly because they are constructed with little attention to the needs of the people who have to live in them. The high rise is a quick answer to a city's embarrassment. "The thing about a slum," Hall said, "is that you can see it. The reason for this particular solution is that it walls off what's behind it. Slums, poor people, dirt and filth—they're not attractive. People don't like to look at them. So you build one of these things and the problem becomes invisible."

The price for making the slum problem invisible is high. Like high-rise office buildings, increased midtown parking facilities, and super-expressways, these buildings permit ever-increasing concentrations of human beings—with results that may be partially reflected in summertime riots and rising crime rates. These developments also destroy the existing community structure. "Our cities have been bombed by urban renewal in as devasting a way and just as effectively as though they had been bombed by an outside enemy," Hall told the Smithsonian symposium. This is allowed to happen, he concludes, because "the members of a dominant ethnic group and class look at the biotope of another group and fail to see its structure. . . . By carelessly destroying entire environments and shifting people around, we wreck the fabric of their social relationships, separate them from friends and relatives and familiar surroundings, and generally destroy everything that gives their life meaning."

For example, Italians and Puerto Ricans tend to center their social lives around the town square. In New York and Chicago they make do with the street. People can chat with friends sitting on the front steps. Children can play stickball and tag within close range of their mothers. By destroying the physical environment that makes social contact easy—by moving these people into high-rise buildings—the whole structure of their interpersonal relationships is altered. They feel trapped and alone.

Besides, Hall says, "We can't accurately measure the psychological effect on small children of growing up in an environment where nothing is permanent. Where there is no tradition. Where nothing has a past." The result could be a neurotic mistrust of their entire environment, contributing to such seemingly unrelated factors as a higher divorce rate or increased suicides.

Hall sees promise in current attempts at "instant re-hab." Rehabilitation of existing structures, which can be accomplished within a few days during which occupants live in hotels, seems a feasible alternative to replacing whole neighborhoods with high-rise prison architecture. When new housing *is* required, however, Hall believes that adequate density can be achieved without resorting to high-rises. He cites the Israeli architect Moshe Safdie's "Habitat 67" in Montreal as an "imaginative, original, and still human" way of handling the problem.

Hall is mystified by the apparent refusal of architects to seek the advice of the people who inhabit their buildings. In seven years of close dealings with architects, he claims, he has "failed to find a single instance of a systematic recording of feedback from users which could later be incorporated in the program or design phase of a new building. All over the United States, rooms have been getting steadily smaller, walls more transparent to sound, views cut off. And what do we know about the consequences? What hard data is there?" Often, Hall says, prizes are awarded for buildings on the basis of two-dimensional representations of structures that have yet to be built and that cannot possibly be judged on the most relevant criterion—human habitability.

On the South Side we came upon neighborhoods that, so

far, had been left intact. Rows of brownstone houses, well cared for, stood behind small, neat yards. Here, although the residents are not much better off economically than the inmates of the public high-rise complexes, a strong sense of community exists. Social pressure in the form of block clubs prevent the piling up of refuse and the destruction of property so prevalent in other low-income sections of the city.

Often, Hall said, one family interested in the appearance of the neighborhood can make a difference. As an example, he pointed out a neighborhood near the new Chicago Circle campus of the University of Illinois. There, a member of the architecture faculty had bought and restored an old brick house. Within weeks, neighbors began to repaint their own houses and to clean up their littered yards. The faculty member painted decorations on his ash cans. The novelty of the idea appealed to his neighbors, who organized an ash-can painting contest of their own and, in the bargain, cleaned up a formerly unsightly alleyway behind their houses.

Painted ash cans in a Chicago back alley may not seem like much of an answer to the complex disease threatening our urban centers, but they are a sign of hope.

The day after our tour of Chicago, Hall met with his students in a course titled "Culture as Communication" at the Illinois Institute of Technology, where he taught until his recent move to Northwestern. The class was made up of about two dozen undergraduates, majoring, for the most part, in design, linguistics, and architecture. "We have badly neglected the training of architects," Hall had told me. "We've got to teach them to think in terms of the total environment and to make them responsive to human requirements." Social sciences, especially ethology and the humanities, must be incorporated in architectural curricula.

Hall's concern in his classes is to train his students to ask the kind of questions he has learned to ask about his environment. Among the projects being discussed were the redesigning of a local restaurant in accordance with its patrons' habitual seating patterns and the rerouting of campus walkways to conform to paths actually followed by the students. For the latter project, diagrams were made the day after a recent snowfall, illustrating pathway patterns left by footprints in the snow. The results were aesthetically more satisfying than the existing grid patterns of walkways, and, as it proved, considerably more sensible.

"A boy in the course last semester noticed that the exit signs out on the Dan Ryan Expressway were placed above the drivers' line of vision, and they came too late," a girl informed me. "He went to work on the problem and submitted his recommendations to the highway department, and they're going to change the signs." My informant was working on traffic-flow problems in her doctor's office and produced diagrams to prove that the existing seating arrangement in the waiting room made some of the patients uneasy.

A young man with a camera walked among the little groups of students, photographing the class in action. "At the beginning of the semester the desks were lined up like soldiers," Hall said. "That boy's project is to study the evolving seating patterns of the class. Maybe we'll learn what kind of desk arrangement works best for an active class like this one, where the teacher is present mainly in advisory capacity and the students do most of the teaching themselves."

Upstairs in the antiquated brick building that housed Hall's classes and his proxemics laboratory, one of his research assistants, a young Negro design student named Marshall Williams, was working on apartment floor plans. "What the ladies in the public housing complain about most," Williams told me, "is that there usually isn't any division between the living room and the dining area. They really hate it when there isn't a separate place for eating." Occasionally, too, he heard complaints that there was too much closet space for the residents' meager possessions.

Hall explained that he and Williams were trying to get the families who live in public housing to make their own suggestions on layout, partly to give them a sense of involvement and partly on the theory that they are the ones who should make such decisions in the first place. "This sort of data is hard to come by," he said. "Poor people have a hard time envisioning the possibility of change." They tend to accept the designs handed down by the city's contractors as immutable.

Hall and his research assistants are gradually teaching their subjects in the housing projects that the environment *can* be changed. Human beings are not like eggs, they argue, to be crated in the most efficient way possible. Human sensory and spatial requirements must be taken into account. Conscious human decisions—ill-advised sometimes—are responsible for the shape of our cities. But conscious human decisions can change that shape, and must, if we are to survive. What is required first, Edward Hall believes, is a revolution in our way of thinking about ourselves.

THE DISPARATE

Racial, Ethnic and Economic Minorities

THE ROLE OF THE UNDESIRABLES

Eric Hoffer

A San Francisco longshoreman sage concludes that one group of society's outcasts bear a remarkable resemblance to America's pioneers.

In the winter of 1934, I spent several weeks in a federal transient camp in California. These camps were originally established by Governor Rolph in the early days of the Depression to care for the single homeless unemployed of the state. In 1934 the federal government took charge of the camps for a time, and it was then that I first heard of them.

How I happened to get into one of the camps is soon told. Like thousands of migrant agricultural workers in California I then followed the crops from one part of the state to the other. Early in 1934 I arrived in the town of El Centro, in the Imperial Valley. I had been given a free ride on a truck from San Diego, and it was midnight when the truck driver dropped me on the outskirts of El Centro. I spread my bedroll by the side of the road and went to sleep. I had hardly dozed off when the rattle of a motorcycle drilled itself into my head and a policeman was bending over me saying, "Roll up, Mister." It looked as though I was in for something; it happened now and then that the police got overzealous and rounded up the freight trains. But this time the cop had no such thought. He said, "Better go over to the federal shelter and get yourself a bed and maybe some breakfast." He directed me to the place.

I found a large hall, obviously a former garage, dimly lit, and packed with cots. A concert of heavy breathing shook the thick air. In a small office near the door, I was registered by a middle-aged clerk. He informed me that this was the "receiving shelter" where I would get one night's lodging and breakfast. The meal was served in the camp nearby. Those who wished to stay on, he said, had to enroll in the camp. He then gave me three blankets and excused himself for not having a vacant cot. I spread the blankets on the cement floor and went to sleep.

I awoke with dawn amid a chorus of coughing, throat-clearing, the sound of running water, and the intermittent flushing of toilets in the back of the hall. There were about fifty of us, of all colors and ages, all of us more or less ragged and soiled. The clerk handed out tickets for breakfast, and we filed out to the camp located several blocks away, near the railroad tracks.

From the outside the camp looked like a cross between a factory and a prison. A high fence of wire enclosed it, and inside were three large sheds and a huge boiler topped by a pillar of black smoke. Men in blue shirts and dungarees were strolling across the sandy yard. A ship's bell in front of one of the buildings announced breakfast. The regular camp members—there was a long line of them—ate first. Then we filed in through the gate, handing our tickets to the guard.

It was a good, plentiful meal. After breakfast our crowd dispersed. I heard some say that the camps in the northern part of the state were better, that they were going to catch a northbound freight. I decided to try this camp in El Centro.

My motives in enrolling were not crystal clear. I wanted to clean up. There were shower baths in the camp and wash tubs and plenty of soap. Of course I could have bathed and washed my clothes in one of the irrigation ditches, but here in the camp I had a chance to rest, get the wrinkles out of my belly, and clean up at leisure. In short, it was the easiest way out.

A brief interview at the camp office and a physical examination were all the formalities for enrollment.

There were some two hundred men in the camp. They were the kind I had worked and traveled with for years. I even saw familiar faces—men I had worked with in orchards and fields. Yet my predominant feeling was one of strangeness. It was my first experience of life in intimate contact with a crowd. For it is one thing to work and travel with a gang, and quite another thing to eat, sleep, and spend the greater part of the day cheek by jowl with two hundred men.

I found myself speculating on a variety of subjects: the reasons for their chronic bellyaching and beefing—it was more a ritual than the expression of a grievance; the amazing orderliness of the men; the comic seriousness with which they took their games of cards, checkers, and dominoes; the weird manner of reasoning one overheard now and then. Why, I kept wondering, were these men within the enclosure of a federal transient camp? Were they people temporarily hard up? Would jobs solve all their difficulties? Were we indeed like the people outside?

Up to then I was not aware of being one of a specific species of humanity. I had considered myself simply a human being—not particularly good or bad, and on the whole harmless. The people I worked and traveled with I knew as Americans and Mexicans, whites and Negroes, Northerners and Southerners, etc. It did not occur to me that we were a group possessed of peculiar traits, and that there was something— innate or acquired—in our makeup which made us adopt a particular mode of existence.

It was a slight thing that started me on a new track.

I got to talking to a mild-looking, elderly fellow. I liked his soft speech and pleasant manner. We swapped trivial experiences. Then he suggested a game of checkers. As we started to arrange the pieces on the board, I was startled by the sight of his crippled right hand. I had not noticed it before. Half of it was chopped off lengthwise, so that the horny stump with its three fingers looked like a hen's leg. I was mortified that I had not noticed the hand until he dangled it, so to speak, before my eyes. It was, perhaps, to bolster my shaken confidence in my powers of observation that I now began paying close attention to the hands of the people around me. The result was astounding. It seemed that every other man had had his hand mangled. There was a man with one arm. Some men limped. One young, good-looking fellow had a wooden leg. It was as though the majority of the men had escaped the snapping teeth of a machine and left part of themselves behind.

It was, I knew, an exaggerated impression. But I began counting the cripples as the men lined up in the yard at mealtime. I found thirty (out of two hundred) crippled either in arms or legs. I immediately sensed where the counting would land me. The simile preceded the statistical deduction: we in the camp were a human junk pile.

I began evaluating my fellow tramps as human material, and for the first time in my life I became face-conscious. There were some good faces, particularly among the young.

Several of the middle-aged and the old looked healthy and well preserved. But the damaged and decayed faces were in the majority. I saw faces that were wrinkled, or bloated, or raw as the surface of a peeled plum. Some of the noses were purple and swollen, some broken, some pitted with enlarged pores. There were many toothless mouths (I counted seventy-eight). I noticed eyes that were blurred, faded, opaque, or bloodshot. I was struck by the fact that the old men, even the very old, showed their age mainly in the face. Their bodies were still slender and erect. One little man over sixty years of age looked a mere boy when seen from behind. The shriveled face joined to a boyish body made a startling sight.

My diffidence had now vanished. I was getting to know everybody in the camp. They were a friendly and talkative lot. Before many weeks I knew some essential fact about practically everyone.

And I was continually counting. Of the two hundred men in the camp there were approximately as follows:

Cripples	30
Confirmed drunkards	60
Old men (55 and over)	50
Youths under twenty	10
Men with chronic diseases, heart, asthma, TB	12
Mildly insane	4
Constitutionally lazy	6
Fugitives from justice	4
Apparently normal	70

(The numbers do not tally up to two hundred since some of the men were counted twice or even thrice—as cripples and old, or as old and confirmed drunks, etc.)

In other words: less than half the camp inmates (seventy normal, plus ten youths) were unemployed workers whose difficulties would be at an end once jobs were available. The rest (sixty percent) had handicaps in addition to unemployment.

I also counted fifty war veterans, and eighty skilled workers representing sixteen trades. All the men (including those with chronic diseases) were able to work. The one-armed man was a wizard with the shovel.

I did not attempt any definite measurement of character

and intelligence. But it seemed to me that the intelligence of the men in the camp was certainly not below the average. And as to character, I found much forbearance and genuine good humor. I never came across one instance of real viciousness. Yet, on the whole, one would hardly say that these men were possessed of strong characters. Resistance, whether to one's appetites or to the ways of the world, is a chief factor in the shaping of character; and the average tramp is, more or less, a slave of his few appetites. He generally takes the easiest way out.

The connection between our makeup and our mode of existence as migrant workers presented itself now with some clarity.

The majority of us were incapable of holding onto a steady job. We lacked self-discipline and the ability to endure monotonous, leaden hours. We were probably misfits from the very beginning. Our contact with a steady job was not unlike a collision. Some of us were maimed, some got frightened and ran away, and some took to drink. We inevitably drifted in the direction of least resistance—the open road. The life of a migrant worker is varied and demands only a minimum of self-discipline. We were now in one of the drainage ditches of ordered society. We could not keep a footing in the ranks of respectability and were washed into the slough of our present existence.

Yet, I mused, there must be in this world a task with an appeal so strong that were we to have a taste of it we would hold on and be rid for good of our restlessness.

My stay in the camp lasted about four weeks. Then I found a haying job not far from town, and finally, in April, when the hot winds began blowing, I shouldered my bedroll and took the highway to San Bernardino.

It was the next morning, after I had got a lift to Indio by truck, that a new idea began to take hold of me. The highway out of Indio leads through waving date groves, fragrant grapefruit orchards, and lush alfalfa fields; then, abruptly, passes into a desert of white sand. The sharp line between garden and desert is very striking. The turning of white sand into garden seemed to me an act of magic. This, I thought, was a job one would jump at—even the men in the transient camps. They had the skill and ability of the average American. But their energies, I felt, could be quickened only by a task that was spectacular, that had in it something of the miraculous. The pioneer task of making the desert flower would certainly fill the bill.

Tramps as pioneers? It seemed absurd. Every man and child in California knows that the pioneers had been giants, men of boundless courage and indomitable spirit. However, as I strode on across the white sand, I kept mulling the idea over.

Who were the pioneers? Who were the men who left their homes and went into the wilderness? A man rarely leaves a soft spot and goes deliberately in search of hardship and privation. People become attached to the places they live in; they drive roots. A change of habitat is a painful act of uprooting. A man who has made good and has a standing in his community stays put. The successful businessmen, farmers, and workers usually stayed where they were. Who then left for the wilderness and the unknown? Obviously those who had not made good: men who went broke or never amounted to much; men who though possessed of abilities were too impulsive to stand the daily grind; men who were slaves of their appetites—drunkards, gamblers, and womanchasers; outcasts—fugitives from justice and ex-jailbirds. There were no doubt some who went in search of health— men suffering with TB, asthma, heart trouble. Finally there was a sprinkling of young and middle-aged in search of adventure.

All these people craved change, some probably actuated by the naïve belief that a change in place brings with it a change in luck. Many wanted to go to a place where they were not known and there make a new beginning. Certainly they did not go out deliberately in search of hard work and suffering. If in the end they shouldered enormous tasks, endured unspeakable hardships, and accomplished the impossible, it was because they had to. They became men of action on the run. They acquired strength and skill in the inescapable struggle for existence. It was a question of do or die. And once they tasted the joy of achievement, they craved for more.

Clearly the same types of people which now swelled the ranks of migratory workers and tramps had probably in former times made up the bulk of the pioneers. As a group the pioneers were probably as unlike the present-day "native sons"—their descendants—as one could well imagine. Indeed, were there to be today a new influx of typical pioneers, twin brothers of the forty-niners only in a modern garb, the citizens of California would consider it a menace to health, wealth, and morals.

With few exceptions, this seems to be the case in the settlement of all new countries. Ex-convicts were the vanguard in the settling of Australia. Exiles and convicts settled Siberia. In this country, a large portion of our earlier and later settlers were failures, fugitives, and felons. The exceptions seemed to be those who were motivated by religious fervor, such as the Pilgrim Fathers and the Mormons.

Although quite logical, this train of thought seemed to me then a wonderful joke. In my exhilaration I was eating up the road in long strides, and I reached the oasis of Elim in what seemed almost no time. A passing empty truck picked me up just then and we thundered through Banning and Beaumont, all the way to Riverside. From there I walked the seven miles to San Bernardino.

Somehow, this discovery of a family likeness between tramps and pioneers took a firm hold on my mind. For years afterward it kept intertwining itself with a mass of observation which on the face of them had no relation to either tramps or pioneers. And it moved me to speculate on subjects in which, up to then, I had no real interest, and of which I knew very little.

I talked with several old-timers—one of them over eighty and a native son—in Sacramento, Placerville, Auburn, and Fresno. It was not easy, at first, to obtain the information I was after. I could not make my questions specific enough. "What kind of people were the early settlers and miners?" I asked. They were a hardworking, tough lot, I was told They drank, fought, gambled, and wenched. They were bighearted, grasping, profane, and God-fearing. They wallowed in luxury, or lived on next to nothing with equal ease. They were the salt of the earth.

Still it was not clear what manner of people they were.

If I asked what they looked like, I was told of whiskers, broad-brimmed hats, high boots, shirts of many colors, suntanned faces, horny hands. Finally I asked: "What group of people in present-day California most closely resemble the pioneers?" The answer, usually after some hesitation, was invariably the same: "The Okies and the fruit tramps."

I tried also to evaluate the tramps as potential pioneers

by watching them in action. I saw them fell timber, clear firebreaks, build rock walls, put up barracks, build dams and roads, handle steam shovels, bulldozers, tractors, and concrete mixers. I saw them put in a hard day's work after a night of steady drinking. They sweated and growled, but they did the work. I saw tramps elevated to positions of authority as foremen and superintendents. Then I could notice a remarkable physical transformation: a seamed face gradually smoothed out and the skin showed a healthy hue; an indifferent mouth became firm and expressive; dull eyes cleared and brightened; voices actually changed; there was even an apparent increase in stature. In almost no time these promoted tramps looked as if they had been on top all their lives. Yet sooner or later I would meet up with them again in a railroad yard, on some skid row, or in the fields—tramps again. It was usually the same story: they got drunk or lost their temper and were fired, or they got fed up with the steady job and quit. Usually, when a tramp becomes a foreman, he is careful in his treatment of the tramps under him; he knows the day of reckoning is never far off.

In short, it was not difficult to visualize the tramps as pioneers. I reflected that, if they were to find themselves in a singlehanded life-and-death struggle with nature, they would undoubtedly display persistence. For the pressure of responsibility and the heat of battle steel a character. The inadaptable would perish, and those who survived would be the equal of the successful pioneers.

I also considered the few instances of pioneering engineered from above—that is to say, by settlers possessed of lavish means, who were classed with the best where they came from. In these instances, it seemed to me, the resulting social structure was inevitably precarious. For pioneering deluxe usually results in a plantation society, made up of large landowners and peon labor, either native or imported. Very often there is a racial cleavage between the two. The colonizing activities of the Teutonic barons in the Baltic, the Hungarian nobles in Transylvania, the English in Ireland, the planters in our South, and the present-day plantation societies in Kenya and other British and Dutch colonies are cases in point. Whatever their merits, they are characterized by poor adaptability. They are likely eventually to be broken up either by a peon revolution or by an influx of typical pioneers—who are usually of the same race

THE ROLE OF THE UNDESIRABLES

or nation as the landowners. The adjustment is not necessarily implemented by war. Even our old South, had it not been for the complication of secession, might eventually have attained stability without war: namely, by the activity of its own poor whites or by an influx of the indigent from other states.

There is in us a tendency to judge a race, a nation, or an organization by its least worthy members. The tendency is manifestly perverse and unfair; yet it has some justification. For the quality and destiny of a nation is determined to a considerable extent by the nature and potentialities of its inferior elements. The inert mass of a nation is in its middle section. The industrious, decent, well-to-do, and satisfied middle classes—whether in cities or on the land—are worked upon and shaped by minorities at both extremes: the best and the worst.

The superior individual, whether in politics, business, industry, science, literature, or religion, undoubtedly plays a major role in the shaping of a nation. But so do the individuals at the other extreme: the poor, the outcasts, the misfits, and those who are in the grip of some overpowering passion. The importance of these inferior elements as formative factors lies in the readiness with which they are swayed in any direction. This peculiarity is due to their inclination to take risks ("not giving a damn") and their propensity for united action. They crave to merge their drab, wasted lives into something grand and complete. Thus they are the first and most fervent adherents of new religions, political upheavals, patriotic hysteria, gangs, and mass rushes to new lands.

And the quality of a nation—its innermost worth—is made manifest by its dregs as they rise to the top: by how brave they are, how humane, how orderly, how skilled, how generous, how independent or servile; by the bounds they will not transgress in their dealings with man's soul, with truth, and with honor.

The average American of today bristles with indignation when he is told that this country was built, largely, by hordes of undesirables from Europe. Yet, far from being derogatory, this statement, if true, should be a cause for rejoicing, should fortify our pride in the stock from which we have sprung.

This vast continent with its towns, farms, factories, dams,

aqueducts, docks, railroads, highways, powerhouses, schools, and parks is the handiwork of common folk from the Old World, where for centuries men of their kind had been as beasts of burden, the property of their masters—kings, nobles, and priests—and with no will and no aspirations of their own. When on rare occasions one of the lowly had reached the top in Europe he had kept the pattern intact and, if anything, tightened the screws. The stuffy little corporal from Corsica harnessed the lusty forces released by the French Revolution to a gilded state coach, and could think of nothing grander than mixing his blood with that of the Hapsburg masters and establishing a new dynasty. In our day a bricklayer in Italy, a house painter in Germany, and a shoemaker's son in Russia have made themselves masters of their nations; and what they did was to reestablish and reinforce the old pattern.

Only here, in America, were the common folk of the Old World given a chance to show what they could do on their own, without a master to push and order them about. History contrived an earthshaking joke when it lifted by the nape of the neck lowly peasants, shopkeepers, laborers, paupers, jailbirds, and drunks from the midst of Europe, dumped them on a vast, virgin continent and said: "Go to it; it is yours!"

And the lowly were not awed by the magnitude of the task. A hunger for action, pent up for centuries, found an outlet. They went to it with ax, pick, shovel, plow, and rifle; on foot, on horse, in wagons, and on flatboats. They went to it praying, howling, singing, brawling, drinking, and fighting. Make way for the people! This is how I read the statement that this country was built by hordes of undesirables from the Old World.

Small wonder that we in this country have a deeply ingrained faith in human regeneration. We believe that, given a chance, even the degraded and the apparently worthless are capable of constructive work and great deeds. It is a faith founded on experience, not on some idealistic theory. And no matter what some anthropologists, sociologists, and geneticists may tell us, we shall go on believing that man, unlike other forms of life, is not a captive of his past—of his heredity and habits—but is possessed of infinite plasticity, and his potentialities for good and for evil are never wholly exhausted.

POVERTY IS A TOUGHER PROBLEM THAN EVER

Robert Bendiner

A political historian discovers that the larger areas in the thirties called Hoovervilles have been replaced by poverty pockets that are smaller but whose victims are more bitter.

If the Johnson administration's war on poverty is ever substantially successful, in spite of a reluctant Congress and a competitive war in Asia, history will have to credit the President with as great a social and political triumph as any brought off by his mentor and idol, Franklin D. Roosevelt. For the poverty of the sixties, though less extensive by far than that of the thirties, is proving considerably harder to deal with. It is, in fact, the poverty that the New Deal scarcely touched—congenital, chronic, and now all the more galling to its victims because of the opulence that surrounds it on all sides. More than that, the *avowed* objective now is not merely relief and amelioration, as it was when Roosevelt took office thirty-five years ago, but the very eradication of poverty.

So great indeed is the difference between the two periods that the most casual comparison will show why popular attitudes toward the poor have changed, why the poor themselves have moved from resignation to the fringes of rebellion, and why their plight calls for more fundamental approaches than were ever dreamed of in the New Deal philosophies.

Although one-third of all Americans, even by President Roosevelt's conservative estimate, were "ill-housed, ill-clad, ill-nourished" in the years of the Great Depression, there was less talk of poverty in the abstract then than there is now—and much more specific talk of making jobs, giving relief and priming the national pump. For that earlier decade was a period of emergency, with all the excitement that a great crisis generates and an intense nationwide preoccupation with the immediate. Now in the sixties, it is "pockets of poverty" that are talked about—deeper and more extensive perhaps than the phrase suggests, but pockets nonetheless—in a landscape of plenty. And it is poverty itself that is the object of attention rather than the poor.

The contrast, in terms of national attention, is roughly the difference between the destruction of a coastline by slow erosion and a dramatic assault on it by a tidal wave. The erosion may be more deadly in the long run but, except for those who live on the disappearing coast, it will excite only the farseeing, the ultrasensitive, and the "cranks," whereas all the resources of the state will be poured, with the blessing of the public, into the proclaimed disaster area left in the wake of the wave.

Just so, the shrinking minority who now live in the "pockets of poverty" do not evoke in the general public or in the run of politicians the kind of passionate interest that practically all politicians in the dramatic thirties were obliged to display toward the poor on pain of seeing their public careers brought to an untimely end. The coolness of the 90th Congress toward the Office of Economic Opportunity and all its works is a far cry from the style of political debate in the early thirties.

Then a Representative Cross from Texas, of all states, could make his tremulous colleagues shudder with talk of "the French Revolution with its guillotine, its Dantons and Robespierres" and warn them that "when the storm breaks, it will be too late, and there will be no cellars in which to hide." Huey Long could shake the nation and make even the triumphant Roosevelt administration jittery with his plans to recarve the economic pie so as to "Make Every Man a King." And Dr. Townsend could send tremors of alarm through politicians who expressed doubts about his scheme to give two hundred dollars a month to every American over the age of sixty.

Today's poor, by contrast, are viewed by most politicians with impersonal detachment. Congress evinces no qualms whatever about taking a stern, even self-righteous, attitude regarding welfare, showing a keener interest in controlling riots than in controlling rats. Few candidates for office feel obliged to make their pitch any more to those below the officially recognized poverty line. And only four years ago a Presidential nominee other than Mr. Johnson could boldly observe that people were poor because they had either "low intelligence or low ambition."

Altogether it is reasonable to suggest that the current drive against poverty is neither politically nor economically inspired, then, but essentially a "cause," a moral crusade, with all the strength and weakness that such crusades are likely to have.

But while this moral concern is the driving force of those who are on the outside looking in, very different sources of power are operating within the dark pockets themselves, where the poor seem to be slowly waking from a torpor, sensing for the first time that they have been locked in a needless misery and that just beyond them are the good things of life they see on television, in advertising and, tantalizingly close, in shop windows. Both drives are significant in giving poverty and the war on poverty a wholly different coloration from that of the thirties, and each rates a little further examination.

The current campaign against poverty owes its beginning not to any sense of national urgency but to the coincidence that a book entitled *The Other America*, by Michael Harrington, fell into the hands of that omnivorous reader, President Kennedy, soon after he had seen, as though for the first time, the gaunt face of poverty in that particular pocket called West Virginia. To be sure, Kennedy had among his advisers several who were keenly aware of the problem and were preparing to press their view on him in any case. But as it happened, he needed no convincing and was planning to advance a major program at the time of his death.

Harrington's thesis was that too much had been made of the country's affluence, as though the poverty of twenty-five percent, or even twenty percent, of Americans was a minor problem, especially since some of them had jalopies and even washing machines (often without running water). "Shall we say to them that they are better off than the Indian poor, the Italian poor, the Russian poor?" Harringon asked with the fervor of an old-time Socialist. "I should put it another way. I want to tell every optimistic and well-fed American that it is intolerable that so many millions should be maimed in body and spirit when it is not necessary that they should be. My standard of comparison is not how much worse things used to be. It is how much better they could be if only we were stirred."

Just as President Kennedy had been stirred, so was his successor, who had known poverty at first hand and who had an active desire to go down in history as the President who completed and extended the work of the New Deal. Harrington's book had a surprisingly good sale, other authors and magazines took up the theme, and soon the poor found themselves not only the subject of major federal legislation but, for the first time since the Depression, a focus of interest for social idealists in search of a cause.

But where social movements in the thirties saw the plight of the poor as a measure of the need for changing the entire economic system, few of today's workers on the antipoverty front take any such drastic view. They are moved not by the messianic hopes of ideologists but by a wistful idealism not unmixed with guilt. For the question of poverty now, at least in the big cities, is tied to the question of race to a degree that would have seemed fantastic in the thirties when at least hardship, if nothing else, was integrated.

"During the W.P.A. days, the day of relief, when every one was undergoing the economic crisis of the nation," Ralph Ellison has said, "there seemed to be a closer relationship between Negroes and whites and between Harlem and the rest of the community." It is typical of the more guilt-ridden present that Mayor Jerome P. Cavanaugh of Detroit, citing the example of West Germany's payments to the victims of Nazism, should call on the federal government to establish the principle of "reparations" to the Negroes "for the deeds of past generations and of our own."

The fact that Negroes actually represent only one-fifth of those in the country who are technically defined as poor—that is, with incomes below 3,000 dollars for a family of four—is immaterial. So is the fact that nearly half the poor families of the country live in rural areas. The steam for the drive on poverty is being generated in the cities. It is there that hundreds of thousands of people whose parents in the thirties were sharecroppers on Tobacco Road, without sufficient knowledge of the world to be desperate, have seen the fruits of middle-class life and want them—immediately.

It is the migration of these 1.5-million Negroes since 1950 that has made most, though by no means all, of the difference between the problems posed by poverty in the two decades. To the wretched tenant farmer of the pre-civil-rights South, rumors and reports from the Harlems of the North were easily converted into dreams of an earthly paradise, complete with jobs, money, schools, electricity, indoor plumbing and human dignity. When it all turned out to be squalor and the misery of supporting a family of seven on sixty-five dollars a week, paradise receded, leaving an intolerable vacuum. And if that was true even for the lucky ones who consistently took home a low wage, how about the ones who soon discovered that in the economic scheme of things they were doomed to be last hired, first fired?

Families, unstable enough to begin with, broke up at an accelerating speed, but the disappearance of fathers did nothing to reduce the swiftly mounting birth rate. On the contrary, sex became often enough a source of income for abandoned mothers and for youth one of the few indulgences to be afforded. Testifying last year before a United States Senate subcommittee on urban problems, a thirty-year-old grandfather and veteran of most of New York's state prisons explained that he had the first of his illegitimate eight children when he was fifteen and his daughter had her first at the age of twelve. Sex, a more literary witness explained, "was the most we had," and everyone knew all about it from the age of six. "By the time we were thirteen we knew it was a great anodyne, you know, before you got to heroin."

While the Southern parents of these witnesses and thousands like them knew little of the material things they were missing in American society, their children quickly learned all about them. Claude Brown, author of *Manchild in the Promised Land*, explained:

> We knew the things that were in the offing, what was out there to be had. It is like our parents' generation didn't have TV, we had it. We came up in school and read the same comic books others were reading. They showed us the same magazines, even though they didn't include us in them. . . . We knew what the good life was supposed to be.

They heard, too, from their teachers about the "American Dream," but those who had come to school without breakfast because there was no food at home were not sufficiently inspired by such fiction to listen to it any longer than the law demanded. Becoming dropouts, they thereby made certain what had before been merely probable—that their share in the dream would be no more than the possibility of a lucky break in the numbers game, or perhaps what could be had from a successful and not too risky crime. Given this preoccupation with the acquisitive, a not un-American emphasis, it is understandable that many impoverished and embittered black Americans came to resent, on the one hand, those middle-class Negroes who have "made it" (they were among the major targets in the Detroit violence) and, on the other hand, those hippie fugitives from the white middle class who affect to despise the very objects of materialism that deprived black youths will smash windows to acquire.

At least eleven percent of all Americans live in families whose income qualifies them for public assistance even under state laws, a standard notoriously short of indulgence. Another nine or ten percent are a shade above that desperation level but still below the 3,000-dollar-a-year poverty line. It is this latter group, owning an occasional television set or a household appliance admittedly beyond the dreams of an Egyptian fellah or a Balkan peasant, who have induced some redefining of poverty.

They are the "psychological poor," who manage to eat enough to keep going but who suffer as keenly as those below them on the economic ladder because they have so little hope of ever enjoying what the rest of American society routinely enjoys—twelve years of schooling for their children, sanitary plumbing, medical care outside of impersonal factory-like clinics, and an occasional jaunt out to the country in bumper-to-bumper traffic.

What is so different about these "psychological poor" of the sixties from the poor of the thirties, to whom resentment was likewise no strange emotion? Indeed, the *nouveaux pauvres* created then by the collapse of the economy were much more aware of what they were missing in the way of bourgeois refinements than those who have never enjoyed them, the genteel poverty of "reduced circumstances" being, after all, among the hardest forms of the curse to endure.

The difference, quite simply, is the difference between a feeling of *temporary* exclusion from the good things of one's society and deprivation as a permanent, even hereditary, way of life. To be sure, many of the temporarily dispossessed in the days of the Depression did give way to despair—too old, too tired or too discouraged to pick up the pieces and start all over again—and their lot was tragic. But there were more who either were certain that with the recovery of the economy their fortunes would rise again or who were perfectly prepared to join some movement or other for trading in that economy for a newer and more workable model. In short, there was hope and spirit, or at the very least the feeling of being in the same boat as half the population of the country.

However low in the mind a jobless man might get, trudging from one shabby employment office to another—and I can testify to the lowness—he did not have to feel that, thanks to some inherent inferiority, he was an exile in his own country, forever fixed in a second- or third-class status. And everywhere he turned there were vivid reminders that the Depression was as bad or worse for others: a mushroom colony of improvised shanties in a vacant lot, a breadline of shabby men waiting impassively along the wire fencing of a shabby building, a row of empty storefronts recalling a departed way of life.

Even the popular culture of the day reflected the great common experience in which he shared, and it took out a little of the sting. Over the radio he could hear Eddie Cantor chirping that what with potatoes being cheaper, "Now's the Time to Fall in Love." He might be reassured by Ethel Merman and Rudy Vallee that "Life Is Just a Bowl of Cherries." Or he could at least feel a bond with all those who sang "Brother, Can You Spare a Dime?" And if he read at all, or even watched the newsreels on Bank Night at the movies, he couldn't help knowing something about the Dust Bowl, the Oakies and the sharecroppers.

Above all, the entire apparatus of government was giving evidence every day in the week that those in high places knew the straits he was in and were trying to do something about it. The President himself came on the air from time to time to confide in him, as no President had ever done before, and to explain what it was he hoped to do. If a man was not himself in the ranks of the W.P.A., the P.W.A. or the C.C.C., he had a friend or relative in one or another of them and knew what those agencies were up to.

And for a time he could not avoid seeing on all sides that sign and symbol of his government's interest, the blue eagle of the N.R.A. Not only did that bird proclaim the will to National Recovery from shop windows, food packages, and factory rooftops, but it rode aloft on banners carried in gaudy parades through the streets of cities by mayors, industrial tycoons, trade-union presidents and folk heroes from Hollywood and Broadway—all to advise their countrymen that in the great campaign for recovery, "We Do Our Part."

To the dispossessed of the thirties, none of this brought joy perhaps, but the atmosphere was one in which the solidarity of disaster did provide a certain warmth—and strength. The contrasting bitterness of the dispossessed today is both striking and understandable. It is one thing to be caught out in the rain with a thousand others and another to be left there while everyone else has gone home to dry off.

Conversely, the comfortable find it increasingly hard to recall the discomfort, the further removed they are from it. This relativity factor in poverty is no less real for being psychological and is both a brake on action by the "haves" and a source of bitterness to the "have-nots." Certainly it feeds those smug reflections on the "rich poor," which run all the way from Will Roger's famous boast about our being "the only nation in the history of the world that ever went to the poorhouse in an automobile" to John Jacob Astor's philosophical reflection that a man who has a million dollars is as well off as if he were rich.

While government *was* doing things in the thirties, it must be pointed out that, except for direct emergency relief, its activity was not aimed at those in the greatest need but at those in need who were most vital to a quick restoration of the economy—the trade-union member, the big-market farmer, the skilled worker, the small pensioner. As it happened—and one will be as skeptical on the subject as his nature dictates—these were also the ones who in spite of hard times still had a large measure of political leverage, who indeed made up the backbone of the administration's electoral support. Those who had no such leverage—the sharecroppers, tenant farmers and migratory workers, the chronically and congenitally poor of the city slums, lacking both the vigor and the organization to exert political pressure—these were helped very little and in a fundamental way not at all.

It is the children and grandchildren of these same long-sufferers who are the hard core of the problem today. The extent to which this is not just figuratively but also literally true is a dismal phenomenon now being faced for the first time: hereditary poverty. What has been regarded for millennia in the Old World as a fact of life, to be meekly accepted as one's divinely ordained lot on earth, has not traditionally been viewed as part of the American Way, but on the contrary a gross violation of the spirit of Horatio Alger.

Now, however, a United States Senate committee can report in passing that ". . . poverty in America has been changing in nature. The American frontiersman knew poverty as he struggled to build a society sufficiently productive to offer a more abundant life. The immigrant knew poverty as he entered a new land and prepared his children to move upward in the economic and social scale. In both cases poverty was a transition stage to better things. Poverty in modern America tends to be a permanent state, concentrated among certain disadvantaged groups and in many cases continuing generation after generation."

This is what the technicians mean by *structural* poverty as opposed to the cyclical variety that hit so many Americans in the thirties. It has little to do with general prosperity or lack of it, because, prosperity or no, there is nothing to do for those whose unskilled services are no longer needed, who cannot acquire new skills for lack of education, and whose lack of education stems in turn from the atmosphere of neglect, apathy and ignorance which their parents' poverty has imposed on them. They are poor, it has been said, not because they are just starting out to be rich but because they have already been rejected—or feel they have, which amounts to the same thing.

Obviously this kind of poverty calls for different approaches from those that seemed applicable to the hardships of the fallen bourgeoisie in the thirties. They had to do with lifting the entire economy. But, as Galbraith and others have pointed out, general prosperity now not only fails to help those trapped in the "pockets" or those who are poor because they are individually handicapped but actually deepens their misery and increases their bitterness.

All of which brings us to two attitudes on the subject of poverty which are gaining a degree of acceptance now and which would have been unthinkable thirty-five years ago. Both serve to give the whole question an emphasis sharply different from anything we knew in the days of the Depression.

The first is that since the poverty of the "structurally poor" is scarcely of their own making, and since they have so few chances to escape through their own initiative, they are as much entitled to a voice in plans for improving their lot as any other element in the citizenry. In principle, the Office of Economic Opportunity and other government agencies recognize that claim, and elsewhere their spokesmen increasingly assert it as a matter of right. They represent their constituents, as it were, on community antipoverty boards, and before legislative committees, much as lobbyists represent war veterans, chiropractors or oil promoters. And they cover professional gatherings, whether invited or not.

Crashing a recent conference of the American Medical Association on health care for the poor, a delegation from a Chicago Negro slum marched up to the platform and demanded a voice at the gathering on the ground that the matter concerned them. "You are interfering with our efforts to help the underprivileged," said the irate chairman, thereby setting up the retort obvious: "We are the underprivileged." Under pressure from the assembled doctors, the chairman allowed the poverty delegates five minutes to denounce the health-care facilities in their district, after which they triumphantly filed out.

If today's spokesmen for the poor are for the most part a pragmatic lot, with an eye on what can be had here and now, the dispossessed also have would-be champions of a more revolutionary bent, just as they did in the thirties. But there are differences. Devotees of the New Left, determined to steer clear of the fatal dogmatism of the Old, carry individual whim to the point where programs are consumed in personal anarchy and a passion for disorder passes for democracy. If the Old Left in its procedures too often suggested Kafka, the New—witness last fall's National Conference for New Politics—often recalls nothing so much as the trial of the Knave of Hearts in *Alice's Adventures in Wonderland*.

More fundamental, the Left could seriously envision a forced change in the whole economic order in the thirties, when a quarter of the working force was idle, when the poverty wave had engulfed a third of the population and was imminently threatening more than that, and when new economic orders were very much in vogue elsewhere in the world. Today's Left has less a program for revolutionary change than a fondness for using revolutionary rhetoric and tactics to extract immediate concessions from the Establishment.

It is possible that the New Left will in time settle down to a more systematic approach to whatever goals it decided upon, but so far it would seem to have considerably less influence on events than the Popular Front had in the thirties—and extremely little in the campaign to abolish poverty. It is worth noting that the most comprehensive and detailed program to this end, the "Freedom Budget" for massive government investment, comes not from the New Left but from such representatives of the relatively Old (and Mild) Left as A. Philip Randolph and Leon Keyserling.

The other major change in attitude which I suggest has occurred raises an equally basic question: Since much of the remaining poverty is of the "case" variety for which jobs are not the prescription—roughly fifty percent of the poor are scarcely in the job market at all—why not face facts and simply subsidize the victims out of their poverty?

Certainly a return to the public-works programs of the thirties is not the answer for this very large segment of today's poor, handicapped as they are by age and health. Even for the young and healthy but poorly educated. Government-provided employment is not the obvious answer it once was. For there is clearly less need for huge pools of unskilled manpower than was the case in the preautomation days of the Depression. By and large, I was told by a former official in the poverty program, such projects would employ the wrong people—"They wouldn't do much for the poor, just mean double time for the building trades."

Clearly this was not true in the thirties, when scores of thousands of highly skilled men were idle. With all the loose charges of "leaf-raking" and loafing, P.W.A. contributions to Hoover Dam, Triborough Bridge and a whole new sewage system for Chicago went all but uncredited, not to mention such other fruits of indolence as the aircraft carriers *Yorktown* and *Enterprise*. The injustice of the criticism was caught fairly enough by a contemporary cartoon showing two lady tourists gazing at a plaque indicating the New

Deal origin of a magnificent bridge. "And to think," one of them says in astonishment, "they did all of this while leaning on shovels."

But that was a time when the unemployed ran as high as twenty-five percent of the nation's working force. The first order of business was clearly to get them back to work and restore the nation's buying power. What we are faced with now is an unemployment rate of less than four percent and a growing number of *unemployables,* people who never will have either buying power or decent lives unless something is done to *give* them income while educating their young to the point where they can earn their own.

What public-works programs were to New Deal critics, namely a red rag, current proposals for subsidizing the poor out of their poverty are to critics of the present administration—or will be if the proposals get beyond the talking stage.

The schemes vary in amount and in mechanics. At their most stringent is Milton Friedman's "negative income tax," which would guarantee each family fifty percent of minimal needs, calculated on the poverty-threshold figure, in exchange for *all* further welfare assistance. This plan of Senator Goldwater's economic adviser would seem to offer the poor only a freer choice of how to spend their lack of money. But through several gradations of generosity, coupled with provisions designed to encourage the recipients to work if possible, the negative-income-tax proposal at its peak is offered as a way to eliminate poverty altogether. For eleven billion dollars a year, which is well under two percent of the gross national product, the entire bottom fifth of the population could be lifted once and for all over the threshold of poverty.

If this is deemed too ambitious, there are several schemes on tap to grant government family allowances, such as Canada and other nations have long provided. Generally these would be paid for by eliminating the present income-tax deduction for dependents, so that the poor, who don't pay taxes, would net ten dollars or so a month for each child, while those who do pay taxes would in effect foot the bill.

These proposals, none of which, again, stems from the New Left, are mentioned here not with any idea of judging them or even discussing their merits but merely to highlight the overriding difference between the two decades. What was done thirty-five years ago was done out of weakness and the demands of an emergency. What is proposed now stems from strength and a growing, though hardly pervasive, sense in the country, if not in Congress, that social decency requires it. For the first time in the long history of man it is possible here and now to wipe out this most venerable plague. And the decision, at last, is more philosophical than economic. As in the thirties, war at the end of the decade has all but eliminated cyclical poverty, while leaving the structural variety untouched. The difference is that the structurally poor know now what their forerunners in the thirties could not know—that their plight is wholly unnecessary.

In this respect the poverty of the sixties in America differs not only from that of the thirties but from that of every period and every society that has gone before. It was all very well for feudal serfs to accept an animal-like poverty as the decree of Providence, or for the Puritans to regard it as a confession of sloth and a mark of disgrace. It was understandable even for the Rev. Henry Ward Beecher, on a yearly income that would be 75,000 dollars in today's currency, to rail at do-gooders in the Gilded Age who thought it hard for a man to support a family of five on a dollar a day. Not pretty but understandable. Because none of these nor any of their contemporaries could eliminate poverty even with the best will in the world.

We can. And that fact poses for us a moral question that no people has yet had to decide—certainly not the Depression-ridden Americans of thirty-five years ago. To execute the required programs would scarcely tax our ingenuity, but to make the required decision, so hostile to the Puritan tradition—that will not be easy.

A NEGRO PSYCHIATRIST EXPLAINS THE NEGRO PSYCHE

Alvin F. Poussaint

A professor of psychiatry warns that the Negro's learned passivity is being replaced by a strong and at times violent drive to correct social injustices.

In recent years social scientists have come to attribute many of the Negro's social and psychological ills to his self-hatred and resultant self-destructive impulses. Slums, high crime rates, alcoholism, drug addiction, illegitimacy and other social deviations have all been attributed in part to the Negroes' acting out of their feelings of inferiority. Many behavioral scientists have suggested that the recent urban Negro riots are a manifestation of subconscious self-destructive forces in black people stemming from this chronic feeling of self-denigration. Noted psychologist Dr. Kenneth B. Clark has even speculated that these riots are a form of "community suicide" that expresses the ultimate in self-negation, self-rejection and hopelessness.

Given the self-hatred thesis, it is not surprising that many people, both white and Negro, champion programs intended to generate a positive self-image in the Negro "masses" as a panacea for all black social problems: "Teach Negro history and our African heritage in the schools so those cats won't be ashamed of being black!" A Negro friend says, "Help those boys develop pride in being black and the riots will stop."

The self-hatred thesis appeals on the one hand to racists, who reason that if Negroes develop enough "self-love" they might wish to remain complacently segregated and stop trying to "mongrelize" the white society, and on the other to Negro militants, including the Black Muslims and Black

Power advocates, who scream from soapboxes, "We must undo the centuries-old brainwashing by the white man that has made us hate ourselves. We must stop being ashamed of being black and stop wanting to be white!" There is also talk of building a Negro subculture based on "a positive sense of identity." Some militant Negroes seek to boost their self-esteem by legitimizing being black. Last year after a sit-in demonstration in Mississippi, a Negro civil-rights worker said to me: "White racism has made me hate white people and hate myself and my brothers. I ain't about to stop hating white folks, but I'm not gonna let that self-hatred stuff mess me up any more!"

No one denies that many Negroes have feelings of self-hatred. But the limitations of the thesis become apparent when one realizes that a Negro with all the self-love and self-confidence in the world could not express it in a system that is so brutally and unstintingly suppressive of self-assertion. Through systematic oppression aimed at extinguishing his aggressive drive, the black American has been effectively castrated and rendered abjectly compliant by white America. Since appropriate rage at such emasculation could be expressed directly only at great risk, the Negro repressed and suppressed it, but only at great cost to his psychic development. Today this "aggression-rage" constellation, rather than self-hatred, appears to be at the core of the Negro's social and psychological difficulties.

Consider the following. Once last year as I was leaving my office in Jackson, Mississippi, with my Negro secretary, a white policeman yelled, "Hey, boy! Come here!" Somewhat bothered, I retorted: "I'm no boy!" He then rushed at me, inflamed, and stood towering over me, snorting, "What d'ja say, boy?" Quickly he frisked me and demanded, "What's your name, boy?" Frightened, I replied, "Dr. Poussaint. I'm a physician." He angrily chuckled and hissed, "What's your first name, boy?" When I hesitated he assumed a threatening stance and clenched his fists. As my heart palpitated, I muttered in profound humiliation, "Alvin."

He continued his psychological brutality, bellowing, "Alvin, the next time I call you, you come right away, you hear? You hear?" I hesitated. "You hear me, boy?" My voice trembling with helplessness, but following my instincts of self-preservation, I murmured, "Yes, sir." Now fully satisfied that I had performed and acquiesced to my "boy status," he dismissed me with, "Now, boy, go on and get out of here or next time we'll take you for a little ride down to the station house!"

No amount of self-love could have salvaged my pride or preserved my integrity. In fact, the slightest show of self-respect or resistance might have cost me my life. For the moment my manhood had been ripped from me—and in the presence of a Negro woman for whom I, a "man," was supposed to be the "protector." In addition, this had occurred on a public street for all the local black people to witness, reminding them that *no* black man was as good as *any* white man. All of us—doctor, lawyer, postman, field hand and shoeshine boy—had been psychologically "put in our place."

The self-hate that I felt at that time was generated by the fact that I and my people were completely helpless and powerless to destroy that white bigot and all that he represented. Suppose I had decided, as a man should, to be forceful? What crippling price would I have paid for a few moments of assertive manhood? What was I to do with my rage?

And if I, a physician in middle-class dress, was vulnerable to this treatment, imagine the brutality to which "ordinary" black people are subjected—not only in the South but also in the North, where the brutality is likely to be more psychological than physical.

Let us briefly look at the genesis and initial consequences of this oppressive behavior and the Negroes' responses to it. The castration of Negroes, and the resulting problems of self-image and inner rage, started more than 350 years ago when black men, women and children were wrenched from their native Africa, stripped bare both psychologically and physically, and placed in an alien white land. They thus came to occupy the most degraded of human conditions: that of a slave, a piece of property, a nonperson. Families were broken up, the Negro male was completely emasculated, and the Negro woman was systematically sexually exploited and vilely degraded.

Whites, to escape the resultant retaliatory rage of black men and women, acted to block its expression. The plantation system implanted a subservience and dependency in the psyche of the Negro that made him dependent upon the goodwill and paternalism of the white man. The more acquiescent he was, the more he was rewarded within the plantation culture. Those who bowed and scraped for the white boss and denied their aggressive feelings were promoted to "house nigger" and "good nigger."

It became a virtue within this system for the black man to be docile and nonassertive. "Uncle Toms" are exemplars of these conditioned virtues. If black people wanted to keep some semblance of a job and a full stomach to survive, they quickly learned "Yassuh, Massa." Passivity for Negroes became necessary for survival both during and after slavery, and holds true even today.

For reinforcement, as if any was needed, white supremacists constructed an entire "racial etiquette" to remind Negroes constantly that they are only castrated humans. In their daily lives, Negroes are called "girl" and "boy"—this in spite of the fact that such "girls" and "boys" as domestics are capable of managing a household with an efficiency and physical endurance that their white middle-class employers seem no longer to possess. Negroes are also addressed by their first names by whites no matter how lowly, but are in turn expected to use courtesy titles when addressing whites. It was sickening for me to hear a Southern white dime-store clerk address a Negro minister with a doctoral degree as "Jimmy," while he obsequiously called her "Miss Joan." If the Negro minister rejected these social mores he would probably be harassed, punished or in some way "disciplined." White racists through the centuries have perpetrated violence on Negroes who demonstrate aggressiveness. To be an "uppity nigger" was considered by white supremacists one of the gravest violations of racial etiquette.

Nonetheless, the passivity to which the black community has been so well conditioned is frequently called "apathy" and "self-hate" by those who would lay the burden of white racism on the black man's shoulders. The more reasonable explanation is that Negroes had little choice but to bear the severe psychological burden of suppressing and repressing their rage and aggression.

Nonassertiveness was a learned adaptation to insure survival. For example, the whole system of Southern legal justice has been designed—and still functions—to inflict severe and inequitable penalties on Negroes showing even minor aggression toward whites. In both the North and the South, Negroes who dare show their anger toward whites are usually punished out of proportion. Negroes who are "too outspoken" about racial injustices often lose their jobs or are not promoted to higher positions because they are considered "unreasonable." The recent unseating of Congressman Adam Clayton Powell and the use of guns and bullets by police and National Guardsmen on rioting Negro college students (white college-age rioters are seldom even tear-gassed) are examples of this inequitable white retaliation.

Black people have learned their lesson well. Both in the North and in the South it is not uncommon to hear young Negro mothers instructing their two- and three-year-old children to "behave, and say, 'Yes, sir,' and 'No, sir' when the white man talks to you."

Similarly, various forms of religious worship in the Negro community have fostered passivity in blacks and encouraged them to look to an afterlife for eventual salvation and happiness. Negroes have even been taught that they must love their oppressor and it is "sinful" to hate or show appropriate anger. It is significant that the civil-rights movement had to adopt passive resistance and nonviolence in order to win the acceptance of white America. But, alas, even in nonviolent demonstrations there was too much "aggression" shown by Negroes. Whites recoiled and accused civil-rights groups of "provoking violence" by peaceful protest.

The lack of self-assertion has had devastating consequences in terms of Negro social behavior and psychic responses. It has been found, for instance, that Negroes are less likely to go into business than are members of other ethnic groups. The most obvious explanation for this (and one missed by Glazer and Moynihan in their *Beyond the Melting Pot*) is that central to the entrepreneurial spirit is assertiveness, self-confidence and the willingness to risk failure in an innovative venture. A castrated human being is not likely to be inclined in any of these ways.

A trained incapacity to be aggressive would also account in large part for Negroes' below-par achievement in school. Negro girls, who are not as threatening to whites and therefore not as systematically crushed as are Negro boys, have been found to exceed boys in achievement in elementary schools. The pattern of behavior set for the young Negro, especially the male, is directly opposed to that upheld as masculine for the rest of American youth. With our country's emphasis on individualism and the idealization of the self-made man, brutalization into passivity leaves the Negro with a major handicap.

Of course, this is also conveniently protective for the white racist, because Negroes who are nonassertive will be afraid to compete with him for education, jobs and status. Studies have reported that even when Negroes are given objective evidence of their equal intellectual ability they continue to feel inadequate and react submissively. Thus their low aspirations may be due primarily to a learned inability to be normally aggressive and only secondarily to an inferiority complex.

Many psychiatrists feel that self-denigration is secondary to the more general castration of the black man by white society. Some believe that the self-hatred should be viewed as a rage turned inward rather than as a shame in being black and a desire to be white. Both my white and Negro colleagues agree that central to whatever specific emotional problems their Negro patients exhibit is how they deal with their feelings of hostility and rage. (This problem is particularly relevant to their behavior in the presence of whites.)

Of course, Negroes react and adapt to the stresses of white racism in a myriad of ways depending upon socioeconomic level, family life, geographical location, etc. Yet the fact remains that Negroes as individuals must deal with the general effects of racism. Since individual Negroes share the common experiences of Negro castration, rage and self-hatred, group trends can frequently be discerned.

What happens then to the accumulated rage in the depths of each Negro psyche? What does the black man do with his aggression?

The simplest method for dealing with rage is to suppress it and substitute an opposing emotional attitude—compliance, docility or a "loving attitude." A colleague told me about the case of a Negro graduate student he was treating for anxiety. The student was engaged to a white girl and circulated primarily in white social circles. He had a reputation for being very ingratiating and accommodating with his white friends, who described him as a "sweet guy" and a "very loving person." The student took a great deal of pride in this reputation and "acceptance" by whites, although he frequently encountered degrading racial prejudices among them. He attempted to deal with bigoted whites by being "understanding" and hoping that they would begin to see him as "just another human being."

At the beginning of treatment, he painted a rosy picture of his social life and particularly of his engagement to the white girl, although her parents had disowned her. He consistently denied holding any angry feelings toward whites or bitter feelings about being Negro. As therapy progressed and his problems were explored, more and more anger toward whites in general and toward his white friends in particular began to emerge. He became less tolerant of the subtle racial bigotry which he saw in his fiancée and began to quarrel with her frequently. For many weeks he became so overwhelmed by rage that he developed nausea and could not face his white friends for "fear of what I might do." He also became quite guilty about his acquiescence to white racial prejudice and slowly recognized that perhaps he himself had anti-Negro feelings. He began to avoid seeing his fiancée, feeling completely alienated from white people. The engagement was finally broken. The student left treatment to take a job in another city and shortly thereafter it was reported to his therapist that he had become a "black nationalist."

As this student exemplified, the greater the repressed rage, the more abject the pretense of love and compliance. Thus feet-shuffling, scraping and bowing, obsequiousness and Uncle Tomism may actually indicate inner rage and deep hatred.

Sometimes rage can be denied completely and replaced by a compensatory happy-go-lucky attitude, flippancy or—a mechanism extremely popular among Negroes—"being cool."

Or the aggression may be channeled into competitive sports, music, dance. Witness the numbers of Negroes who flock to these activities, among the few traditionally open to them by white society. Negro males in particular gravitate to sports as a means for sublimating their rage and aggression.

Another legitimate means of channeling rage is to identify with the oppressor and put all one's energy into striving to be like him. The most obvious example of this is the Negro who feels that the most flattering compliment his white friends can pay him is, "You don't act like all the other Negroes," or "You don't seem Negro to me." Such blacks usually harbor strong, angry anti-Negro feelings similar to the white racists. They may project their own self-hatred onto other Negroes. This mechanism is indicated in the high incidence of impulsive violence of Negroes toward each other: assaults and homicides by Negroes are more often against Negroes than against whites.

It is also legitimate and safe for the oppressed to identify with someone like himself who for one reason or another is free to express rage directly at the oppressor. This phenomenon would account for the immense popularity among Negroes of Congressman Adam Clayton Powell and Malcolm X. They were both willing to "tell the white man like it is" and did so, for a while at least, with apparent impunity —something which many of their followers could never do.

Another technique for dealing with rage is to replace it with a type of chronic resentment and stubbornness toward white people—a chip on the shoulder. Trying to control deep anger in this way frequently shows itself in a general irritability and it always has the potential of becoming explosive. Thus the spreading wave of riots in Negro ghettos may be seen as outbursts of rage. Although these riots are contained in the ghetto, the hatred is usually directed at those whom the rioter sees as controlling and oppressing him economically, psychologically and physically—store owners and policemen.

The same hostility which is expressed in a disorganized way by a collection of people in a riot can be expressed in an organized way in a political movement. In this connection the Black Power movement is relevant.

In the South I observed many civil-rights workers struggling with suppressed rage toward whites until it culminated in the angry, assertive cry of "Black Power!" I remember treating Negro workers after they had been beaten viciously by white toughs or policemen while conducting civil-rights demonstrations. I would frequently comment, "You must feel pretty angry getting beaten up like that by those bigots." Often I received a reply such as: "No, I don't hate those white men, I love them because they must really be suffering with all that hatred in their souls. Dr. King says the only way we can win our freedom is through love. Anger and hatred has never solved anything."

I used to sit there and wonder, "Now, what do they really do with their rage?"

Well, after a period of time it became apparent that they were directing it mostly at each other and the white civil-rights workers. Violent verbal and sometimes physical fights often occurred among the workers on the civil-rights projects throughout the South. While they were talking about being nonviolent and "loving" the sheriff who just hit them over the head, they rampaged around the project houses beating up each other. I frequently had to calm Negro civil-rights workers with large doses of tranquilizers for what I can describe clinically only as acute attacks of rage.

As the months progressed and Negro workers became more conscious of their anger, it was more systematically directed toward white Southern racists, the lax federal government, token integration and finally the hypocrisy of many white liberals and white civil-rights workers. This rage was at a fever pitch for many months before it became crystallized in the "Black Power" slogan. The workers who shouted it the loudest were those with the oldest battle scars from the terror, demoralization and castration which they experienced through continual direct confrontation with Southern white racism. Furthermore, some of the most bellicose chanters of the slogan had been, just a few years before, exemplars of nonviolent, loving passive resistance in their struggle against white supremacy. These workers appeared to be seeking a sense of inner psychological emancipation from racism through self-assertion and release of aggressive, angry feelings.

Often the anxiety, fear and tension caused by suppressed emotion will be expressed in psychosomatic symptoms. Tension headaches, diarrhea and low back pain are conditions frequently linked to repressed hostility. Whether these symptoms occur more frequently among Negroes than among whites is an important question that has yet to be explored.

Rage is also directed inward in such deviations as alcoholism, drug addiction and excessive gambling. These escapist expressions are very prevalent among poorer Negroes and often represent an attempt to shut out a hostile world. In psychiatric practice it is generally accepted that a chronic repressed rage will eventually lead to a low self-esteem, depression, emotional dullness and apathy.

It appears that more and more Negroes are freeing themselves of suppressed rage through greater outspoken release of pent-up emotions. Perhaps this is an indication that self-love is beginning to outbalance self-hate in the black man's soul. A report this June by the Brandeis University Center for the Study of Violence said: "Although most Negroes disliked violence and had mixed feeelings about its effect, even moderates were shifting to the opinion that only intense forms of social protest would bring relief from social injustice."

The old passivity is fading and being replaced by a drive to undo centuries of powerlessness, helplessness and dependency under American racism. It is not uncommon now to hear Negro civil-rights leaders as well as the teen-ager in the ghetto say such things as, "White America will have to give us our rights or exterminate us." James Meredith echoed the sentiments of many Negroes after his "march against fear" in Mississippi when he said. "If Negroes ever do overcome fear, the white man has only two choices: to kill them or let them be free."

The implication of all this seems to be that black people can obtain dignity only through continued assertive social and political action against racism until all of their just demands are met. It also appears that old-style attempts to destroy the natural aggression of the black man and to fail to give him his full rights can only provoke further outbreaks of violence and inspire a revolutionary zeal among Negro Americans.

The behavior of young Negroes today implies their recognition that racial pride and self-love alone do not fill the bellies of starving black children in Mississippi. Nor does being proud of one's African heritage alone bring jobs, decent housing or quality education. Perhaps the emphasis by social scientists on self-hatred problems among blacks is just another thesis that is guilt-relieving for whites and misguides the Negro. It's as if many white Americans are saying, "From now on when we oppress you, we don't want you to hate being black, we want you to have racial pride and love each other."

For the fundamental survival problems of black Americans to be dealt with, a variety of social, economic and political forces controlled primarily by whites must be challenged. "Positive-sense-of-identity" programs are relevant only insofar as they generate greater constructive aggressiveness in Negroes in their struggle for full equality. Since this assertive response appears to be growing more common among Negroes, the implications for American society are clear: stop oppressing the black man, or be prepared to meet his expressed rage.

THE NEGRO AS AN AMERICAN

Robert C. Weaver

The first Negro member of the Cabinet and an outstanding economist lists the responsibilities of Negro leaders.

When the average well-informed and well-intentioned white American dicusses the issue of race with his Negro counterpart there are many areas of agreement. There are also certain significant areas of disagreement.

Negro Americans usually feel that whites exaggerate progress; while whites frequently feel that Negroes minimize gains. Then there are differences relative to the responsibility of Negro leadership. It is in these areas of dispute that some of the most subtle and revealing aspects of Negro-white relationships reside. And it is to the subtle and less obvious aspects of this problem that I wish to direct my remarks.

Most middle-class white Americans frequently ask, "Why do Negroes push so? They have made phenomenal progress in one hundred years of freedom, so why don't their leaders do something about the crime rate and illegitimacy?" To them I would reply that when Negroes press for full equality now they are behaving as all other Americans would under similar circumstances. Every American has the right to be treated as a human being, and striving for human dignity is a national characteristic. Also, there is nothing inconsistent in such action and realistic self-appraisal. Indeed, as I shall develop, self-help programs among nonwhites, if they are to be effective, must go hand-in-glove with the opening of new opportunities.

Negroes who are constantly confronted or threatened by discrimination and inequality articulate a sense of outrage. Many react with hostility, sometimes translating their feelings into overt antisocial actions. In parts of the Negro community, a separate culture with deviant values develops.

To the members of this subculture I would observe that ours is a middle-class society and those who fail to evidence most of its values and behavior are headed toward difficulties. But I am reminded that the rewards for those who do are often minimal, providing insufficient inducement for large numbers to emulate them.

Until the second decade of the twentieth century, it was traditional to compare the current position of Negroes with that of a decade or several decades ago. The depression revealed the basic marginal economic status of colored Americans and repudiated this concept of progress. By the early 1930s Negroes became concerned about their *relative* position in the nation.

Of course, there are those who observe that the average income, the incidence of home ownership, the rate of acquisition of automobiles, and the like, among Negroes in the United States are higher than in some so-called advanced nations. Such comparisons mean little. Incomes are significant only in relation to the cost of living, and the other attainments and acquisitions are significant for comparative purposes only when used to reflect the Negro's relative position in this nation or other nations' relative position in the world. The Negro here—as he has so frequently and eloquently demonstrated—is an American. And his status, no less than his aspirations, can be measured meaningfully only in terms of American standards.

Viewed from this point of view what are the facts?

Median family income among nonwhites was slightly less than fifty-five percent of that for whites in 1959; for individual incomes, the figure was fifty percent.

Only a third of the Negro families in 1959 earned sufficient to sustain an acceptable American standard of living. Yet this involved well over a million Negro families, of whom 6,000 earned 25,000 dollars or more.

Undergirding these overall figures are many paradoxes. Negroes have made striking gains in historical terms; yet their current rate of unemployment is well over double that among whites. Over two thirds of our colored workers are still concentrated in five major unskilled and semiskilled occupations, as contrasted to slightly over a third of the white labor force.

Despite the continuing existence of color discrimination even for many of the well prepared, there is a paucity of qualified Negro scientists, engineers, mathematicians, and highly trained clerical and stenographic workers. Lack of college-trained persons is especially evident among Negro men. One is prompted to ask, why does this exist?

In 1959, nonwhite males who were high-school graduates earned, on the average, thirty-two percent less than whites; for nonwhite college graduates the figure was thirty-eight percent less. Among women a much different situation exists. Nonwhite women who were high-school graduates earned on the average some twenty-four percent less than whites. Nonwhite female college graduates, however, earned but slightly over one percent less average annual salaries than white women college graduates. Significantly, the median annual income of nonwhite female college graduates was more than double that of nonwhite women with only high-school education.

Is it any wonder that among nonwhites, as contrasted to whites, a larger proportion of women than of men attend and finish college? The lack of economic rewards for higher education goes far in accounting for the paucity of college graduates and the high rate of dropouts among nonwhite males. It also accounts for the fact that in the North, where there are greater opportunities for white-collar Negro males, more Negro men than women are finishing college; whereas in the South, where teaching is the greatest employment outlet for Negro college graduates, Negro women college graduates outnumber men.

There is much in these situations that reflects the continuing matriarchal character of Negro society—a situation which had its roots in the family composition under slavery where the father, if identified, had no established role. Subsequent and continuing economic advantages of Negro women who found steady employment as domestics during the post-Civil War era and thereafter perpetuated the pattern. This, in conjunction with easy access by white males to Negro females, served to emasculate many Negro men economically and psychologically. It also explains, in part, the high prevalence of broken homes, illegitimacy, and lack of motivation in the Negro community.

The Negro middle class seems destined to grow and prosper. At the same time, the economic position of the untrained and poorly trained Negro—as of all untrained and poorly trained in our society—will continue to decline. Nonwhites are doubly affected. First, they are disproportionately concentrated in occupations particularly susceptible to unemployment at a time when our technology eats up unskilled and semiskilled jobs at a frightening rate. Secondly, they are conditioned to racial job discrimination. The latter circumstance becomes a justification for not trying, occasionally a lack of incentive for self-betterment.

The tragedy of discrimination is that it provides an excuse for failure while erecting barriers to success.

Most colored Americans still are not only outside the mainstream of our society but see no hope of entering it. The lack of motivation and the antisocial behavior which result are capitalized upon by champions of the status quo. They say that the average Negro must demonstrate to the average white that the latter's fears are groundless. One proponent of this point of view has stated that Negro crime and illegitimacy must decline and Negro neighborhoods must stop deteriorating.

In these observations lies a volume on race relations. In the first place, those who articulate this point of view fail to differentiate between acceptance as earned by individual merit, and enjoyment of rights guaranteed to everyone. Implicit, also, is the assumption that Negroes can lift themselves by their bootstraps, and that once they become brown counterparts of white middle-class Americans, they will be accepted on the basis of individual merit. Were this true, our race problem would be no more than a most recent phase in the melting-pot tradition of the nation.

As compared to the earlier newcomers to our cities from Europe, the later ones who are colored face much greater impediments in moving from the slums or from the bottom of the economic ladder. At the same time, they have less resources to meet the more difficult problems which confront them.

One of the most obvious manifestations of the Negro's paucity of internal resources is the absence of widespread integrated patterns of voluntary organizations. The latter, as we know, contributed greatly to the adjustment and assimilation of European immigrants. Both the Negro's heritage and the nature of his migration in the United States militated against the development of similar institutions.

Slavery and resulting post-Civil War dependence upon

whites stifled self-reliance. Movement from the rural South to Northern cities was a far cry from immigration from Europe to the New World. This internal migration was not an almost complete break with the past, nor were those who participated in it subjected to feelings of complete foreignness. Thus the Negro tended to preserve his old institutions when he moved from one part of the nation to another; the immigrant created new ones. And most important, the current adjustment of nonwhites to an urban environment is occurring at a time when public agencies are rapidly supplanting voluntary organizations.

Although much is written about crime and family disorganization among Negroes, most literate Americans are poorly informed on such matters. The first fallacy which arises is a confusion about what racial crime figures reflect. When people read that more than half the crime in a given community is committed by Negroes, they unconsciously translate this into an equally high proportion of Negroes who are criminals. In fact, the latter proportion is extremely small.

In a similar vein, family stability, as indicated by the presence of both husband and wife, which is very low among the poorest nonwhites, rises sharply as income increases.

Equally revealing is the fact in all parts of the country that the proportion of nonwhite families with female heads falls as incomes rise. A good steady pay check appears to be an important element in family stability. Those Negroes who have been able to improve their economic position have generally taken on many of the attributes of white middle-class Americans.

But poverty still haunts half of the Negroes in the United States, and while higher levels of national productivity are a *sine qua non* for higher levels of employment in the nation, they alone will not wipe out unemployment, especially for minorities. The labor reserve of today must be trained if it is to find gainful employment. Among nonwhites this frequently involves more than exposure to vocational training. Many of them are functionally illiterate and require basic education prior to any specialized job preparation.

The very magnitude of these problems illustrates that society must take the leadership in solving them. But society can only provide greater opportunities. The individual must respond to the new opportunities. And he does so, primarily, in terms of visible evidence that hard work and sacrifice bring real rewards.

Many white Americans are perplexed, confused, and antagonized by Negroes' persistent pressure to break down racial segregation. Few pause to consider what involuntary segregation means to its victims.

To the Negro, as an American, involuntary segregation is degrading, inconvenient, and costly. It is degrading because it is a tangible and constant reminder of the theory upon which it is based—biological racial inferiority. It is inconvenient because it means long trips to work, exclusion from certain cultural and recreational facilities, lack of access to restaurants and hotels conveniently located, and, frequently, relegation to grossly inferior accommodations. Sometimes it spells denial of a job, and often it prevents upgrading based on ability.

But the principal disadvantage of involuntary segregation is its costliness. Nowhere is this better illustrated than in education and housing. By any and all criteria, separate schools are generally inferior schools in which the cultural deprivations of the descendants of slaves are perpetuated.

Enforced residential segregation, the most stubborn and universal of the Negro's disadvantages, often leads to exploitation and effects a spatial pattern which facilitates neglect of public services in the well-defined areas where Negroes live. It restricts the opportunities of the more successful as well as the least successful in the group, augmenting artificially the number of nonwhites who live in areas of blight and neglect and face impediments to the attainment of values and behavior required for upward social and economic mobility.

The most obvious consequence of involuntary residential segregation is that the housing dollar in a dark hand usually commands less purchasing power than in a white hand. Clearly, this is a denial of a basic promise of a free economy.

For immigrant groups in the nation, the trend toward improved socioeconomic status has gone hand-in-hand with decreasing residential segregation. The reverse has been true of the Negro. Eli Ginzberg, in his book *The Negro Potential*, has delineated the consequences:

> It must be recognized that the Negro cannot suddenly take his proper place among whites in the adult

world if he has never lived, played, and studied with them in childhood and young adulthood. Any type of segregation handicaps a person's preparation for work and life. . . . Only when Negro and white families can live together as neighbors . . . will the Negro grow up properly prepared for his place in the world of work.

Residential segregation based on color cannot be separated from residential segregation based upon income. Both have snob and class appeal in contemporary America. Concentration of higher-income families in the suburbs means that many of those whose attitudes and values dominate our society do not see the poor or needy. But more important, cut off by political boundaries, it is to their interest *not* to see them.

Yet there are over thirty million Americans who experience poverty today. For the most part, we resent them and the outlays required for welfare services. They are a group which is separate from the majority of Americans and for whom the latter accept only the minimum responsibility. Thus we have, for the first time, class unemployment in the United States.

I happen to have been born a Negro and to have devoted a large part of my adult energies to the problem of the role of the Negro in America. But I am also a government administrator, and have devoted just as much energy—if not more—to problems of government administration at the local, the state, and the national levels.

My responsibilities as a Negro and an American are part of the heritage I received from my parents—a heritage that included a wealth of moral and social values that don't have anything to do with my race. My responsibilities as a government administrator don't have too much to do with my race, either. My greatest difficulty in public life is combating the idea that somehow my responsibilities as a Negro conflict with my responsibilities as a government adminstrator: and this is a problem which is presented by those Negroes who feel that I represent them exclusively, as well as by those whites who doubt my capacity to represent all elements in the population. The fact is that my responsibilities as a Negro and a government administrator do not conflict: they complement each other.

The challenge frequently thrown to me is to go out into

the Negro community and exhort Negro youths to prepare themselves for present and future opportunities. My answer is somewhat ambivalent. I know that emphasis upon values and behavior conducive to success in the dominant culture of America was an important part of my youthful training. But it came largely from my parents in the security and love of a middle-class family. (And believe me, there is nothing more middle-class than a middle-class minority family!)

Many of the youths I am urged to exhort come from broken homes. They live in communities where the fellow who stays in school and follows the rules is a "square." They reside in a neighborhood where the most "successful" are often engaged in shady—if not illegal—activities. They know that the very policeman who may arrest them for violation of the law is sometimes the payoff man for the racketeers. And they recognize that the majority society, which they frequently believe to be the "enemy," condones this situation. Their experience also leads some of them to believe that getting the kind of job the residents in the neighborhood hold is unrewarding—a commitment to hard work and poverty. For almost all of them, the precepts of Ben Franklin are lily-white in their applicability.

Included in the group are the third generation of welfare clients. It is in this area—where they learn all the jargon of the social workers and psychologists—that they demonstrate real creativity. It is in activities which "beat" the system that they are most adept—and where the most visible rewards are concentrated.

All youth is insecure today. Young people in our slums are not only insecure but angry. Their horizons are limited, and, in withdrawing from competition in the larger society, they are creating a peculiar, but effective, feeling of something that approaches, or at least serves as a viable substitute for, security. In the process, new values and aspirations, a new vocabulary, a new standard of dress, and a new attitude toward authority evolve. Each of these serves to demonstrate a separateness from the dominant culture.

As a realist, I know that these youths relate with me primarily in a negative sense. They see me in terms of someone who has been able to penetrate, to a degree, the color line, and to them I have bettered the "enemy." If I should attempt to suggest their surmounting the restrictions of color, they cite instances of persons they know who were qualified —the relatively few boys or girls in their neighborhood who finished high school or even college, only to be ignored, while white youths with much less training were selected for good jobs. And such occurrences are not unique or isolated in their experience.

The example which will be an inspiration to the Negro boys and girls whose antisocial behavior distresses most whites and many Negroes is someone they know who has experienced what they have experienced, and who has won acceptance in the mainstream of America. When the Ralph Bunches, William Hasties, and John Hope Franklins emerge from *their environment*, the achievements of these successful Negroes will provide models which have meaning for them.

This is reflected in the occupations which provide the greatest incidence of mobility for slum youth. One thinks immediately of prizefighting and jazz music. In these fields there is a well-established tradition of Negroes, reared in the ghetto areas of blight and poverty, who have gone to the top. For youth in a similar environment, these are heroes with whom they *can* and *do* identify and relate. And in these fields, a significant proportion of the successful are nonwhites. For only in those pursuits in which excellence depends largely on native genius (if indeed it does not profit from lack of high-level training) does the dominant environment of the Negro facilitate large-scale achievement.

For many successful older colored Americans, middle-class status has been difficult. Restricted, in large measure, to racial ghettos, they have expended great effort to protect their children from falling back into the dominant values of that environment. And these values are probably more repugnant to them than to most Americans. This is understandable in terms of their social origins. For the most part, they come from lower-middle-class families, where industry, good conduct, family ties, and a willingness to postpone immediate rewards for future successes are stressed. Their values and standards of conduct are those of success-oriented middle-class Americans.

It is not that responsible Negroes fail to feel shame about muggings, illegitimacy, and boisterousness on the part of other Negroes. Many—particularly the older ones—feel too much shame in this connection. Accordingly, some either repudiate the "culprits" in terms of scathing condemnation or try to escape from the problem lest it endanger their none-too-secure status.

These attitudes, too, are shifting. The younger middle-class Negroes are more secure and consequently place less stress upon the quest for respectability. But few Negroes are immune from the toll of upward mobility. Frequently their struggle has been difficult, and the maintenance of their status demands a heavy input. As long as this is true, they will have less energy to devote to the problems of the Negro subculture. It is significant, however, that the sit-ins and Freedom Marches in the South were planned and executed by Negro college students, most of whom come from middle-class families.

Middle-class Negroes have long led the fight for civil rights; today its youthful members do not hesitate to resort to direct action, articulating the impatience which is rife throughout the Negro community. In so doing they are forging a new solidarity in the struggle for human dignity.

There are today, as there always have been, thousands of dedicated colored Americans who don't make the headlines but are successful in raising the horizons of Negroes. These are the less well-known leaders who function at the local level, the teachers, social workers, local political leaders, ministers, doctors, and an assortment of indigenous leaders —many among the latter with little formal education—who have familiarized themselves with the environmental factors which dull and destroy motivation. They become involved with the total Negro community, they demonstrate—rather than verbalize—a concern for the Negro youth's problems. They are trying to reach these young people, not by coddling and providing excuses for failure, but through identification of and assistance in the development of their potentialities. Both genuine affection and sufficient toughness to facilitate and encourage the development of self-reliance are involved.

Those, white and black alike, who reach the newcomers in our urban areas, avoid value judgments relative to cultural patterns. When they suggest thrift, good deportment, greater emphasis upon education and training, they do so as a pragmatic approach. For them, it is not a matter of proselytizing, but rather of delineating those values and patterns of behavior that accelerate upward mobility in contemporary American society.

Such a sophisticated approach enables them to identify deviations from dominant values and conduct which are not inconsistent with a productive and healthy life in modern urban communities. The latter are left undisturbed, so that there will be a minimum adjustment of values and concepts and the maximum functional effectiveness on the part of individuals who will not soon become middle-class America.

What are the responsibilities of Negro leadership?

Certainly the first is to keep pressing for first-class citizenship status—an inevitable goal of those who accept the values of this nation.

Another responsibility of Negro leadership is to encourage and assist Negroes to prepare for the opportunities that are now and will be opened to them.

The ultimate responsibilities of Negro leadership, however, are to show results and maintain a following. This means that it cannot be so "responsible" that it forgets the trials and tribulations of others who are less fortunate or less recognized than itself. It cannot stress progress— the emphasis which is so palatable to the majority group—without, at the same time, delineating the unsolved business of democracy. It cannot provide or identify meaningful models unless it effects social changes which facilitate the emergence of these models from the environment which typifies so much of the Negro community.

But Negro leadership must also face up to the deficiencies which plague the Negro community, and it must take effective action to deal with resulting problems. While, of course, crime, poverty, illegitimacy and hopelessness can all be explained, in large measure, in terms of the Negro's history and current status in America, they do exist. We need no longer be self-conscious in admitting these unpleasant facts, for our knowledge of human behavior indicates clearly that antisocial activities are not inherent in any people. What is required is comprehension of these—a part of society's problems—and remedial and rehabilitation measures.

Emphasis upon self-betterment, if employed indiscriminately by Negro leaders, is seized upon by white supremacists and their apologists to support the assertion that Negroes—and they mean all Negroes—are not ready for full citizenship. Thus, because of the nature of our society, Negro leadership must continue to stress rights if it is to receive a hearing for programs of self-improvement.

Black Muslims, who identify the white man as the devil, can and do emphasize—with a remarkable degree of success—morality, industry, and good conduct. But the Negro leader who does not repudiate his or his followers' Americanism can do so effectively only as he, too, clearly repudiates identification with the white supremacists. This he does, of course, when he champions equal rights, just as the Black Muslims accomplish it by directing hate toward all white people.

Most Negroes in leadership capacities have articulated the fact that they and those who follow them are a part of America. They have striven for realization of the American dream. Most recognize their responsibilities as citizens and urge others to follow their example. Sophisticated whites realize that the status of Negroes in our society depends not only upon what the Negro does to achieve his goals and prepare himself for opportunities but, even more, upon what all America does to expand these opportunities. And the quality and nature of future Negro leadership depends upon how effective those leaders who relate to the total society can be in satisfying the yearnings for human dignity which reside in the hearts of all Americans.

DISPATCH FROM
WOUNDED KNEE

Calvin Kentfield

A successful fiction writer analyzes the very real problems of the red man in America caused by white man's legislation.

WOUNDED KNEE, S.D. From time to time over the years, since long before the frigid Plains winter of 1890 when United States forces armed with Hotchkiss machine guns mowed down men, women, children and some of their own soldiers in the final slaughter at Wounded Knee, the Congress of the United States has become guiltily concerned about the condition and fate of the native American Indian. The most recent manifestation of that concern was the House of Representatives Bill 10560, also known as the Indian Resources Development Act of 1967, sponsored by Representative Wayne N. Aspinall of Colorado, chairman of the Committee on Interior and Insular Affairs with which the bill now resides.

The bill would allow the Indians greater freedom in selling, mortgaging, and developing what lands they still possess, encourage them through government loans to bring industry to the reservations, and enable them with the approval of the Interior Department's Bureau of Indian Affairs to obtain loans from private sources. Indians in general, after years of bitter experience with Congressional maneuvers and of watching the depletion of their lands despite federal largesse, were wary of the bill's benevolence, but most of their tribal councils chose to go along with it, chiefly because they hoped that this time around the economic provisions would really work and because they figured that this was as good a bill as they could get at this time.

Out where the battle of Wounded Knee took place, however, the tribal elders are decidedly unenthusiastic about such bills and their government backers. "We know they mean well," said Johnson Holy Rock, the chairman of the Tribal Council of the Oglala Sioux at Pine Ridge Reservation in South Dakota. "Their intentions in putting forth this bill are undoubtedly of the best, but they don't understand the Indian mind, and we here at Pine Ridge have simply said we won't accept it, we want to be left out, we're not ready for it, we know we'd lose more than we'd gain and we've lost too much already."

And Brice Lay, the chief of the Pine Ridge Agency of the Bureau of Indian Affairs to which an Indian must apply in order to sell or lease his land, said, "We here at the bureau know, and the council knows, that if a piece of land comes up for bids, a non-Indian's going to get it." He pointed to a chart of the reservation that showed forty-two percent of the land already in white hands. "The Indians have first choice," he went on, "but very few of them can afford it, not even the council acting for the tribe as a whole. It's simply going to go out of Indian hands, and there's nothing on earth we can do about it."

The ever-diminishing land is almost the sole source of subsistence for the inhabitants of the Pine Ridge Reservation—or, more colorfully, the Land of Red Cloud—which is the seventh largest of the three-hundred-odd reservations in the United States. It stretches for ninety miles east from the Black Hills and about fifty miles from the northern Badlands south to the Nebraska line.

In the eastern part some of the land is fertile enough to bear wheat, oats, safflower and the like, but ninety-nine percent of this farmland is now and forever in the hands of the white man. The rest of the reservation consists of rolling short-grass prairie land, an enormous landscape divided into four parts: endless green grass, tall blue sky, low ridges of ponderosa pine, and a constant rustling, sighing wind. Through these great plains wander cottonwood-shaded creeks such as Bear in the Lodge, Potato, Wounded Knee, and the twisted White and Cheyenne Rivers. In the summer, thunderclouds build up towers on the far horizons and the uninhibited sun may produce temperatures of 120 degrees; in the winter, the creeks become ice and blizzard winds such as those that froze the bodies at the massacre of Wounded Knee into such baroque and unusual shapes can bring the thermometer down to forty below.

U.S. Highway 18 passes east-west through the southern edge of the reservation. There are miles and miles of good black-top roads kept in repair by Indians working for the Interior Department road service; and there are miles and miles of roads that are no good at all. There are modern boarding schools exclusively for Indian children as well as local public schools and a Catholic mission school, outlying clinics and a good free hospital with doctors, surgeons, dentists and a psychiatrist. There are churches of all kinds (forty percent of the Indians profess to be Catholics and more to be Protestants, but the old beliefs still lie heavily in their souls). There is an American Legion Post, a Lions Club, a Ladies' Aid, a P.-T.A. and a Boy Scout troop. Nearly all of the Sioux (or Dakotas, their own prereservation name for themselves) speak English as well as their native Lakota dialect, and there are still a few medicine men around, like old Frank Fools Crow who usually presides over the annual Sun Dance. The center of nearly everything—government, society, law and order, education—is Pine Ridge, a town of 1,256 people close enough to the state line to have a "suburb" in Nebraska, Whiteclay, center of shopping (three supermarkets) and entertainment (bars and dance halls).

On this reservation live, in one fashion or another, nearly 10,000 Teton Sioux of the Oglala tribe. They are not the poorest or the richest of the country's Indians. The Hopis and some of the Apaches of the Southwest are poorer, and the inhabitants of the Aguacaliente reservation in Southern California, who more or less own Palm Springs, are richer, to say nothing of those few tribes that have oil wells. But the Oglalas range from a state of imminent starvation to fair affluence.

On the reservation itself, unemployment is forty-three percent, so some of the younger people go elsewhere for summer work. There is a new factory at Pine Ridge that employs about a hundred people to make "handmade" moccasins. A fishhook factory near Wounded Knee employs nearly two-hundred more, and a few more work for the Bureau of Indian Affairs. Most of the businesses—filling stations, grocery stores—are owned by whites, and the rest of the Indians work for white ranchers or live off the land which they work themselves or lease to white ranchers. The land, though it belongs to the Indians, is held in trust by the Department of the Interior, which takes care of all the leasing arrangements and issues checks to the owners each month from a computer in Aberdeen.

Aside from Interior Department employees and a few Indian ranchers, the average annual income per family is less than nine hundred dollars. The thirty-four members of the Tribal Council, however, have voted themselves a yearly salary of 7,500 dollars, paid out of proceeds from tribal lands under grazing leases. "Those earnings are supposed to be divided up amongst us all," one man told me, "but we ain't none of us seen a pinny of it for years." Most of the money, of course, goes into the operation of the tribal government, which has charge of all municipal services—police, fire and courts—as well as the maintenance of lawyers in Rapid City and Washington to represent the tribe in all higher dealings with the government. Though technically wards of the federal government under the guiding thumb of the Bureau of Indian Affairs, the Indians, since 1924, have enjoyed the rights and privileges of full American citizenship, including the right to serve in the armed forces and the privilege of paying income taxes. They enjoy some extra privileges as well, such as untaxed land.

"We try to help them," said Brice Lay in his office in the new air-conditioned bureau headquarters in Pine Ridge, "to make the best possible use of the land they have, but it's very hard." Like most of the non-Indian (the bureau does not use the term "white man") employees of the bureau, he is intensely sincere in his desire to help the Indian become a white man. "Here in Pine Ridge most of the people live fairly well, but you go out on the reservation—the way some of those people live!" He made a gesture of despair. "No one should have to live that way."

And, indeed, out on the windy treeless tracts of the reservation, at the end of two dirt ruts across the prairie, will be a one-room shack, possibly a log cabin, possibly a frame house walled in tarpaper, for a family of six, eight, ten people and surrounded by a circle of old car bodies that, like the bodies of U.S. soldiers killed in a battle of olden times, have been stripped and mutilated and left to rot where they lay. An outhouse nearby. No electricity, no running water. A monthly ration of rice, flour, powdered milk, peanut butter, margarine, lard, raisins, oatmeal, cornmeal, potted meat, dried beans, dried peas, bulgar and rolled wheat, plus fifty dollars in cash from Welfare. This kind of poverty engenders horror, pity and disgust in the Anglo-Saxon breast, but all the Oglalas are not that badly off, and many of them simply don't want some of the amenities that the Great White Father insists they must have, if possible, for their own good.

"We had one old woman out on the reservation," Brice Lay said, "that was all by herself and living in a tent, so we found a house for her, but she wouldn't move in. She said she'd die if she lived in a house, that the air in a house was bad air. Oh, she was stubborn. But finally," he concluded with a tone of great satisfaction, "we got her in there."

Out at Wounded Knee about two miles from the general store and post office lives a man in his late fifties, his wife, two married sons, six grandchildren, three dogs, two cats, some hens and a rooster. He is a full blood, very dark, though his wife is not. He owns a section of land (640 acres) through which runs Wounded Knee Creek and on which graze about two hundred head of cattle and sixty or seventy horses. He has a field of alfalfa which, this year, because of the late rains, is exceptionally rich and high and, when I visited him, was ready for cutting. There are tall shade trees along the creek, plenty of water, and a small field of sweet corn nearby.

He and his wife and one orphaned grandchild live in a very old, one-room log cabin with a shade, or "squaw cooler" (though "squaw" is an insulting word these days), a kind of summer house made of poles and pine boughs that keep off the sun but let the breeze come through, making it a comfortable outdoor kitchen and sleeping place during the hot months. His sons and their families live in small asphalt-shingled houses on either side of the parental house. One son is a cowboy and works the section, the other works at the fishhook factory over the hill. Standing to one side at the edge of the alfalfa is a two-hole outhouse.

They carry their water from the creek, build their fire with wood and light their lamps with kerosene. They walk to the store and back, as they have no car. They are well and presumably happy. They are members of the Native American Church who use peyote, the hallucinatory cactus, in their services, during which, under the spell of the drug, they chant and sing and pray to God that the day will come when all men will be at peace and all men will be brothers. Not half a mile from this man's house reside the bones in a mass hilltop grave of the victims of the massacre of Wounded Knee.

Though a Peace Sacrifice was the climax of 1967 Sun Dance—"Richard 'Buddy' Red Bow," the posters read, "seventeen years old, member of the Oglala Sioux tribe, will pray for worldwide peace by performing the traditional Sun Dance worship. Red Bow will pierce his flesh and offer his blood, praying for the safety of American Servicemen and a peaceful speedy end to war in Vietnam"—the Sioux were not always a peaceable people.

"Sioux" is short for "Nadowessioux," which is French for "Nadowessi," which is Chippewa meaning "little snakes" or, in other words, treacherous enemies. The Sioux fought everybody—the Chippewa, the Crow, the Cheyenne, the Kiowa and the white man after he came pushing onto the plains, stealing, pushing, lying, slaughtering the buffalo, always pushing. In 1866, Red Cloud, "the first and only Indian leader in the West to win a war with the United States," said to a Colonel Carrington, come to open a road to the Montana goldfields, "You are the White Eagle who has come to steal the road! The Great Father sends us presents and wants us to sell him the road, but the White Chief comes with soldiers to steal it before the Indian says yes or no! I will talk with you no more. As long as I live I will fight you for the last hunting grounds of my people."

Red Cloud and Crazy Horse, Custer's Last Stand, Sitting Bull and Big Foot, and the final slaughter at Wounded Knee! After all that misery, bravery, and bloodshed, the Sioux, romanticized by the white man, became the Ideal Indian, the Mounted Warrior in War Bonnet, the End of the Trail, the Indian at the Medicine Show, the All-American Buffalo-Nickel Indian.

The last treaty the Sioux made with the United States Government (1868–69) set aside nearly half of South Dakota, including the sacred Black Hills, and part of North Dakota as the "Great Sioux Reserve." But white men discovered gold in the Black Hills (as Johnson Holy Rock said to me, "The Indians still don't understand gold, it's a white man's concept and the white man just can't understand that"), so an Act of Congress in 1877 removed the Black Hills from the Indians' reserve. Later, another act divided what was left of the "Great Sioux Reserve" into five reservations with still more loss of land, settling the Oglalas at Pine Ridge. It is no wonder, indeed, that the Indian leaders look twice and twice again at Acts of Congress.

The Indian Bureau demands at least one-quarter Indian blood as a prerequisite for donating its paternalistic blessings —but the Pine Ridge Tribal Council has *never* been able to decide upon who is and who is not an Indian.

"The Tribal Council is ridiculous," said a man I shall call Edgar Running Bear because he has asked me not to use his real name. "Two of them are stupid women who have not even had a sixth-grade education, one of them is a hopeless alcoholic, and they're all prejudiced."

We were sitting in Edgar Running Bear's house in one of the several new Pine Ridge subdivisions financed by the Public Housing Authority and built by Indian labor against the fierce objections of half a dozen union leaders. It is a two-bedroom house, pink and white, with a carport and a front lawn like millions of others all over America. In the living room were two modernistic armchairs, a huge radio-phonograph-television combination set in the corner. On top of the TV stood a vase of plastic flowers and on the wall opposite the picture window hung a small imitation tapestry of a roaring tiger printed in lurid colors on black velvet.

It was a hot day and through the open windows we could hear the drumming and amplified chanting of one of the bands, the Oglala Juniors or the Sioux Travelers, who had gathered at the nearby campground for the four-day Sun Dance celebration, a kind of county fair, carnival and tribal get-together combined with ancient ritual which was just then beginning. The celebration is an annual rite that Edgar, at one point in our conversation, referred to scornfully as a reversion to primitivism, though he later took his children over to the campground to ride the Space-Mobile.

"Why do you say they're prejudiced?" I asked. "Against whom?"

"Against the mixed bloods."

Both Edgar and his wife, and indeed most of the population of the reservation, are mixed bloods. The classic face of Red Cloud is seldom seen. Johnson Holy Rock himself is three-quarters Oglala and one-quarter Scotch-Irish. I mentioned this fact and elicited only a shrug from Edgar.

"Do you find," I asked, "that white people on the reservation or off it show prejudice toward you because you're Indians?"

"Oh, yes," Edgar's wife said quickly. "They move onto our land, look down their noses at us, and complain about our laws and our dogs and—"

"When I go off the reservation," Edgar broke in, "I expect to abide by the ways of the people there. It doesn't bother me, if we don't get served one place, we'll go someplace else, but *you* could go staggering drunk down the main street of Rushville [Rushville, Nebraska, the nearest town of any size] and nobody'd look at you, but if *I* did—well, not me because being a policeman they know me—but if an ordinary Innun did the same thing he'd be in jail so fast . . ."

I related an incident I had witnessed in a restaurant-bar in Rushville. The television had been giving news of the aftermath of the Negro riots in Detroit and the waitress had said, "I know it's a funny attitude to take, but if one of them come in here, I just couldn't serve him. I don't know what it is, but—" Then she had given a little laugh and said, "But nobody kin accuse me of racial prejudice because I feel the same damn way about the dirty Indians."

There was a moment of silence while the drums beat at the Sun Dance grounds.

"Well," Edgar said, "that's the kind of thing you run into."

"Well, us Innuns aren't prejudiced against the niggers," Edgar's wife said. "Of course, I wouldn't want my daughter to marry one any more than I'd want her to marry a full blood."

Edgar, slouching deeply in his armchair, gave the living-room wall a kick with the side of his foot. "Look at this damn house," he said. "It's coming apart already."

"That's why we send our kids to public school instead of the B.I.A. Innun school," his wife went on, "because we don't want them to grow up with nothing but Innuns."

"To live here, to live this life we live here," Edgar said, shaking his head, "you have to be half-drunk all the time.

Until 1953, it was, as a Klamath Indian friend of mine once explained, "against the law to feed liquor to Indians." It's still against the law on Pine Ridge because the members of the tribe voted for a dry reservation, though in the "suburb" of Whiteclay there are bars and dance halls that get quite lively on a Saturday night or just after the computer has issued the Mother's Aid or Welfare check.

In those resorts, there is, as well as drunkenness, a great deal of laughter and joking and horseplay; the Oglala is a friendly and, at times, very witty creature. He loves athletic games and plays them well, and his manual deftness makes him an excellent carpenter, machinist or technician if he takes the trouble to develop his talents and possesses the courage to go into the outside world and exercise his skills. One of the commonest reasons, of course, for Indian apathy toward government training programs is that once an Indian learns a white man's trade there is no place on the reservation where he can exercise it. He has to leave his home and relatives and work in some foreign place, and he doesn't want to.

In one Whiteclay bar, I met a fat, jolly Oglala lady who, although she has an excellent secretarial job with the bureau, also creates fine tomahawks for the ever so slightly increasing tourist trade. She has three daughters who are or are becoming registered nurses, one son who has a Ph.D. in sociology and is working with other Indians in Nebraska, and a young son who is a good-for-nothing drunk. She knows Edgar Running Bear very well.

"Pooh! You can't believe a word Ed says," she said, although she allowed that the council was, in fact, incompetent and overpaid and that Johnson Holy Rock was unfair in his recommendations for loans. In general, she felt, the Innuns on the reservation were a passably contented lot and pretty much satisfied with the way the bureau was handling their affairs.

"This is our place," she said. "Some of us go away, but an awful lot of us come back. See those two boys over there in the ball caps? They've been in Oakland, California, making good money, but they've come back."

I asked them why they had come back. One of them laughed and said, "Hell, *I* don't know. I guess to play baseball."

Johnson Holy Rock told me that he had been to Washington and explained to the Interior Department people that the chief complaints they have against the government were that the government treated them like digits instead of human beings, that it didn't understand the Indians' attachment to their people and their land, and that the Indians themselves didn't yet understand the white man's notion of business and money and private property. "We're not ready to be let out on our own," he had told them, "but treat us like people instead of numbers."

I remarked that all of us, not just the Indians, were victims of the official digital computer, that we were all cards full of little holes. *"We've* given up," I said, but this time he didn't understand, because he means to go right on trying to keep his people what they are, more so than any other Americans I know—human beings. But I'm sure that one day he, too, will give up just as Red Cloud, in spite of his vow to fight for his lands forever, gave up, finally telling his people in tones of scornful irony:

"You must begin anew and put away the wisdom of your fathers. You must lay up food and forget the hungry. When your house is built, your storeroom filled, then look around for a neighbor whom you can take advantage of and seize all he has."

That was the way, he said, to get rich like a white man.

THE LAST HOLDOUTS

Patricia Lynden

A young reporter exposes the alienation of a Gypsy tribe who must manipulate and reject the rest of society in order to live by their own rules.

In a land of assimilation they are the last holdouts. They have roamed this country for over 250 years, but they show no signs of joining us; nor are they ever likely to. They are the Gypsies, and they have been at home away from home since the first unrecorded moment of their exodus from India.

They meet with the rest of the world, the non-Gypsies, or the "Gajay" in their language, only to steal our money. Then they disappear behind the doors of their *ofisas,* dingy storefronts where they live and "work," and laugh endlessly at their latest trick. While they are a people apart, they are infatuated by our status symbols and exploit our credit economy to buy Cadillacs, color television sets, diamonds, and the services of some of the nation's best medical specialists. They rarely pay, however.

Most of us—who do not seek Gypsies out for magic solutions to problems—are dimly aware of their existence, have perhaps caught glimpses of them emerging from a rented hall after a celebration, or calling out to "suckers"— their term—from *ofisa* doorways. But try to ask a Gypsy about his way of life, and you will meet with vague answers, lies, an uncomprehending though well-meaning expression, or an appallingly servile manner. One loses interest quickly, and that is their intent.

I had the good luck one day, while on a routine reporting assignment at the New York City Police Department's Pickpocket and Confidence Squad, to discover that the detective I was interviewing was one of the few people in this country who know about Gypsies. He is Lieutenant Allen

Gore, who had at that time spent ten years as the department's sole Gypsy expert. The same season on Broadway he became the basis of the male lead in *Bajour*, a musical about Gypsies. Over the years, Lieutenant Gore had gotten to know them well, and even learned an impressive amount of their language, Romany, which is difficult because it is an unwritten tongue. He said I could go with him on his investigations for as long as I needed to get a story.

Our visits were restricted to Gypsies living in New York City, where the best estimates put the population at around 12,000; but American Gypsies are the same whether you see them in San Francisco or New York. Indeed, they are literally the same, because the American Gypsy population (probably about 200,000) is in constant slow flux from one place to another. Any middle-aged Gypsy has likely camped for months or even years in fifteen or more cities across the country from Portland to Miami, from Provincetown to Los Angeles.

To know the Gypsies, one must practically live among them. So few have that the literature is scant, and much of it marred by untruths. Jan Yoors, a New York artist, did live with them during his adolescence in Europe, and his recent book, *The Gypsies,* is an account of that life. Lieutenant Gore solved the problem by spending much of his working day and all his free time visiting their *ofisas,* talking, listening, and watching. It took him five years before he was fully able to distinguish their lies from the truth and the myths from the realities. I was told by Lieutenant Gore that an extended visit at a Gypsy home would be out of the question for me. No Gypsy would ever consent, he said. However, there was one family I had come to know whose members were anxious to cultivate Lieutenant Gore. When he suggested, after a year, that they allow me to visit them for a week, the woman of the house immediately agreed.

My hostess was a woman in her sixties named Peppa, and she set up only one condition to my visit: she would answer all questions except any about the *boojo*. In Romany the word means "bag" (it was incorrectly called "bajour" in the musical). It is also the name of the most elaborate of Gypsy confidence games. At its culmination, the customer's money is sewn into a small bag, and by means of a deft switch, the victim is given a bag of plain paper and the Gypsy keeps the one that contains the money. Many content themselves

THE LAST HOLDOUTS 119

with lesser forms of confidence tricks because, while they don't get rich, they also don't have to take big risks or work many weeks for results. But my hostess "made *boojo*," as the Gypsies say, and made 50,000 dollars a year at it. She was worried that my professed desire to know more about Gypsy life, their beliefs and customs, was just a pretext for learning the mechanics of the *boojo*.

I had, however, already learned how the *boojo* is carried off from listening to Lieutenant Gore and suckers tell about it. A typical Gypsy customer was a fashionable New Jersey matron who told how she sought out a Gypsy to work black magic so she could get a divorce and large alimony settlement from her husband. The Gypsy assured her she could solve the problem, and it developed after many consultations that the problem was caused by a "curse" on the customer's money and valuables. She was told to bring 7,000 dollars in cash, some diamond jewelry, and several fur pieces to the *ofisa* to have the curse banished. The jewelry and furs were left there for further "work," and the customer returned home with the bag she thought contained her money. Later in the evening she became suspicious, opened the bag to find plain paper, and returned to the *ofisa* to confront the Gypsy. The Gypsy and her family had, of course, disappeared, and next day the woman went to the police. Her money was never recovered, and the Gypsy was never captured.

It is rare that a Gypsy gets caught. Many of their clientele never realize they are being bilked; others are too embarrassed to tell. As often as not, they get caught because other Gypsies inform on them. As one Romany woman said: "Everybody know it when somebody make a score." That knowledge is used when the Romany legal system—the only one they recognize—breaks down because a Gypsy refuses to follow its dictates. If he, for example, refuses to pay a penalty imposed on him by a Romany court, his adversary often takes revenge by going to the Gajo law. (Gajo is the masculine singular and Gajee the feminine singular form for "non-Gypsy.") He simply informs to the police about one of his enemy's thefts, and the police make an arrest. Gypsy law, or *crees*, has no enforcement machinery. Corporal punishment is not part of the Romany tradition; obeying the law is voluntary. Jurors at a trial do no more than arrive at a decision on who is right and wrong in a case, and name the penalty, usually a fine. After that, if one party refuses to comply, the other takes the law into his own hands by going to the Gajo law.

The Romany life is concerned almost solely with itself. World affairs are Gajo affairs, and thus of no interest to the Gypsies. What really absorbs them are their own feuds, marriages, divorces, births, deaths, illnesses. A New York internist who was called in for consultation on a Gypsy case said afterward that no patient was ever so difficult to treat. The entire clan arrived from all over the country and encamped at the hospital to assume *en masse* the anxiety for the patient that is usually reserved, in the Gajo world, only to the patient and his immediate family. Day in and day out they dunned the doctor and the hospital staff for reassurances that the patient would recover, fretting with extravagant intensity, which the doctor found inordinate and felt was a hindrance to his attempts to treat the patient.

In a similar way, a divorce also becomes a community preoccupation. During my stay at Peppa's, the family was the center of interest because one of the daughters was about to have a divorce trial. Day and night, Gypsies were in and out of the house, learning the background of the case, arguing it endlessly. Since it was the major topic of conversation for the week, I too became familiar with its details and nuances. Complicated as it may seem, what follows is a very abbreviated version of a situation all the local Gypsies familiarized themselves with in preparation for the impending trial.

One of Peppa's six daughters, a woman of thirty-two called Maleva, had left the *ofisa* she shared with her husband, taken their daughter, and returned to her mother's house. She claimed that her husband had abandoned her, and was determined to have custody of their daughter. She was prepared to go to the Gajo court if need be to keep the child, since Gypsy law does not necessarily favor the mother in custody disputes. Wanya, the estranged husband, was countercharging abandonment, and also wanted the child, as well as the return of more than the customary one half of his wife's purchase price at marriage.

The dispute had become a feud between the two families, since by Romany custom marriages are arranged between the fathers of a couple, and the bride is purchased by the groom's father. It is not unusual to pay 5,000 dollars for a girl who is a virgin, healthy, well mannered, and adept at the confidence game.

Things had been somewhat unusual in the marriage of Wanya and Maleva. For one thing, Peppa knew her daughter felt an attraction for Wanya, although it would have been scandalously improper for Maleva to say so. But Wanya's family did not have enough money to pay for such a girl who possessed all the Gypsy virtues. So Peppa let her go for only 2,500 dollars, and she let her go on credit until Wanya's mother could make the money to pay the price.

By strict custom, the credit arrangement was a compromise of the bride's family's honor. However, Peppa exacted in return a commitment from Wanya's father that because of the low price, Maleva would not be required to spend the usual first years of her marriage living with her in-laws and giving her earnings to them. Peppa herself had been very unhappy as a young wife taking orders from her mother-in-law and didn't want her daughter to suffer the same. Wanya's family agreed to the condition, and the couple was married.

The trouble started when Wanya's father began demanding money from Maleva. Maleva supported Wanya (which seems to be an American innovation among Gypsies) better than Wanya's mother kept his father. The father became so envious at his son's good fortune that he refused even after his wife did make a large sum of money to pay Peppa what he owed her. Not until a year later did he finally pay 2,000 dollars, and Maleva had to put up the remaining 500 dollars herself—another compromise of honor.

By then the two families were well into a feud; the couple had begun to quarrel, and the parents to exchange insults. Wanya's mother threatened to make Maleva's father *marimay*, or unclean—the worst thing a Gypsy can do to another. An object or a person unwillingly exposed by a woman to her own genitals is considered *marimay*, and unfit to associate with other Gypsies. A man and his family are ostracized for many months should it happen to him. Wanya's mother threatened to make Maleva's father *marimay* when, one day during a quarrel, she cursed him and pointed to her genitals to indicate that if she got any angrier, she would touch them, and then touch him with the "tainted" hand. When recalled, the incident brought disgrace so near in the minds of Maleva's family that it was spoken of only in whispers and tones of dread.

By the time the two families were ready to make a *crees*, there was much "dishonor" and "disgrace" that had been suffered by Maleva's family, and they wanted the jurors to rule that none of the marriage price be paid back, and indeed, they said, Wanya's family should pay them for their suffering. The trial was held a week after my visit, lasting all one evening and through the night. The principals, their families, and other Gypsies who held an opinion about the couple shouted for hours, coming away hoarse from the rented hall. Maleva got custody of the child, but her father had to pay back 1,500 dollars to Wanya's father.

One of the reasons Gypsies hold the Gajay in contempt is, they say, because we are materialistic and attached to our possessions. But the Gypsy is also materialistic, almost a caricature of us in his buying of Cadillacs, diamond rings, mink coats, and color televison sets. The difference, the Gypsy maintains, is that he doesn't become attached to what he owns. To prove it, he takes no care of his possessions. Gypsy Cadillacs, even when they are still new, characteristically have torn upholstery and dented fenders.

Peppa makes 50,000 dollars a year and owns an apartment building in Miami Beach that provides additional income, but one would not suspect it by looking at members of her family or the outside of their little pink 18,000-dollar house in a lower-middle-class section of Queens. But inside the house, all the walls have been ripped out to make one big room following Gypsy preference. Expensive gilt and brocade sectional couches, on which the family sleeps, contrast wildly with the florid red and black carpeting and ornate lamps. On all the furniture and walls were stains, marks, and tears to which no one paid attention. In the center of one wall was a huge color televison set. A broken one stood next to it; rather than fix the old set, they had purchased a new one. The closets bulged with clothes, many of them never worn, especially the traditional long skirts and low-necked tops that American Gypsies now wear only to Gypsy gatherings. (On the streets they are unrecognizable except to an experienced eye because their dress is American.) There were several mink coats. The bureau held a large collection of gold-coin necklaces, antique jewelry, and diamond rings. Peppa's husband, Nicola—also known as "Deaf Nick" according to the Romany custom of nicknaming for a characteristic—had many drawers full of handmade silk shirts, and in a closet were as many baggy but custom-tailored suits. His daily attire included large topaz cuff links, a diamond tie clip, and a solid-gold belt buckle with gold coins soldered to it. He wore two gold watches, one on the wrist and one on a chain in his waistcoat. Since, as the Gypsies say, "the woman makes the man," Peppa kept Nicola always in a new Cadillac. A large portion of the family's money also seemed to go to innumerable medical specialists, since American city-bred Gypsies are hypochondriacs.

It is characteristic of Gypsies, rich or poor, to be often without money, since they respect spending, not saving. And there was no embarrassment on Peppa's part when, moneyless, she had to borrow from me. Over the week I loaned money to her, Nicola, and their daughters on many occasions (and was punctiliously paid back each time). Once, when a plumber was summoned in an emergency, Peppa at first tried to get out of paying him. "Just send me a bill, Mister," she said, with a cavalier wave of the hand. But the plumber wanted cash. "I thought you came to help us out, Mister, but I see you just came to take our money," she shouted. Cowed, the plumber took what he could get, which was my five dollars, and left. When he was gone, Peppa said: "It's a good thing he didn't know I'm Gypsy or he never would have gone away without all the money." It is a lesson increasingly being learned by landlords, doctors, and stores that cater to the Gypsy trade.

Among themselves, Gypsies recognize differences of tribe. There are basically four tribes throughout the world: Muchwaya, Calderash, Churura, and Lovara. The Muchwaya and Calderash are the two that have come to this country in the largest number. The Muchwaya are the smaller of the two, and have adapted in such a way that they have become the richer. It is generally the Muchwaya women who make *boojo*, although some Calderash—such as Peppa, who is married to a Muchwaya—practice it too. The difference between tribes is small. There are variations in a few words they use. The Muchwaya, for instance, say *lovay* for money, and the Calderash say *loy*. Marriage tends to be within the tribe, but this is not a fast rule.

Contrary to the popular belief, there are no kings or queens among the Gypsies. In fact, there are no rulers. They are governed by the *crees*, which represents the general will, and their traditions. Some Gypsies become more powerful than others by playing politics and having a wife who makes a good deal of money. These Gypsies cultivate the police, local politicians, lawyers at the district attorney's office, and judges. When another Gypsy gets into trouble, the Gypsy politician uses his pull to get him off and his wealth to cover any expenses involved. Sometimes he can even exact "taxes" for the protection he offers. Gypsies who balk at payment, or become competitive, are informed on.

Although they live surrounded by the Gajay, and get to know the most intimate secrets of some, Gypsies surprisingly understand very little about us. They make generalizations from what they observe of their customers, from what they see on television, and random experiences. The picture is distorted. Since they do not send their children to school, or attach any value to the kind of education we prize, there are great gaps in their understanding of Gajo institutions and culture. I was in Washington, D.C., one day and happened upon a Gypsy family taking a guided tour through the Capitol. It was unusual, so I followed to eavesdrop on them. Near the Senate chamber they smiled and nodded appreciatively as the guide told the dimensions and other statistics of a mural. But they did not understand what the Senate chamber was about. "Who sits there?" the Gypsy woman asked her husband. "The jury," he replied. During my visit at Peppa's, she asked one night, "Who is Gromyko?" I replied that he was once the Russian ambassador to this country, and she wanted to know what an ambassador does. I explained that he watches over his country's interests in another country. She could understand why they would be necessary to try to keep the peace in unfriendly countries, but she could not understand why the Gajay need an ambassador in a country they get along with. She soon tired of my attempts to explain Gajo ways, and changed the subject.

As the visit wore on, the hostility that attended my initial presence—as an outsider who would not make them richer —subsided, and the family began to speak less guardedly. Sonia, one of Peppa's daughters, asked one night, as we shared a plate of fish and potatoes—eating the Romany way, with our fingers—what I thought of the Gypsies, having seen them up close. I said I thought them nice. She replied: "You know what I mean. What do you think about, you know, the way we make our living? You think it's bad that we do that . . . make *boojo,* don't you?" she pressed. "You have to, those are your people. I would if I was you." If she was sympathetic, I asked, why didn't she stop? "I have to do it. It's in the blood. If you've got the blood, you have to do it," she answered with finality. Did she ever feel guilty? "You don't feel bad. It's not something to feel bad about. You feel good when you make *boojo.* That's something good. You don't think about the woman," she replied. Did she ever wish she were a Gajee? "Sometimes I wish I was a Gajee. You have a nice life. But we're different people. A Gypsy, he doesn't murder, he doesn't kidnap, he doesn't rob banks . . ."

The religion was the most difficult of all to pin down, and in that respect it tells the most about them. Although they claim to be Catholic, the Gypsy religion is actually a confusing mixture of Christianity and ancestor worship. The latter is perhaps a surviving remnant from their Indian origins. As the Gypsies arrived and spread into the Western world, beginning around the fourteenth century, they picked up smatterings of Christianity and assorted local folkways. All these make up their religion today, a creed that is without an organized dogma. When they do go to church, which is rarely, the Gypsies generally choose an Eastern Orthodox one, and they usually bury their dead in Eastern Orthodox cemeteries. Their forays into church are casual, and the one I witnessed was also raucous, although no disrespect was intended. Early in January five members of one family were killed in a fire at their Brooklyn *ofisa.* Some twelve hundred shocked members of the Muchwaya tribe came from all parts of the country to mourn, and as they entered the church, many wailing with grief, they ignored the No Smoking signs that the experienced priest had put up for the occasion. Seating was a noisy business, with much yelling and changing of seats to join friends and console one another. Later, at the gravesite, still crying, they showered the coffins with liquor and money to give the departed a start in the next life, as the priest stood by praying aloud but being ignored. Again no disrespect was meant. And, while they seem to take their religion seriously, they are not averse to using it to fool the Gajay. Each *ofisa* has a small corner with an altar—a cross surrounded by candles and photographs of any recently deceased relatives. It is used by the family for its own infrequent observances, but also as a prop to convince the Gajay of their spiritual powers and closeness to God.

While at Peppa's, I persistently questioned members of the family in an attempt to grasp a body of dogma that I later learned does not exist. Tired of my questions and amused at my confusion, one of Peppa's daughters repeated a story her grandmother had once used to answer her questions: The Gypsies once had a church, she said, but it was made out of cheese. One day the Gypsies got hungry and ate it, and that was the end of their church.

There is another tale they tell—the only hint I heard of an attempt to rationalize and explain the Romany life. Some Gypsies say they believe it, others wink when asked if they do. When Christ was on the cross, the story goes, His persecutors were preparing a fourth spike made of silver to pierce his heart. Some Gypsies stole the spike, and Christ was spared the additional agony. God was so grateful that he gave the Gypsies permission to steal thereafter. I asked my hostess whether she believed the story. "How else can you explain it?" she replied. "Why can a Gypsy steal but he'll never get caught? The Gypsies don't have a church, and they don't have a country, but God made them free and He watches over us."

THE DIVIDED

Estranged Generations

TO ABOLISH CHILDREN

Karl Shapiro

A modern poet admonishes adults to wage war on the current concept of "youth," which, he feels, is destroying America.

Betrayal is an act of vengeance, obviously. But in an age of betrayal, when men of authority traduce their office and violate the trust placed in their hands, betrayal becomes the official morality. "Official morality" shortly becomes "public immorality"; whereupon the fabric of a society rots before one's eyes. In the years since the end of the Second World War, announced by the drop of the first Ultimate Weapon, the world has been stunned, horrified, and ultimately cajoled and won over to the official morality of America and its corollary of public immorality and anarchy. Hardly a leader, whether President, general, public-relations man, professor, publisher, or poet, can be held to be honorable in his intentions. Everywhere lies the hidden premise and the calculated betrayal, the secret and chauvinistic lie.

To what end? Who is the betrayer, and why? Who are the betrayed? In a pyramidal society, a hierarchy, one would know the answers. But in a jungle there are no answers, only cries of victory or death. In the modern American jungle there are no answers.

Must America give birth to facism? Or can it survive its pristine Constitution? Both issues seem doubtful. Can the economic motive live with the mass monster it has created? Can the poor white who has sacrificed his brain to television, or the poor Negro who loots a TV set from the store ever again cross the line from somnambulism to wakeful joy? Can only the modern artist discover beauty in the twentieth century?

The entire world has become aware of the pervasiveness of American violence. The Americans were the last to discover it. This is as it should be. A betrayed husband is the last to know his situation. America is shocked at itself; someone has handed it a mirror. Instead of the young and handsome heir of all the ages, with his bathing-beauty consort, winners of Olympic Games, we see the soft and rotten killer (almost Hemingway style) with his call-girl W.A.S.P. girl friend, wearing a tiny crucifix between her scientifically measured bosoms. Wars are staged and televised on the battlefield; all sports are openly and avowedly big business; all books sell according to the amount of money deposited for advertising; countries are bought and sold in the stock market like cattle. Not that any of this is particularly new. What is new is that it is all now *public* knowledge. And what is awesome is that nobody cares. Everyone wants a share of the rot, the *faisandage*. Ours is a gamy culture from top to bottom. Books about the gaminess are best sellers.

The goal of any writer or professor nowadays is to defend his—there is an old-fashioned word—honor. Can a writer write what he wants and in his manner? Can a teacher teach what he was hired to teach, in his own manner? Or must he give way to some form of blackmail from above or below, some Big Brother, who reinterprets his role for him? But we have heard enough of this structural mechanism from Aldous Huxley, Orwell, McLuhan, and so forth.

At the bottom of the spectrum of betrayal are the "Movements," the pseudo-revolutionary insurrections without goals. The purest of these aim at simple theft and sabotage, such as occur during and after hurricanes. The more complicated are identified with civil rights and sex, freedom of drugs and pills of various forms, the right to unlimited travel vouchers and hospitalization. These are the heirs to the kingdom of Wall Street—the latest generation of betrayers and destroyers. This is the generation that uses the word Love as a synonym for Hate, that practices infantilism on a scale which has never been seen.

In between are the always-duped bourgeoisie, playing both ends against the middle. The bourgeois pays his children off to stay away, horrified at his mistake of educating these freewheeling organisms equipped with electric guitars.

Possibly because the economic structure has reached the saturation point, the old order of social development is defunct. The pattern roughly used to be: immigrant (or settler), bourgeois, professional man, and artist (or patron). The child enacts the pattern in reverse: the young man or woman aspires to be artist *first,* deploring professionalism and education itself, condemning the standards of safety of the bourgeois (while exploiting the material wealth of the bourgeois exchequer), and eventually achieving the role of pseudo-immigrant or "native." The Beats and Hippies are products of the American aesthetic which has always preached disaffiliation and single combat with the forces of nature and of society. All American dissident movements tend to fall apart as soon as they are organized. Each artist and pseudo-artist is his own Huckleberry Finn, a moral expatriate. All of our best artists have been recluses of one kind or another, Melville, Faulkner, Hemingway, Cummings. The American artist who does not shun the Center is suspect. The dissident, however, misunderstands the commitment of the artist and thinks of this commitment only in terms of rebellion. The failure of the masses of dissidents to evolve a politic is inherent in the national aesthetic of individualism. And because the dissidents offer no organized threat to the existing order, the existing order continues to consolidate its gains and to ignore the threat of blackmail. The dissidents simply supply additional dry rot to the cultural fabric. The burning and looting of slums signify the abysmal failure of imagination of the would-be revolutionaries, who in fact have no goals. Their only goals are pillage and revenge. The intellectual infantilism of the American radical makes him a figure of fun or of affection (or disaffection, as the case may be). The most one can say of an Allen Ginsberg or a Timothy Leary or a LeRoi Jones is that they are sincere. Children are always sincere.

Dissidence spread to the professoriat with the installation of artists and writers on the campuses of the nation. (I am one of the writer-professors who encouraged the moral-intellectual dropout philosophy for about a decade.) It was easy and sometimes necessary to equate the mass university with other forms of the bureaucratic organism, but the vagueness of the issues involved and the failure to clarify them simply added up to an abstract dissent. That a university can be a democracy is patently absurd. The prattle about Free Speech at Berkeley which thrilled the sophomores of all ages served simply to debase whatever issues were at hand. Professors such as myself had already fought this issue in the courts, and won. The campus rioters were betraying these gains and taking a little private revenge on the side.

Vietnam itself is a falsified issue in the dissident "revolutions." The war is one of the most evil adventures in our history and its evil effects on the American character are incalculable, but the dissent is largely hypocritical. The "Underground" did not raise its voice against the Russian suppression of Hungary; it pursues a hands-off policy *vis à vis* Castro, even to the endorsement of antique Marxist slogans; it does not agitate for the overthrow of the last big brother of the Axis, Francisco Franco. On the contrary, the dissidents are to be found disporting themselves as frequently in Spain as in other exotic places, pursuing their careers, and brushing up on the guitar. If it is laudable to avoid a draft, it is despicable to moralize about it.

The importation of mysticism and pseudo-mysticism into the West was an early strategem of withdrawal from the known modes of communication. Mysticism is simultaneously an insult and a threat to communal behavior. Mystical evidence is by definition hearsay and inhibits communication. The conveniences of Zen and the Sutras to the dissidents (who were rarely if ever "believers") were that they opened the door to a counterculture, one in which consciousness was superseded by unconsciousness, and provisioned their minds with a counterliterature. The literature of the Orient has never been and cannot be naturalized in the West, but the stratagem of the haiku, for instance, is supposed to put the quietus on Western poetry.

But neither poetry nor any of the other arts is essential to the existence and furtherance of the "Movement," as its members refer to it with typical mystification. The Beat poets were the only dissidents who maintained even diplomatic relations with poetry, but their poetry was openly propaganda for the Movement. The planks of the primitive dissident platform were simple and narcissistic: pot, homosexuality, and doom-prophecy, a tame and almost Baptist program. The poetry lacked ambition to rise above these themes.

Because poetry was meaningless as a vehicle or an aesthetic to the Movement, the early Beat poetry took to the drum and trumpet (nineteenth-century symbols of slave revolt). The mixture of jazz and verse laid the groundwork for the dissident aesthetic: volume of noise, mass hypnotism, pure size, all canceled out the possibility of dialogue or even thought. Nor did hatred of the electronic world preclude the utmost exploitation of the amplifier. Herewith began the invasion of parks.

The deliberate and mischievous inversion of modes (anything "adult" was proscribed) opened a Pandora's box for the child mentality which would have driven Lewis Carroll to suicide. The wave of male and female hysterics with guitars and brotherhood lyrics turned into a mass industry, on the one hand, and, on the other, a generation of *révoltés* without goals. The dissident music is verbal—both the music and the language descend to levels of callousness and insensitivity heretofore unknown—but the contents are those of the infant banging its fists on the high chair. It is an amazing phenomenon that this art, pitched directly to the level of the five- or six-year-old, should also be the level of the college student. (Dissidence appears to taper off thereafter.) Dissident sartorial fashion also abolishes distinctions between the sexes; the not very subtle transvestism of the dissident costume situates the Movement in the years prior to puberty. The burlesque Edwardianism of The Beatles expresses a nostalgia for the age of aristocracy and unlimited wealth.

Throughout human history the fine arts have provided the nexus between intuitional insight and civilized hindsight. That is what the arts have been for. But at times when intuition usurps the more wakeful states of mind, the arts plunge into the playpen and the cry of "immediacy" fills the air. Immediacy (as in D. H. Lawrence's "immediate present" or the Zen Now!) cripples hindsight and deliberation and prevents criteria from coming into existence. The failure of the Beat community to create poetry or any of the other arts is the most significant fact about the Movement. The hidden aesthetic premise of the Movement is that art is evil and must be hamstrung. Only states of unconsciousness are valid: drug-states, violence in bed and on the street, secret languages, political nihilism. These are the *lingua franca* of the Movement.

The drug agitprop of the Movement is widely misinterpreted. The Movement does not want drugs to be legalized for their own use; it wants to convert others to drugs. The drug propaganda is entirely evangelistic: take acid and you will be saved is the same message of Jesus Saves. The counterviolence of the police and the drug authorities is not so much opposed by the drug propagandists as it is courted. Legalization of the drugs would remove the thrill;

without the official opposition and the melodrama of rebellion, LSD would be about as attractive as ice cream. But the uses of hallucinogenic materials also provide the necessary escape from creativity, from the action of writing a poem or painting a picture. If you have been to the artificial paradise, why write about it? There all the poems and paintings and music are ready-made. There everyone is a Michelangelo, a Mozart, and a Shakespeare. The Movement maintains its puritanical aversion to alcohol ("Scotch is for fathers"), for alcohol confers only a temporary nonactivity upon the psyche. Hallucinogens show you the Promised Land.

As students of medieval and Oriental mysticism know, only about one in a hundred thousand mystics has ever recorded his or her "trip" in even mildly impressive prose or poetry. The jottings of drug-takers are even less engaging. The taker of drugs may be trying to force the gates of the imagination, as perhaps was the case with Coleridge, but the mass movement for freedom of unconsciousness is clearly an aesthetic draft-dodge. The aesthetic arrogance of the drug-user in any case lacks the substantiation of visible works. Pot-head, show me your book!

The nihilistic mind is a runaway horse. The Movement blots out literature without ever having cracked a book. Or rather, it burns all literature to the ground. The Movement cultivates cultural brainwashing; even advanced university students pretend to be ignorant of what they know. The fear of cultural infection and the demand for "immediacy" immunize their minds to any responses except to the latest fad or artifact. Their speech and writing degenerate into code (at the moment it is the underworld argot of the slum Negro, a genuine proletarian dialect for him which is, however, awkward and inapplicable to well-wishers and fellow travelers). The Movement's adulation of the Negro slum dweller as hero-victim leads it with characteristic naïveté to adopt his sublanguage as a generalized medium of communication. The very mystery of this language gives it credence: the terminology and metaphors of jazz, sex, drugs, double-speak, and revenge supply the necessary circuits of sympathy to the adolescent of the upper worlds. You dig?

The jazz put-on is a major form of cultural blackmail by the Movement. Anyone not "with" the jazz is a marked man. The hagiography of jazz is as immense as the Vatican Library. It is all phony, a conglomeration of the Music Corporation of America and the masses of delayed and permanent adolescents. Jazz is only a minor facet of modern folk music. What is beatified about jazz is that it is Negro. The Negro, as the most obvious victim of society since the latest massacre of the Jews, is thought to be universalizing about the human condition in jazz. Nothing could be further from reality. Negro jazz is—Negro jazz: charming, entertaining, hot, cool, abstract, evangelistic, white, black, blue, but never revolutionary. Negro jazz is masochistic, and that is precisely its failure and its appeal to the adolescent. What it lacks in content it makes up for in sentimentality, sexuality, and volume.

The blotting out of language in jazz lyrics, the accommodation by skillful musical improvisers to cranked-out dollar-making stanzas, many of them half a century old, attests to the deliberate destruction of language as a medium. The nostalgia of the horn takes over; there is a vague reminiscence of language, unbelievably debased to begin with, whether it came from Tin Pan Alley or from Hollywood. The insistence on jazz, as taken over by the Movement, is the insistence on hysteria as a Way of Life. As such it appeals to the American joy in violence.

The Movement nominates Bob Dylan as great poet. The whining puerilities of this phenomenon are not to be taken lightly in the stock market or in the hearts of millions of children bursting with vitamins and cash. Is he the Leader?

The open release of violence is always a surprise to intellectuals. Rebellion without goals is the most fascinating spectacle of all. The media intone with relentless stupidity: Why? Why? Congresses mourn. Whole cities are put to the torch while children dance and scream as at a jazz festival or an Ice Capade. Yet violence is inculcated by the elders and is exactly predictable. Violence is the answer to the question, Why?

It is quite natural and expectable in psycho-politics that Negro looters should espouse white genocide and Nazi anti-Semitism. It is quite natural that W.A.S.P. children in posh suburbs should play Nazi, instead of Cowboy and Indian. In a child society the only authentic emotion is hate. In Hippie language Hate is spelled Love; any four-letter word will suffice.

America is the child society *par excellence*, and possibly the only one ever politically arrived at. It is the society of all rights and no obligations, the society of deliberate wreckage and waste, the only society that ever raised gangsterism to the status of myth, and murder to the status of tragedy or politics. The American adulation of the child mentality leads to an industrialized hedonism, on the one hand, and a chauvinistic psychology of greed, on the other. In advertising, anyone over the age of twenty-one or twenty-five is portrayed as a idiot who has got behind in the science and commerce of rejuvenation. This "adult" is appealed to by an almost invisible Big Brother (Mad-Ave or the Executive in the White House) because the "adult" has made the mistake of legal and contractual obligation. Therefore he is an idiot. The costuming of the so-called radical population is a form of jeering: the beard is not only a red flag with certain flickering political messages; it is also the ultimate taunt at the man in the suit. Arson, looting, and murder are also gentle reminders to the fathers that the tumbrels are rolling. (In many of my creative-writing classes the students sit in judgment on their parents and make specific judgments about which of the elders will be allowed to live. When they are confronted with the fact that the elders and the state are paying their way through education, the students snort and sneer at the stupidity of authorities.)

Humanities departments, notoriously the most deprived segment of the American university system, have been powerless to halt the invasion of the child psychosis in higher education. The effeminate backstairs aggressiveness of the Humanities gives way to the Creative Writing Gestalt. "Creative Writing" is to the Humanities as strychnine is to the horse. Any symptom of guilt discerned by the undergraduate on the part of its elders is parlayed into immediate sabotage —a sabotage which stops short of the curtailment of personal benefits, however. The gangsterism of the American youth mind makes it as easy a prey to the Marine recruiter as it does to the Creative Writing instructor. The goals are not education but theft, generally theft of scholarships and undeserved preferment. As American literature heroizes the outlaw, so the outlaw student gains advantage over his more serious companions; the style of contempt, the "cool," determines to a large extent the amount of loot acquired and the length of absolution from the institutions which threatened his freedom of operation.

The cultivation of Youth with a capital Y has kept the

growth of the American mind off balance since perhaps the early nineteenth century. The trashy frontier mythology, hand-to-hand combat, Horatio Alger, Alger Hiss, spy psychology, advertising, Hell's Angels, Beats, Hippies, Beatles, dropouts, assassins, amnesiac mass murderers, pseudo-mystics, lately from Kyoto or Benares, C.I.A., Black Muslims and Black Nazis, these are all part and parcel of the American dream of Youth. The dream was dreamed by the fathers, now on the proscribed list.

As Negro anti-Semitism is Christian (the only political training the Negro was ever given was the flaming cross), so anti-adultism is American flag-waving in reverse. For this state of affairs there would seem to be no remedy. And indeed there is not. Should one suggest a program to slow down or stop the strangulation of American life by children, it might read:

1. Cut off all sources of economic supply to Youth except what they earn by physical or observable mental labor.

2. Deny all higher education except on absolute proof of ability. No student should be admitted to a college or university unless he or she has earned a scholarship or has otherwise demonstrated unusual ability. Public universities should be more stringent in this respect than private, rich universities (the private school is unsupervisable).

3. Deny free travel privileges to children. For instance, raise the age minimum of drivers' licenses to thirty or forty. Deny foreign travel except to those who have been granted the privilege from their school.

4. Set aside a large land area for all dissidents to reside in, with ingress but no egress. As children think the world is their personal property, give them their acre of personal property. Keep them there.

5. Discourage the cowardice and intimidation of parents and "authorities" by reeducating them to the nature of the Yahoo. Encourage construction of housing, especially suburban housing, to delimit or exclude the child, and to suit the needs and requirements of adults.

6. Abolish the child. Deliberate the intelligent society in which the infant is loved and cared for and controlled

until he is ready to be shipped to a place of education, should he be worthy. Consider two types of human beings: the infant and the adult. Destroy all concepts of the adolescent.

Whereupon his "literature" will wither away, his "music," his drugs, his revolutions and murders, his terrorism of everything he lacks the understanding and knowledge to comprehend.

The power shift lies in this direction. Man is an aesthetic animal. His greatest works are slashed to ribbons by "Youth" and will continue to be until Grown Man relinquishes his image of the advertised profile of Youth. As long as Grown Man apes Youth, he will remain the victim of his seed.

The American adult must battle "Youth" to the death. "Youth" is a figment of the American imagination which is destroying America itself.

THE EARLY RESIGNED

Paul Goodman

A popular interpreter of contemporary mores investigates the so-called Beat Generation of the late fifties, and demonstrates that teenage dissenters, no matter what they are called, share the same reaction to the establishment.

1

The Beat Generation, in our model, are those who have resigned from the organized system of production and sales and its culture, and yet who are too hip to be attracted to independent work. They are a phenomenon of the aftermath of World War II, and even more of the Korean war. Their number is swelled by youths whose careers, hesitant at best, have been interrupted by the draft.

This group is socially important out of proportion to its numbers and it has deservedly and undeservedly attracted attention and influenced many young people. The importance of the Beats is twofold: First, they act out a critique of the organized system that everybody in some sense agrees with. But second—and more important in the long run—they are a kind of major pilot study of the use of leisure in an economy of abundance. They are not, as such, underprivileged and disqualified for the system; nor are they, as such, emotionally disturbed or delinquent. Some young men might be driven to this position by personality disturbances, but the subculture they have formed has made sense and proved attractive to others without those disturbances, but who have the identical relation to the organized society.

In many ways the Beat subculture is not merely a reaction to the middle class or to the organized system. It is natural. Merging with the underprivileged, the Beats do not make a poor go of it. Their homes are often more livable than middle-class homes; they often eat better, have good records, etc. Some of their habits, like being unscheduled, sloppy, communitarian, sexually easygoing, and careless of reputation, go against the grain of the middle class, but they are motivated by good sense rather than resentment: they are probably natural ways that most people would choose if they got wise to themselves—at least so artists and peasants have always urged. Their rejection of the popular culture, Broadway theater, status commodities, bespeaks robust mental health. (It is, oddly, just these reasonable and natural ways that have won undeserved attention as outrageous. For Madison Avenue boys are miffed and fascinated that the Beats get away with it, and so they keep writing them up.)

The Beat culture shares specific traits of the "outside" class to which they have appointed themselves. Some of these are accidental, belonging to the particular minorities who form the present-day poor—just as in France, it is the North Africans who set the tone. Others are essential, pertaining to being "outside" of society, such as being outcast and objects of prejudice; defying convention rather than just disregarding it; in-group loyalty; fear of the cops; job uselessness.

Besides these natural traits and present-day poor traits, Beat culture is strongly suffused with the hipsterism that belongs to the middle status of the organized system. This appears in some of the Beat economic behavior; in a defensive ignorance of the academic culture; and in a cynicism and neglect of ethical and political goals.

Balked in their normal patriotism and religious tradition, the Beats seek pretty far afield for substitutes, in D. H. Lawrence's red Indians or feudal Zen Buddhists. (But I was delighted, the other night, to hear Allen Ginsberg, one of their best spokesmen, speak with wonder about visiting the Grand Canyon and boast of going to Walt Whitman's house. Soon, I trust, he will take the cruise up our lordly Hudson to Bear Mountain.)

As a typical genesis for a Beat Generation we have suggested (1) attachment to a middle-class home but (2) withdrawing from its values, (3) without growing into other worthwhile values. They are on speaking terms with their families but dissent from all their ways. They experience the university, for instance, as a part of the worthless organized system rather than as Newton and Virgil.

Finally, we saw that the Beats regard themselves as in a

metaphysical crisis: they have to choose between the system and eternal life; and therefore their more philosophic utterances are religious and strewn with references to the apocalypse and saints of yore, as when Allen Ginsberg, again, calls *Time* "the Whore of Babylon"—but indeed she *is* very like the Whore of Babylon.

This is not, on the whole, a strong position: to be resigned and still attached, and therefore to have recourse to apocalyptic means. But let us see what can be made of it, and turn first to the jargon, a variant of a Negro jargon of English, jive.

2

In this talk there is a phrase "make it," meaning "to establish oneself in some accepted relation to something." One can make it as a writer, as a counter boy, with a girl. The word comes from the common English "make it against difficulties," as, "They kept shooting at him but he made it across the field." It is akin to "make good as a lawyer, a writer," but it is not so strong and positive. (We should not say, "Make good as a counter boy.") The difficulties overcome are those that confront anyone who has dropped "out" of the ordinary social functions when he tries to establish himself as anything at all, to be a *something*, a something or other. The usage is an acceptance of withdrawal. (The notion of Norman Mailer, in *The White Negro*, that this and most other jive terms express positive energy or manliness, is quite idiotic.) Consider the series: "He wrote the book—he was a writer—he made good as a writer—he made it as a writer." Very common is the encouraging, or self-encouraging exclamation, "You've got it made!" or "I'll have it made!" This refers almost exclusively to the future-improbable. When it is said in the past perfect, "He had it made," it refers, somewhat wistfully, to some other third person. To express a neutral or proud past fact about oneself, one says simply, "I wrote the book."

This usage, of establishing an acceptable social relation against obstacles, draws from the Role Playing that is the chief function of the middle status of the organized system (just as, in any period, a Negro would see the white society as a closed system with roles to be aped). One can say, "He made it, I made it, with IBM," indicating no specific job, for that is unimportant.

Now a more general withdrawal, from experiencing altogether, is expressed by the omnicapable word "like." E.g., "Like I'm sleepy," meaning "if I experienced anything, it would be feeling sleepy." "Like if I go to like New York, I'll look you up," indicating that in this definite and friendly promise, there is no felt purpose in that trip or any trip. Technically, "like" is here a particle expressing a tonality or attitude of utterance, like the Greek μέν, *verily*, or δή, *now look*. "Like" expresses adolescent embarrassment or diffidence. Thus, if I talk to a young fellow and give him the security of continued attention, the "like" at once vanishes and is replaced by "You know," "I mean," "you know what I mean," similarly interposed in every sentence.

The vocative expletive "Man," however, has different nuances in different groups. Among the Beats it is used diffidently and means, "We are not small children, man, and anyway like we are playing together as like grownups." Among Negroes it is often more aggressive and means, "Man, now don't you call me boy or inferior." Among proper hipsters it means, "We are not sexually impotent." So far as I can hear, it never means acceptance of the speakers as adult males, nor does it have the ring of respect or admiration *(Mensch)*, as a woman or hero worshipping boys might use it. When the interlocutor is in fact respected or feared, he would not be called "man." (Perhaps "boss"?)

"Cool," being unruffled and alert, has the same nuances. In standard English a man "keeps cool in an emergency." If there is *always* an emergency, it must imply that the danger is internal as well as external: the environment is dangerous and feeling is dangerous. As spoken and enacted by a young Beat, maintaining a mask-face and tapping his toe quietly to the jazz, it means, "I do not feel out of place, I am not abandoned and afraid, I am not going to burst into tears." In the original Negro the nuance is rather, "I'll stay unruffled and keep out of trouble around here; I won't let on what I feel, these folk are dangerous." With the hipster, the jaw is more set and the eyes more calculating, and it means, "I'm on to your game, you can't make me flip." In general, coolness and mask-face are remaining immobile in order to conceal embarrassment, temper, or uncontrollable anxiety.

To make a remark about the language as a whole as used

by the Beats: Its Negro base is, I think, culturally accidental; but the paucity of its vocabulary and syntax is for the Beats essentially expressive of withdrawal from the standard civilization and its learning. On the other hand, this paucity gives, instead of opportunities for thought and problem solving, considerable satisfaction in the act and energy of speaking itself, as is true of any simple adopted language, such as pig Latin. But this can have disadvantages. One learns to one's frustration that they regard talk as an end in itself, as a means of self-expression, without subject matter. In a Beat group it is bad form to assert or deny a proposition as true or false, probable or improbable, or to want to explore its meaning. The aim of conversation is for each one to be able, by speech, to know that he is existing and belonging. So among perfectly intelligent and literate young men, some movie or movie star will be discussed for an hour, giving each one a chance to project his own fantasies; but if someone, in despair, tries to assert something about the truth or worth of the movie, the others will at once sign off.

(Among all American adolescents and even fellows in their late twenties, however, there is an embarrassment about "what to say"—"I never have anything to say to a girl," or "They keep talking about painting and I have nothing to contribute." Speaking, that is, is taken as a role. They do not have confidence that if they are interested in the subject, they'll say something, and if they're not, why bother? Here too the Beats have helped formalize and make tolerable a common difficulty; one contributes just by saying, "Like," "Cool," and "Man.")

3

Let us interrupt discussing the jargon and look at the related problem of the artistic activities that are carried on in resignation. These are multifarious and voluminous, including painting, poetry, reading to jazz, decorating the pads, and playing on drums. Everybody engages in creative arts and is likely to carry a sketchbook, proving what the psychologists and progressive educators have always claimed, that every child is creative if not blocked. Resigning from the rat race, they have removed the block.

They work at these arts honestly, with earnest absorption,

and are not too immodest about the modest products, even if they do continually subject one another and passersby to listening to readings, and encourage the community by exclaiming, "It's the greatest!" Such creative activity sharpens the perceptions, releases and refines feelings, and is a powerful community bond.

In itself it has no relation to the production of art works or the miserable life of sacrifice that an artist leads. It is personal cultivation, not much different from finger painting. Like the conversation just described, its aim is action and self-expression and not the creation of culture and value or making a difference in the further world. There is, of course, no reason why it should be. All men are creative but few are artists. Art making requires a peculiar psychotic disposition. Let me formulate the artistic disposition as follows: It is reacting with one's ideal to the flaw in oneself and in the world, and somehow making that reaction formation solid enough in the medium so that it indeed becomes an improved bit of real world for others. This is an unusual combination of psychological machinery and talents, and those who, having it, go on to appoint themselves to such a thankless vocation, are rarer still. These few are not themselves Beat, for they have a vocation, they are not resigned. (My observation is that if artists are blocked in their vocation, they *cannot* resign themselves to seeking other experiences, and certainly they do not do finger-painting, for if they can do finger-painting, they can make art.)

Nevertheless, living among the Beats, there will be a disproportionate number of artists, for the same reason that artists gravitate to any bohemia. Also, some of these genuine unresigned artists will make works that *speak for* the Beat community that they live among. That is, the "Beat" artists are not themselves Beat, for they are artists; but their art works tell us about the Beat.

This situation raises interesting questions about the relation of an artist and his immediate audience, and it is worth exploring.

It is both an advantage and a disadvantage for an artist to have around him an intensely creative gang of friends who are not rival artists. They provide him an immediate audience that helps assuage the sufferings of art loneliness and art guilt. On the other hand, it is a somewhat sickening audience because it has no objective cultural standard, it is not in the stream of ancient and international tradition. So its exclamations, "It's the greatest!" or, "Go, man, go!" don't give much security. The artist finds that he is a parochial group hero, when the reassurance that he needs, if he is diffident, is that he is a culture hero for the immortal world. Let me tell a few anecdotes to illustrate this fascinating dilemma of the relation of the "Beat" artist both to the Beats and to the objective culture in which he must finally exist.

An incident at a party for Patchen. Patchen is a poet of the "previous" generation, of long-proven integrity, with an immense body of work, some of which is obviously good, and the importance of the whole of it (may much still be added!) not yet clear. The point for our anecdote is that Patchen has the respect of writers but has received no public acclaim, no money, no easy publication. Now at this party, one of the best of the "Beat" writers, a genuine young artist, came demanding that the older poet give some recognition to the tribe of Beat poets, to "give them a chance." This was ironical since, riding on the Madison Avenue notoriety that we have mentioned, they had all got far more public acclaim, invitations to universities, nightclub readings, than all of us put together. But Patchen asked for the names. The Beat spokesman reeled off twenty, and Patchen unerringly pointed out the two who were worth while. This threw the younger poet into a passion, for he needed, evidently, to win artistic recognition also for his parochial *audience,* among whom he was a hero, in order to reassure himself that he was a poet, which he was and as Patchen would at once have said. So he insulted the older man. Patchen rose to his height, called him a young punk, and left. The young man was crushed, burst into tears (he was drunk), and also left. At this, a young woman who often accompanied him came up to me and clutched me by the knee, pleading with me to help him grow up, for nobody, she said, paid him any attention.

That is, the Beat audience, having resigned, is not in the world; yet being an eager creative audience, it wins the love and loyalty of its poet who becomes its hero and spokesman. But he too, then, doubts that he is in the world and has a vocation. As a Beat spokesman he receives notoriety and the chance of the wide public that every poet wants and needs; but he cannot help feeling that he is getting it as a pawn of the organized system.

Here is a simpler illustration of the relation of the spokesman-artist to the objective culture. This fellow is a much weaker poet, more nearly Beat himself, and quite conceited. At a reading of some other poet who is not a Beat spokesman, he tries to stop the reading by shouting, "Don't listen to this crap! Let's hear from X." His maneuver is to make the parochial the *only* existing culture; then, by definition, he himself is an artist.

And here is an illustration of the most elementary response. A Beat spokesman, not ungifted but probably too immature to accomplish much, gives a reading in a theater. During the intermission, he asks a rather formidable and respected critic what he thinks of a particular poem, and the critic says frankly that it's childish. At this the outraged poet, very drunk, stands in the lobby screaming, "I hope you die! I hope art dies! I hope all artists die!"

These illustrations and the analysis of Beat conversation bring out the same point: In a milieu of resignation, where the young men think of society as a closed room in which there are no values but the rejected rat race or what they can produce out of their own guts, it is extremely hard to aim at objective truth or world culture. One's own products are likely to be personal or parochial.

4

Shared creative expression has a therapeutic effect, and so results in transference, unconscious attachment. The striking, and often amusing, example of this is the young ladies who take modern dancing, with its beautiful exercises that release tense muscles; they are all head over ears in love with Martha or Doris, and fiercely loyal and sectarian.

The same occurs among the young Beats, except that, since there is no "leader," the emerging love attaches either to the community or to each one's self-image narcissistically. This makes for a powerful warmth of life—"the warmth of assembled animal bodies," as Kafka said—but it makes it even harder to get into the world. It gives the young men a daily interpersonal excitement, more satisfactory than the empty belonging or conformity of the organization, and happier than the loneliness of art. But it does not give them "something to do."

5

So we return to our crucial problem: What to do that is self-justifying when the great social world is pretty unavailable?

The essential Beat answer is: to heighten experience, and get out of one's usual self.

To heighten experience is a common principle of Beat, Hipster, and Delinquent, but the differences are marked. Among the Hipsters, as Mailer points out, the craving for excitement and self-transcendence is darkly colored with violence and death wish, and they therefore dread flipping, which they interpret as weakness, castration, and death. Among the younger delinquents, we shall see, it is fatalism, the wish is to get caught and be brought back into society. But for the Beats, it is a religious hope that something new will happen, a revival.

In my observation, the Beats do not seem to be self-destructive. The risks of delinquency, criminality, and injury rouse in them a normal apprehension, and they express a human amazement at the brutality and cruelty of some with whom they keep company. In taking drugs for the new experience, they largely steer clear of being hooked by an addiction. On the other hand, if the aim is to get out of this world, one can hardly play it safe. So it is not surprising if they push their stimulants, sleeplessness, and rhythmic and hallucinatory exercises to the point of having temporary psychotic fugues, or flipping. In his book, Lipton speaks touchingly of someone who goes off to the municipal psychiatric hospital as an expected and regular occurrence. Perhaps *this* is the feudal support which I have claimed to be lacking in Beat Zen Buddhism: the young sages seek enlightenment, and the city hospital succors them when they break down.

Let us now go back to the jargon. The supreme words are "crazy," "far out," "gone," "high," "gas," "sent." These mean not in this world but somewhere, not rational but something. "Flip" is generally used with enthusiastic self-deprecation.

When the crazy or far-out moment can be maintained for long enough to be considered a something and somewhere, it is "groovy," that is, one is like somebody else's phonograph record. One is "with it" or "falls in." The "it" or the understood "where" is not, of course, definite, for pure being has no genus and differentia. "Swinging with it" is the condition of passing from here and now to the heightened experience of "it."

Contrariwise, it is bad and painful to be "nowhere," to "fall out" (take an overdose), to be "drug" (dragging).

The way of being-in-the-world, that is, is to be either cool and mask-faced, experiencing little; or to be sent far out, experiencing something. However, since the cool behavior of these usually gentle middle-class boys looks like adolescent embarrassment and awkwardness rather younger than their years, one wonders whether ordinary growth in experience would not be a more profitable enterprise and ultimately get them much further out.

A possibility that has interestingly dropped from Beat culture is the exploitation of shared athletic or wildly physical agitation, which belonged grandly to the old jazz-for-dancing and revival meetings. This is certainly an important truth in Mailer's proposition that jive is energetic, in words like "go" and "dig."

(To the jazz-for-listening one is not supposed to respond overtly by more than a quietly tapped toe. It can then be hypnotic and speak to the listener like a crystal ball or a fountain or a hearth fire. As music it is remarkably thin gruel [no doubt I am tone deaf]. For the performer, of course, it provides the deepening absorption of any simple improvised variations, plus the solidarity of the group.)

I can think of two reasons why the overtly shared crazy physical rhythms are spurned. First is that this motion is in fact too much in the extremities of the body rather then in the solar plexus, it is too superficial an excitement and more fit for teenagers. The difference is between the lostness in juvenile jitterbugging and the "central" experience of Oriental dance or Mary Wigman. Some young men have taken to the Oriental dance, but most Beats do not practice this physiological yoga either, just as their Zen is without breathing-exercises or correction of posture. So perhaps another reason for their dropping the old physical jazz and revival is just the opposite, that the display of energy would upset their coolness, it would be embarrassing and make them feel too young. I wonder if this is not the simple explanation of their disdain of social dancing as "dry" sex; for certainly one of the reasonable uses of social dancing is body contact and sometimes sexual foreplay. But these boys are embarrassed to get an erection, to betray feeling, in public, though they are more than willing to take their clothes off and exhibit themselves, or to beat a drum wildly in public as an exhibition for the others, but not as contact with them.

6

An awkward consequence of heightening experience when one is inexperienced, of self-transcendence when one has not much world to lose, is that afterward one cannot be sure that one was somewhere or had newly experienced anything. If you aren't much in the world, how do you know you are "out of this world"? This problem has been fateful for Beat literature. (The classical mystic who loses this world knows well, on returning to it, that it is a poor thing; and also that it is pointless to try to describe the Reality in terms of this world.)

The Beat novelist does not say, "Like when we left Chicago, we went to like New York." (Samuel Beckett does, of course, do just this in principle, and mighty strange and dull his novels are.) The Beat novelist wants to say that we did leave Chicago and did go to New York. But how would one know? When there is not much structure for the experience —no cause to leave Chicago, no motive to go to New York— these things become very doubtful and it is hard to make the narrative solid. So incidents are multiplied without adding up to a plot; factual details are multiplied that do not add up to interpretation or characterization; and there are purple passages and exclamations. The point of the perseveration is to insist that *something* happened.

(This narrative difficulty of more or less articulate grownups is important in reminding us of what might otherwise be dark about the juvenile delinquents: that in the immense multiplicity of their exploits and kicks, including even horrifying deeds, it is not necessarily the case that they experienced what they were doing. It is therefore beside the point to judge or treat them as if they were performing acts.)

Similarly the Beats make a social ritual of reminiscing and retelling. Meeting in a group, they retell exactly what happened, each one adding his details, with the aim of proving that something indeed happened, and perhaps they can recapture the experience of it, if indeed anything was experienced; just as at a later date, this meeting at which the retelling is occurring will be retold. It is like a man who dreams in exact detail of the fight he had with the boss; what could be the wish in such a dream? It is that when the event occurred he failed to get angry, but dreaming it he is angry. Except that in the Beat retelling, they are not angry this time either.

In such circumstances, it seems to me inevitable that heightened experiences too will pall, for they do not transform enough natural and social world to create experience and new experience. They do not accumulate knowledge, establish better habits, make hypotheses probable, and suggest further projects, all the things that constitute seasoned experience. A Beat will tell you a remarkable vision that he had under peyote, but you do not feel that it was a vision for *him;* it is as useless as the usual experience of extrasensory perception that is irrelevant to anybody's practical affairs. So in their creative activity young Beats compile thick notebooks of poems and drawings, but since there are no problems of art, these do not add up to a body of work. What might then occur, unfortunately, is that, when the flesh is not better nourished, the spirit fails. Since better habits are not developed, the young men simply succumb to bad ones, relying more and more on the drugs, and becoming careless about meaning anything. Then other young fellows who chose this way of life because it suited and solved a problem, quit it because of the bad company.

The word "angry," we saw, was a misnomer for "bitter and waspish." The word "Beat," however, is exquisitely accurate, meaning "defeated and resigned." Public spokesmen of the Beats have, as the result of various visions, assured us that the word means *Beatus, blessed;* but this too soon comes to the same thing, "punchy."

7

Lawrence Lipton tells us that the word "work" always means "copulate." (A job of work is a "gig.") This is a good thought, for it means that the sex is feelingful and productive, even though effortful.

My impression is that—leaving out their artists, who have the kind of sex that artists have—Beat sexuality in general is pretty good, unlike delinquent sexuality, which seems, on the evidence, to be wretched. Animal bodies have their own rhythms and self-limits; in this, sex is completely different from taking drugs; so if inhibition is relaxed and there is the courage to seek for experience, there ought to be good natural satisfaction. One sees many pretty young Beat couples. (*I* think they are pretty; some people think they are hideous.) Since conceit and "proving" are not major factors, there is affection. Homosexuality and bisexuality are not regarded as a big deal.

But the question remains, What is in it for the women who accompany the Beats? The characteristic Beat culture, unlike the American standard of living, is essentially for men, indeed for very young men who are "searching." These young fellows are sweet, independent, free-thinking, affectionate, perhaps faithful, probably sexy—these are grand virtues, some of them not equally available among American men on the average. But Beats are not responsible husbands and fathers of children.

There are several possible sexual bonds. Let us recall the woman at the Patchen party, who pleaded for someone to help the young man. Her relation to him is maternal: she devotes herself to helping him find himself and become a man, presumably so that he can then marry her. (Typically; I do not mean actually in this case.)

Another possible relation is Muse or Model: her Beat is her poet and artist and makes her feel important. This is a satisfaction for her feminine narcissism or penis envy. But it comes, often, to ludicrously overestimating the young man's finger-painting and laying on him an impossible burden to become the artist that he is not.

One sometimes sees a pathetic scene in a bar. Some decent square young workingmen are there, lonely, looking for girls or even for a friendly word. They feel that they are "nobodies"; they are not Beats, they are not artists. They have nothing to "contribute" to the conversation. The girls, meantime, give their attention only to the Beats, who are sounding off so interestingly. But these Beats will not make any life for the girls, whereas the others might make husbands and fathers. If a square fellow finally plucks up his courage to talk to a girl, she turns away insultingly.

Lipton suggests that women follow Beats as they followed roving Gypsies. But this makes no sense, for the Gypsy was an independent who moved with his tribe, his wife, his kids, his animals, and he was (in the ballads) a masterful character. A Gypsy is not a resigned young man, searching.

Finally, of course, there are the young women who are themselves Beats, disaffected from status standards. Perhaps they have left an unlucky marriage, have had an illegitimate child, have fallen in love with a Negro, and found little support or charity "in" society. They might then choose a life among those more tolerant, and find meaning in it by posing for them or typing their manuscripts.

8

To repeat, Beat is not a strong position and it can hardly work out well. The individual young man is threatened either with retreating back to the organized system or breaking down and sinking into the *Lumpenproletariat*. Nevertheless, culturally there is a lot of strength here; let us try to see where it is.

Considered directly, their politics are unimpressive. They could not be otherwise since they are so hip and sure that society cannot be different. Explicitly, they are pacifists, being especially vocal about the atom bomb. The Bomb is often mentioned by themselves and other commentators as an explanation of their religious crisis; but it's not convincing. Their own diatribes seem to be mostly polemical self-defense, as if to say: "You squares dropped the atom bombs, don't you dare criticize my smoking marijuana." In the play *The Connection* this is openly stated as a defense for heroin. On the whole one does not observe that the Beats are so concerned about nuclear weapons as many mothers of families or squares who have common sense. One of the Beat spokesmen wrote a long dithyramb about the Bomb, of which the critic George Dennison remarked: "He seeems miffed that people pay attention to the atom bomb instead of to him."

At the same time, their peacefullness is genuine and their tolerance of differences is admirable, extending also to the squares, except for loathesome class enemies like *Time*, Housing, or gouging employment agencies. Their ability to occupy themselves in poverty on a high level of cultural and animal satisfaction is remarkable, with paperback books, odd records, and sex. Their inventing of community creativity is unique. If we consider these achievements, we see that they are factual evidence for a political proposition of capital importance: *People can go it on their own,* without resentment, hostility, delinquency, or stupidity, better than when they move in the organized system and are subject to authority. (To be sure, the Beats were not among the underprivileged to begin with; they had some useful education and their poverty is in part voluntary; but these are not circumstances unavailable to others.) They do not go far, they invite degeneration, they seem hard put to assume responsibility; but they do exist interestingly and peacefully.

In one important respect, their community culture could be made far more effective. I am referring to the jazz and drums in a community setting. They have chosen too primitive a model, e.g., Haiti. If they would ponder on the Balinese dances, they might learn something—not the Bali dances on a stage on Broadway, but as they exist in their home villages where, to the music of the gamelan, the onlookers suddenly become entranced and fall down or become possessed and would do violence to themselves, except that they are rescued one and all by their friends of the community. (Cartier-Bresson has excellent pictures of these sessions; and of course Artaud, who is becoming scriptural among the Beats, was an ardent champion of them.)

9

Beat literature and religion are ignorant and thin, yet they have two invaluable properties. First, they are grounded in the existing situation, whatever the situation, without moralistic or invidious judgment of it. It is in this sense that Henry Miller is their literary father. Their experience is admittedly withdrawn. (Miller's too does not add up.) Their religion is unfeasible, for one cannot richly meet the glancing present, like Zen, without patriotic loyalty, long discipleship, and secure subsistence. Nevertheless, their writing has a pleasant bare surface, and it *is* experience. It is often bombastic, but on the average it is more primary than other writing we have been getting in America.

A second valuable property of the Beat style is that it tries to be an action, not a reflection or comment. We saw that, in both their conversation and heightened experience, this action doesn't amount to much, for they do not have the weight or beauty to make much difference. But their persistent effort at the effective community reading, appearing as themselves in their own clothes, and willing to offend or evoke some other live response; and also their creative playing (especially if it would become more like the Bali dances), are efforts for art and letters as living action, rather than the likeness to literature that we have been getting in the *Kenyon Review* and the *Partisan Review*.

Religiously, they are making a corrigible error. What they intend, it seems to me, is not the feudal Zen Buddhism, which is far too refined for them and for our times, but Taoism, the peasant ancestor of Zen. Tao is a faith for the voluntary poor, for it teaches us to get something from the act of wresting a living with independent integrity. It is, as Beat intends to be, individual or small-group anarchy. If the Beats would think this through, they would know how to claim their subsistence under better conditions, and perhaps they would have more world. Tao teaches, too, divine experience from the body and its breathing. In this it is like the doctrine of Wilhelm Reich, much esteemed by the Beats but not followed by them. The magic they are after is natural and group magic, and they need not be so dependent on ancient superstitions and modern drugs.

Most important, Tao teaches the blessedness of confusion. Tao is not enlightened, it does not know the score. Confuson is the state of promise, the fertile void where surprise is possible again. Confusion is in fact the state that we are in, and we should be wise to cultivate it. If young people are not floundering these days, they are not following the Way.

The sage is murky, confused. As it says, "Block the passage. Shut the door. . . . I droop and drift as though I belonged nowhere. . . . So dull am I. All men can be put to some use, I alone am intractable and boorish."

It's square to be hip.

The basic words of our jargon are "Search me," "Kid," "I couldn't give you a clue," "I'm murky." "Creator spirit, come."

WHAT'S HAPPENING, BABY?

Paul C. Harper, Jr.

A successful business executive assesses today's adolescents and finds that, despite superficial differences, they are really only replicas of his own generation.

A short time ago I was standing in a pub in London with one of my colleagues enjoying a beer. The name of the pub was "The King's Head and Eight Bells" and it is headquarters for the local pack of Mods. Four Mods were standing near us, two boy Mods in the new bellbottom trousers and bee-waist coats—and two girl Mods with hair in their eyes. Then a fifth Mod with both bellbottom trousers and hair in his eyes walked up and asked casually, "What's happening, Baby?"

As nearly as I can reconstruct it, the reply from one of the girls was, "Pip's topkick just gummed his mini. We all think that's fish."

After eavesdropping a little more, it became clear that what she was reporting was that Pip's father had removed his driving privileges, which they all thought was very stuffy. The meeting at the pub was a protest rally.

The language and problems of Teens are universal. The whole subject of youth and its problems is a close one to me because there are six youths in our family, ages nine to eighteen, three boys and three girls, and three of them teenagers—and while they do not classify as underprivileged—they do, of course, share in the real problems faced by all the youths of our time.

Let's focus on teenagers.

Dinner-table conversations at our house are not orderly discussions. The talk will be frequently interrupted by cries of rage from the victim of a furtive pinch—or by the tinkle of breaking glassware. But the conversations do have a pat-

tern. Sooner or later at the teenage end of the table one of five subjects almost always comes up:
1. *Money*
2. *Sex*
3. *Automobiles (ours)*
4. *Education*
5. *The War*

Now you might ask—well, what else is there to talk about anyway? And honestly, I guess I can't think of many other really interesting subjects.

But these five subjects are actually an inventory of the problems—the big deals—facing teenagers today, and for many reasons they're worth taking a look at. It's worth asking the question, "What's happening, Baby?"

Many people today say that teenagers are a different breed from what they were a generation or two, or three ago. Whole issues of magazines are written about them, books are dedicated to them, and the movies and TV, in their time-honored way, tend to establish teenage stereotypes, thus separating them still further from the normal everyday world.

Now my proposition is very simple and it has three points:

1. It is just as dangerous to lump teenagers as teenagers as it is to lump adults as adults. Each teenager is different, and each is following his own unwritten calendar toward maturity. No two teenagers mature at the same second in time.

2. Teenagers are the most colorful and persistent faddists in our society, but a fad is a symptom, not a disease. They wear funny clothes, funny haircuts, say and do strange things. But the fads they adopt are not to be confused with the immutable law which rules every generation of teenagers. This law says, "Thou shalt be different, but for pretty much the same old reason." No matter how odd their behavior, they are responding to the same age-old urge for independence.

3. In spite of all this, we have to face the fact that teenagers today do face a world that has changed far more between generations than at any time in history. And this has produced an unprecedented lack of understanding and sympathy between generations.

Unless we try to understand these things a little better, we won't do very well as fathers, citizens or advertising men.

These changes get back to the rather basic things discussed at our dinner table. They are:

Money—Teenagers today have enough money to make them a real economic force.

Sex—Teenagers are reaching physical maturity at a somewhat earlier age—and there are more sexual stimuli around than ever before.

Mobility—Teenagers today have a new dimension of independence—the automobile. They can get around. They can get away.

School—Teenagers today are under more pressure from the educational establishment than ever before.

War—Teenagers long-term, like the rest of us, have the bomb hanging over their heads; short-term, they've got Vietnam.

And on top of that—Mom and Dad aren't around as much as they used to be. Mom is more apt to be working and Dad is apt to be away.

Given the teenage appetite for kicking up—showing he's adult, when he isn't—showing he doesn't care, when he really does—given these leanings, he has today more opportunity for colorful behavior than *ever* before.

So if we are ever to approach closing the gap between generations—and understanding this vast, seething mass of highly charged individuals—we'd better take a closer look at each of these points.

There are today 25 million teenagers with 27 million due in five years. The nation's official median age is 27.9 and declining. Forty-eight percent of our population is under twenty-six. Fifty percent of brides today are teenagers; more have their first child in their nineteenth year than any other. Teenagers represent thirteen billion dollars in disposable income. Twenty percent of them own cars.

Let's talk first about *money*. A great majority of teenagers are certainly a reflection of the affluent society they live in. As pollster Louis Harris points out: "High school Americans have never known drastic economic depression or wartime shortages—they're happy now and believe the future can only get better." Generally, youth has no worry about the basic necessities—food, clothing, housing. Their newfound wealth is available for luxuries, recreation and impulse purchases. Recent research indicates that teenage girls buy twenty-seven percent of the cosmetics sold in the U.S., fifty percent of all records, twenty percent of all cars. They own a million TV sets, ten million record players and twenty million radios. They buy forty-five percent of all soft drinks, twenty-four percent of all wristwatches, thirty percent of all low-priced cameras.

David Yunich, president of Macy's, New York, points out that "there are really two markets—the teenager per se and the young marrieds—both with money in their overstuffed wallets, both at peak periods of spending when they want more, need more, buy more." And Yunich points out that the youth market controls upwards of thirty billion dollars' worth of family purchasing aside from its own spending money. The influence of teenagers on family purchases has by no means been lost on giant manufacturers. Ford Motor Company has based a recent advertising campaign on the approval parents will get from their teenagers if they bring home a Mustang.

Since teenagers make up the decisive market for so many products—guitars, motorbikes, sports equipment and movies, for example—and a very lucrative secondary market for countless other categories, they are bombarded with commercial messages. But even without this commercial assault, teenagers would probably be big spenders. Response to questions on how they feel when shopping reveals that "they're buying not so much material things but adulthood; in their way they are trying to be like grownups." Money, to teenagers is a liberating force. Spending it is an expression of adulthood. And in spending it in vast quantities they have institutionalized their tastes. We now have a teenage market.

Sex is, of course, a subject in itself. It must be if those scientists out in Kansas City could spend five years behind a one-way mirror without getting bored. But I really prefer the remark of the mayor of a little New England town as he addressed a group of aldermen worried about town morals. "Now, gentlemen," he said, "there's always been sex in this town—there's just a new crowd takin' over." Nevertheless, some of the data shows real changes in this area, too.

There is no doubt that there is an earlier and more intense focusing on sex. Dates in fifth and sixth grades are commonplace. One survey shows that forty-five percent of teenage girls go steady. Teenage marriages have increased six hundred percent since 1940, accounting for half the marriages in the U.S. More than fifty percent are known to have resulted from pregnancy. The Connecticut Health Department estimates that one of six teenage girls in the state was illegitimately pregnant last year.

There has been no large-scale study of premarital sex among teenagers and sources differ on its extent. Some indicate that it is on the increase, at least in certain areas and among certain social strata. Others say that the public is confusing the known increases in premarital sex among college students with increased sex in high schools. Mervin P. Freedman in *The Young Americans* states his opinion that young men and women need to find security in marriage and a family and that this need far outweighs tendencies toward promiscuous sexual behavior. He believes that this is a reaction against the depersonalization of modern life and sees in the trend to early marriage an indication that family ties will be strengthened rather than weakened in the next several decades. And I think this is the key to the matter. Kids may mature earlier. They may get more stimulation from books, magazines, and movies. But the key fact is that the other pressures he is under force him to seek the security of an intense companionship—the ultimate expression of which is sex.

This brings us to my third point, *Mobility*—It's no news that teenagers today live in cars. Cars have become the standard projection of ego and virility for the boy and give him a dimension of independence he never had before.

According to *Newsweek's* penetrating essay, "It is a car, not truth, that sets them free, gives them a sense of romance. The automobile is this century's riverboat." Teenagers own nine percent of all new cars and an estimated twenty percent of all cars. And, of course, a good many family cars are driven, if not owned, by teens.

The auto manufacturers are also heavily involved encouraging those little-recognized cultural phenomena of postwar United States: drag racing, stock-car racing and their logical extension, the demolition derby. The brilliant young social critic Tom Wolfe, author of *The Kandy-Kolored Tangerine-Flake Streamline Baby,* points out that sports writers have managed to ignore these new automobile sports despite their enormous popularity because "there are too many kids in it with sideburns, tight Levis, and winklepicker boots." Yet he points out that they attract five to ten million more spectators than football, baseball and basketball each year and that stock-car racing is now the number one sport in the South. He sees these sports as symbolizing the emancipation of the young people of the lower social orders in the South from the old social order.

The title of Wolfe's collection of essays, *The Kandy-Kolored Tangerine-Flake Streamline Baby* refers to the postwar teen passion for customizing cars and/or hopping them up for more speed. He says that thousands of kids before they get married put all their money into this.

> Things have been going on in the development of kids' formal attitude toward cars since 1945, things of great sophistication that adults have not been even remotely aware of, mainly because the kids are so inarticulate about it. It is true to say that among teenagers the automobile has become the symbol and in part the physical means of triumph over family and community restrictions.

The fourth big change in the teenage environment is *Education*—how you get it, how long you go to school, what you do when you get there, what happens to you if you don't get there.

With every year that goes by, the long-term penalties for dropping out increase. And the pressures to get into college and stay there, therefore, increase, too.

Why this pressure? *Newsweek* says:

> High school separates the teenager's world as cleanly as if the United States were riven by the Grand Canyon instead of the Continental Divide. On one side are the blessed, who have earned the right to go to college and probably prosperity. On the other are the damned, who drop out, stop short or, at best, go to vocational training schools and sharply circumscribed earning potential.

College is no longer the sanctuary of the privileged, however. The democratization of college through scholarships, the increased ability of more Americans to pay their way and the general recognition that you need college to get ahead holds out a mighty inducement. Never before have teenagers been offered such educational opportunities or been put under such pressure to take advantage of them.

But the pressure and the increase in the academic pace have made millions of young Americans more thoughtful than they have ever been before. Issues are discussed at our dinner table that two generations ago were reserved for lecture halls and coffeehouses. And through the din some pretty penetrating thoughts come through—reflections of real concern with what is going on in the world.

And this brings us to our fifth point—*the Bomb* and *the War*. Every generation has faced the prospect of going to war—in France, in Nicaragua, in the Pacific, in Korea. But no generation until the current one has faced the fact that all of society as he knows it, everything he has been taught was worthwhile, can be blown up in thirty seconds. All generations have had to face the possibility of premature death, but this is the first generation to face the possible death of society.

This produces deeply religious attitudes in some and impresses others with the absurdity of human life. In a recent poll, more than half the teenagers interviewed saw the principal problem confronting the nation as avoiding war. Some commentators have read into this a new emphasis on the enjoyment of pleasures "now," but this is belied by the fact that most teens are more interested in their future than ever before. If they were seriously concerned that there will be no tomorrow, they wouldn't be so motivated to succeed in high school, to get into college, to assure themselves of material success in the future. The net effect of the Bomb has been sobering. It has brought a responsible reaction from our youth, not a wild flight from reality.

But there is much evidence to support the notion that what the kids are afraid of is not so much the Bomb as the adults who have the power to trigger it.

The young are increasingly questioning grownup goals and purposes. Edgar Z. Friedenberg, professor of sociology at the University of California, says:

> Our youngsters do not hate us adults, or even dislike us particularly and even the most militant of them are not primarily interested in putting us down . . . but they have learned that they cannot trust us, because we

have never had any respect for them and very little for the principles by which we pretend to govern our lives and theirs.

Parental authority is diminishing because in all too many cases one or both of the parents simply aren't around. The reasons vary. At one end of the economic scale, father may have long since left his family to their own resources. At the other, he may be providing materially for his family but, in so doing, he may be away more than he is home. Absent fathers and mothers can't swing the kind of moral weight they might if they were on the scene.

Teenagers are not unaware of the world around them. They know that many parents who are shocked at car swiping, exam cheating and teen vandalism are themselves engaging in such higher orders of immoral behavior as tax cheating, price fixing, expense padding and worse. They wonder why parents don't invest the time to discuss the meaningful things of life; counsel them on their education and their future. Instead, they get hung up over the superficialities and fads that every generation goes through.

Professor Friedenberg says:

> Regulations governing dress and grooming may be trivial. What is not trivial is that submission to such regulation teaches students that they have no rights or dignity. The very triviality of the regulations makes them more effectively humiliating. Most adolescents would accept and even welcome adult direction in matters of grave consequence. But I would maintain that the real function of these regulations is to humiliate, to show any adolescents with too much autonomy what happens to wise guys and trouble makers.

The fact is, it doesn't work. It is well known that parental opposition is the surest way to entrench a fad. The fad which starts out as a symbol of identity with the group soon becomes a full-fledged healthy symbol of rebellion against adult authority. The Louis Harris survey shows that almost half the girls and one-third of the boys bought certain clothes against the express wishes of parents. The extent to which this rebellion can go is seen in the current fad for German helmets and iron crosses, the principal function of which seems to be to bug adults.

The other side of the coin is the parent who imitates. This is the pitiful spectacle of the adult trying to proclaim that he thinks young by emulating the dress, the language and the fads of teenagers.

This drive to prove their youthfulness to their children and themselves succeeds in fact in making them look ridiculous to those for whom they should be trying to set an example. There is strong reason to believe that most teenagers have *enough* peers and may need an honest-to-goodness parent who is something more than pseudo-teen.

Teenagers hold a jealous possession of their folkways. When adults took over the twist, young people dropped it like a hot pizza and moved on to dances that were exclusively their own—at least for a while. There is a dedicated effort to create dance steps so exhausting that no adult in his right mind would try them.

The surest way for an advertiser to assure being turned off or turned out is for him to portray an obsolete fad, dance or mode of dress. Since these things can change overnight or at least much faster than advertisers want to change commercials, it's best to avoid these transitory aspects of teen existence.

The same is true of language. We may not understand the language and we certainly shouldn't try to make ourselves understood in it. The language is designed for the exclusive use of teenagers in communicating with one another; similar to the dialects and language variants that such species as lawyers and advertising men create to keep it in the family.

Those of us who are required to establish some form of communication with teenagers had better stick to our own particular idiom of American English, or risk making damn fools of ourselves.

It won't work for parents—and it might be disastrous for advertisers—to try to get chummy with teenagers by telling them that their products are "boss," "tough," "out of sight," "fab" or "dyno." Even though "bad" means "good" in teen, it could prove confusing and downright embarrassing for a client to have to say his product is "bad."

Teenagers are certainly as susceptible to advertising as the rest of us, but they are good shoppers who want to have a good reason why before they buy. They resent being exploited by the adult world and according to Fred and Grace Heckinger "there are signs that sophisticated youths are turning sour on advertising that tries to pull adult rank on them by just calling a product terrific."

Another trap into which advertisers, or anyone else who tries to generalize about teenagers, can easily fall is to lump teenagers as a group. To try to ascribe rigid characteristics to twenty-four million people in an open society that talks a lot about individual achievement is playing a dangerous game. What is a typical American teenager?

A boy or a girl? A thirteen-year-old or an eighteen-year-old? A farmer, a surfer in California, a Groton prep schooler, a Negro in a Detroit slum, a Mexican-American in Arizona, a peace marcher, a drag racer, and on and on.

It's no wonder that teenagers resent being classified as a group. To their everlasting credit and despite their instinct for groupness, teenagers want to be accepted as individuals. Their desire to have a greater say about how their world is run, their questioning of their society, and their rebellion against parents are all indications that they think for themselves. They are, according to Harvard Professor Jerome Bruner, "the most competent generation we have ever reared in this country—and the most maligned."

So—What's happening, baby? Well, it's a tragedy or a comedy, depending upon how you look at it, but in spite of all the new pressures and in spite of all the new outlets, the teenager remains fundamentally the same.

None of these influences—*Money, Sex, Mobility, Education* or *the Bomb*—can mature him faster as a whole person. Nature must take its course. It cannot be speeded up. Society is providing teenagers with many new devices to make them look mature sooner, but basically each one of them has to bumble and fumble his way to adulthood according to his schedule, which applies to him alone and which even he only dimly senses. You can't buy emotional maturity; you can't teach it; and you certainly can't bottle it.

THESE ARE THREE
OF THE ALIENATED

Steven Kelman

A Harvard undergraduate presents the profiles of three youthful outsiders.

"If I had been brought up in Nazi Germany—supposing I wasn't Jewish—I think I would have had an absolute set of values, that is to say, Nazism, to believe in. In modern American society, particularly in the upper middle class, a very liberal group, where I'm given no religious background, where my parents always said to me, 'If you want to go to Sunday School, you *can*,' or 'If you want to take music lessons, you *can*,' but 'It's up to *you*,' where they never did force any arbitrary system of values on me—what I find is that with so much freedom, I'm left with *no* value system, and in certain ways I wish I had had a value system forced on me, so that I could have something to believe in."

The speaker is a sophomore at Harvard University, describing his sense of alienation and its causes. His words may surprise most adults, who tend to view the alienated youth as someone who has no respect for the values of society and who therefore seeks to destroy those values and even society itself—a sort of intellectual descendant of the Luddites. This is only one of the stereotypes that abound in the conventional literature about alienation. All the stereotypes, however, miss one central point: There is a very wide range of attitudes, activities, opinions and experiences among those young people who call themselves "alienated." The alienated are both committed and uncommitted, present-oriented and future-oriented, political and apolitical, even happy and unhappy.

That such varied people are all *self-proclaimed* "alienated youths" could be an indication that alienation is becoming a sort of modern party game, without any real meaning. But I don't feel this is the case. The alienated kids I have spoken with were going through too much real anguish to make the "game" worth it. Adults may confine their alienation to cocktail commiseration; for young people its generally a total thing.

Actually, it should not really be surprising that there are so many different types of alienation, because alienation in itself is only a negative reaction. It is not a set of beliefs—like Socialism, Republicanism or vegetarianism—but a rejection of or even simply an inability to accept the conventional attitudes, mores or way of life of society, a rejection that is essentially emotional and only secondarily, if at all, intellectual. There is every reason to expect, contrary to the typical adult monistic view of alienation, that from such a start the alienated can go into many worlds.

And they do.

GENE

Gene lives in Roxbury, Boston's black ghetto. He is seventeen, a high school dropout, has served a year in prison for car theft and armed robbery committed when he was fifteen. He is about to complete his parole period. Gene will refuse to go to Vietnam if drafted. "I ain't going to fight nobody's war that don't belong to me. That ain't none of *my* fight. I'd go to jail first."

But Gene is not, as one might think, a Black Power activist or even a Muslim. In fact, he is not particularly bitter about American society, or about white America's treatment of Negroes. "I'm not saying we're being treated *wrong,* but it ain't *right* either. You know, part's right and part's wrong." Gene's equivocation is not the hesitant moderation of an Uncle Tom. The simple fact is that it is not so much injustice he feels as separation from the society at large, the world outside. Thus, when I asked him what he thought about America, he answered simply and sincerely, "I don't know too much about the place. I just *live* here."

What he meant is that, while subject to the institutions of society, he is outside when the time comes to draw up the rules of the game, and is even to an extent ignorant of what those rules are. He is, in his own words, "not where the action is." Like Meursault in Camus's *The Stranger*, a character of whom Gene strongly reminded me, the trial goes on without his participation. But this doesn't mean that he hates or flouts the rules or conventions. Consider his attitudes toward school: "School's all right. I ain't got nothing against school; I just don't like to go. I just can't sit up there in no classroom and listen to the teachers blah all afternoon."

Conventions and rules are foreign, and sometimes incomprehensible. Gene was puzzled, for example, that a person could be acquitted of a crime and yet his arrest might still be used against him if he were arrested a second time. "I don't even understand nothing like that," he said. "That's why I said I don't know too much about the place; I just *live* here." Gene's is an alienation in the most nitty-gritty sense of separation from the very day-to-day mechanisms of "normal" society.

Gene nonchalantly and matter-of-factly described how he and his friends stole an automobile and robbed a service station. ("It wasn't so much money, but what could you do?"), a description devoid even of pride of accomplishment. It was as if he were telling me about going to the grocery to buy a loaf of bread. He started his story with, "You see, it was really nothing." He ended it with a description of his capture: "I forgot. You know, I meant to tie the guy at the gas station up, and all this sort of jive. But I forgot." As I was talking to him, trying to get across how I would have had great feelings of compunction and fear before even being able to attempt a robbery, I realized that my scruples sounded as strange to him as his nonchalance did to me. Then I saw that we were part of worlds more separate than those that separated me from the farthest-out, freakiest hippie. He was alienated, and I was not—because my world set the official rules by which his must live.

Nobody should fool himself by trying to explain Gene on any grounds other than those of alienation. His crime was not, for instance, the imperative of a "delinquent subculture" that demands lawbreaking as a condition for acceptance. He never admitted, although I asked him about it, any exalted feelings of power or defiance while committing a crime. His parents certainly disapproved of his getting into trouble. I had no feeling I was sitting next to a "criminal"—and, indeed, I guess I wasn't. For society's law, like society in general, is something *separate* from Gene. He recognizes it, but he is not in formal rebellion against it: "They caught me, and I served time," he noted calmly. It was like a Monopoly game—"Go directly to jail. Do not pass 'Go.' Do not collect two hundred dollars." Nothing more serious than that.

Gene does not identify with any "black community" or even with the civil-rights movement, for which he has nothing but contempt: "They don't gain nothing by doing that but making a fool out of themselves. What are they trying to prove? That's what white people want to see anyway—see niggers making a fool of themselves. You gotta mind your own business." Would he participate in a civil-rights demonstration? "No," Gene answered, drawing it out contemptuously. "I wouldn't even bother to join." Stokely Carmichael? "Who's that? I forgot who that is." After a brief reminder: "Oh, that Black Power junk. White power, Black Power. I don't believe in that."

Although certain theorists have explained the civil-rights movement as the Negro's quest for the middle-class glamour he sees on televison, Gene feels no such pull from the society outside. "That's a lot of bull," Gene said slowly and with disdain for the world pictured on TV. "I don't even believe in nothing like that. That's them old dumb niggers who say, 'Look at that. I'm going to get me some of that.'"

Not everyone in Gene's surroundings is as detached as he. One of his friends wants to go to college, maybe; he thinks that the idea of "stopping Communism" in Vietnam is "a good motive" and even, in hawkish terms, calls for escalation. But Gene has always been different. He remembers his reaction as a child to his mother's explanation of the problems of being black. "She told me that I got to be extra nice, 'cause you know how these whities are. Well, I said, 'Forget it, man. If one says something to me, I'm going to kill him, that's all.'" For a black person, the rules of the game were to be "extra nice" so as not to offend anybody. Gene never accepted those rules.

Because his alienation was, in a sense, imposed on him; because—unlike the middle-class alienated student—he never *left* "normal" American society, Gene is open, serene and completely without the hangups and up-tightness that afflict all the other alienated kids I spoke with. Asked if he ever thought about whether he was happy, he replied quickly, "Yeah, I think about it all the time. Of course I'm happy. I have nothing to be sad about." Would he ever leave Roxbury? "Never. Here it's just the way I like everything, wild and crazy." It was a statement that would fill most alienated students with envy.

BILL

Bill is the very unhappy, very alienated Harvard sophomore quoted earlier. At times he leads a kind of nonlife: "I'll find myself sitting in a chair for hours on end, doing nothing—reading until I get tired of reading, listening to the radio until I even get tired of listening (which is the most passive action I know). Then I'll just sit in the seat doing absolutely nothing, in a certain way wishing there was something I felt like doing, but with nothing being very appealing to me. I'll just sit there for hours, not even caring about getting happy."

As an intellectual, Bill is very verbal about his condition and very precise in defining his alienation: "In my own terms, alienation is my lack of commitment to or even interest in any one position. I hold opinions in politics, philosophy and esthetics, and I suppose also ethical opinions, but I'm not really strongly committed to any position. I can intellectually understand, hold and even approve of both sides, or all sides. Because I can appreciate more than one way of looking at things, I don't really find myself in strong approval or disapproval."

Although this may suggest to the unalienated person merely a healthy skepticism, the question of commitment has become for Bill a central and obsessive concern. Few people would view the rah-rah, "I'm all right, Jack" student, whose horizon extends no further than the comforts available to the upper middle class, as being committed. Yet to Bill, such a student is committed, if "only" to making money. "To me," he said, "the difference between the kid who wants to make a pile and the kid in the New Left is a very minor one. Their commitments to me are of equal merit. One is committed to getting through school; the other is committed to overthrowing the government."

Bill spoke of the things in his life that have molded him. He grew up in "a typical, loving, middle-class home," living in the same house for almost seventeen years. He never had many friends or a close relationship with older brothers and sisters. He recalled that he never did much work in school, partly because he was intelligent enough to get along without working, but mainly because he could only worry about immediate problems, and grades were usually too far in the future, as he put it, to "motivate" him. After losing an earlier interest in physics and math, he decided in the ninth grade that he wanted to be a writer. "I'm not sure," he said, "whether it was more writing or the idea of being a writer which excited me. At any rate, this was a value, a commitment."

Also, shortly after this time, he developed a few very close friendships: "I could always rely to some extent on what friends thought for an arbitrary value system." But at the start of his senior year, Bill had to move from his old home, "which made me feel a little insecure," and last fall he and his friends were spun off to the several corners of the collegiate world.

Nor does Bill draw any solace from association with girls. He never had a girl friend until the middle of the twelfth grade, and this year he has had only one date. Thus he has no emotional ties that might provide commitment to *something* in the day-to-day world, lacking as he does any commitment to beliefs or goals.

Bill's life history may have the ring of a rather unoriginal freshman English theme, but it seems to me to say something about the limits and dangers of intellectualism and intellectualization. The existentialist insight was that, if life were in the abstract meaningless, a person could give it meaning by consciously choosing an absolute commitment and sticking by it.

"But I just find it impossible," said Bill, "to pick something and feel committed to it any other way but intellectually, and that's not enough to motivate me. I don't think you can take something and *decide* to feel committed to it, and genuinely feel committed. I have had a very strong reaction against intellectualism. If I could avoid using my mind at all, I would avoid using it. I would depend on emotional reactions, which are arbitrary and real. But if I put my mind to it, I become *aware* that they're arbitrary, and aware that on an absolute scale, they're not real or valid—and that *nothing's* valid on an absolute scale, and that takes me right into not being able to function."

"Not being able to function": for Bill, unhappily, his alienation means just that. He is extremely present-oriented and, as he described it, the stimuli which most frequently move him to "action" are hunger and sleeplessness. Whatever preferences he has are determined by his mood: "Imagine, my whole *Weltanschauung* is determined by how I feel when I get up in the morning." Like Hamlet, his sin is "thinking too precisely on the event"; for Bill, its wages—as, almost pathetically, he realizes, since he is still, in spite of himself, an intellectual—is an acceptance of nothing but emotion. And he even, although hesitantly, curses his ever having started to think and envies those who have never thought or questioned. "But I guess," he added almost ritualistically, "once you've started to think, there's nothing you can do about it."

Bill takes drugs. He has "turned on" with pot many times, often swallowed pep pills and—once—taken LSD. He thinks only of the moment and is not concerned about the consequences of his act. Moreover, drugs fill one of his essential needs: "When you're left with no values you believe in, it's a comforting thing to know you can take a pill, and it will give you an arbitrary set of values. Anything that comes up to do, you'll want to do." In fact, this is the way Bill gets through exams. He takes pep pills, not to keep awake, but to give him the motivation to get in some cramming.

What about the psychedelic drugs? "It'll make you feel good, that's the first thing. It'll impose a good mood on you. You'll see how pointless things are, but it'll give you so many beautiful things to see that you'll say, 'What difference does that make? Let's have a good time anyway.'" Marijuana? "Pot doesn't really give you any set of values. Pot just serves after a while to turn off your mind if you're feeling bad, to give you a completely neutral feeling."

How long can the drug "thingie" last? As with his alienation, itself, Bill hopes that it's not forever. First, there's just a limit to what drugs can do. "There are times," he commented, "when I'm so demobilized that I don't even have the motivation to turn on." After a while, too, "kicks get harder to find," in the words of a popular teenage song. Three months ago, Bill said, he never would have taken LSD. Now he was talking about a psychedelic drug called STP, which he describes as "so powerful that you either flip out for life or you die." He adds, more seriously, that "if someone put some heroin under my nose today, I wouldn't hesitate to sniff some."

Despite adult myths about the supposed fashionableness of alienation, the truth is that for Bill alienation is hell, and he is hoping for out. Reading about it in books, intellectually understanding it, Bill said, is easy enough, but emotionally experiencing it is something else. Talking with me in *my* world, Bill could intellectually describe his emotions; but in his own world, he can't apply his mind to solving his problems. He spoke of returning to writing again, "when I get out of this," but he cannot get "out of" it by telling himself intellectually to do so. Instead, he almost mystically holds onto those few commitments he has made. At the age of twelve he swore not to commit suicide. Recently he promised an old friend not to take LSD for three months. Mainly, he hopes.

"Strange though it might seem," he said, "I think I'm the only person I know in this school who's basically religious. I happen to believe in God, I think. I'm not definite about it, and that's why I'm not committed to it. But that strikes me as vaguely important." Could be.

HANK

Bill would not call Hank alienated at all, for Hank is an activist in Students for a Democratic Society and therefore "committed." In fact, although they are both Harvard sophomores, Hank is the opposite of Bill in many ways. Bill is from a big Northern city; Hank is from a city in the Deep South. Bill grew up, so he says, with no values forced on him; Hank grew up a practicing Christian and was president of his teenage church group. Yet Hank, too, is very conscious of his own alienation. One day when I was speaking with him he commented: "I think that the basic difference between the New and the Old Left is in their degree of alienation."

A comment lifted out of Jack Newfield's book on the New Left? But Hank hasn't read it. It is rather something really felt, for alienation is both the first step in the process of the making of a radical and a condition that coexists with political commitment later on. And I think that Hank is right about alienation's being a somewhat larger component in the radicalism of the New Left than of the Old. In the thirties one did not need to be alienated from American society as a whole—revulsion for American capitalism, which could safely be separated from the society in general, was enough.

For Hank, the emotional act of alienation was based on his rejection of Christianity. Although, in explaining the genesis of his alienation, he went at length into political reasons for it (the conventional ones: Southern racism, the war in Vietnam, poverty of whites and blacks), the first thing he talked about was his disillusionment with Christianity.

"Around tenth grade in high school," he said, "I started wondering about Christianity, wondering if all this they were feeding me for all these years wasn't a bunch of bull. I seriously questioned for a few years, but I was president of my church group through my junior year in high school, and I went through all the motions. I was actually the epitome of hypocrisy. But I finally came to the decision that I couldn't find any meaning in Christianity. I read a good deal of Camus and Kierkegaard, and I got hung up on some type of existential philosophy, seeing that no broad dogma could be adhered to by everyone and that each person has to find his own truth. This is part of my alienation now. I'm sort of withdrawing philosophically and religiously from the established religion, and I'm trying to grapple with myself and find some philosophy to suit my own needs."

In a sense, Hank was lucky to have such a clear-cut, primitive set of dogmas to rebel against—racism, hypocrisy, what he calls the "contradictions" of the particular society around him. He spoke of the contradictions between Southern hospitality ("It's not mythical what they say about that. People really are very nice—if you're white") and Southern attitudes ("These nice people then turn around and do atrocious things —like beating up Negroes or starting to shout for bombing Hanoi three years ago"). There are also the contradictions which Hank feels in American society in general, and which any radical would sense, such as between the principle of free speech and its stifling, according to Hank, as soon as it becomes "effective," that is to say, a clear and present danger. And there are the contradictions posed by his liberal parents, who constantly told him, "We only want what's best for you," but "You'd better do what we want you to do," or "We want you to say what you believe in," but "You've got to be realistic." Fortunately for Hank, many of *his* contradictions can be resolved by embracing an activist political philosophy. Perhaps because he's had enough to feel alienated from in the society around him, he hasn't had the time or inclination to become, like Bill, alienated from life in general.

Hank's mixture of alienation and commitment is easy enough to maintain at school, away from the "real world," especially when one is a member of a sizable group like S.D.S. (which at Harvard numbers almost two hundred). His problem comes when he goes home; up to now, he has solved it by "cooling it" on some of his alienation while back, figuratively, at the Manse. Up North, he speaks boldly of the need to work outside the "Establishment" while at home he works for liberal Democratic candidates. This doesn't mean that Hank becomes a sell-out at home. Last year he was the only voice in an entire state Key Club convention to come out against acceptance by acclamation of a resolution calling for escalation of the war. The resolution was adopted 177–1.

Hank also tries to mix radicalism and more conventional social action. This summer at home he tutored Negro high-school students. Meliorism? "No, because I was tutoring them in a radical critique of American society."

How does someone from the South become alienated, in the face of the pressures there for conformity (Hank remembers chanting as a child, "Two, four, six, eight—we don't want to integrate!")? Hank explained it this way: "My parents were sort of an initial cause of my alienation, but in an unconventional way. Their being liberals sort of caused me to question at first. They got the ball rolling, but from there it just took off."

These alienated young people suffer from their alienation, but it may be that they will be the better for it. I have the feeling that, when they finally figure out "where they're at," they'll be far ahead of many adults who never went through the painful process.

One alienated student made this point in strong terms. He had been telling me of a student he called Mr. Joe Straight ("the guy who never thinks about these problems, who's oblivious of his own existence"), and then he brought up the story of another student's father:

"He's made a lot of money, and at the age of sixty he's finally found out that, as far as he's concerned, his life is nothing. Because he sees that in five years or ten years he's going to die, and he sees that he's got all his 'goal,' and he's still nowhere. Life itself was just a vehicle for him to attain these exterior goals. So now what is he going to do? How does he handle life? Because he has no goals to preoccupy his mind, what's preoccupying his mind now is *life*, and he can't handle that.

"This cat at sixty is where I am at twenty. When I'm sixty, I don't know where he's at. Being desperate at twenty, you still feel you can know yourself, but at sixty—where do you go from there?"

THE SPLENDID OLD

Gabriel Fielding

A British prison doctor and brilliant novelist considers old age a graduation to rather than a progressive subtraction from life's possibilities.

On the morning of my last birthday I went to a funeral. The friend who had died was fifty-two and I was never very involved with him while he was alive. He was good-looking in the high Italian fashion, very evasive, with a habit of sliding out of situations like some shy marine animal. I used to think of him as a very beautiful limpet on a shelf of rock below the surface, moving imperceptibly along its face whenever the tide was high and clamped there immovable when it was low.

I don't know how it happened but somehow I became intensely involved in his dying. The solitude he had always sought seemed to have caught up with him and the thought of him made me feel lonely. I kept on going to see him in the local hospital where he had a private room, filled like an undergraduate's with the small objects that had always pleased him: an oil painting of a boat putting out on a lake, a Chinese vase, a little statue. I expected always on these occasions that he'd suddenly start talking to me—really talking, because I thought we both knew that he was dying.

I knew it for certain but now I don't think he had an idea of it; in the midst of death he was in life. He couldn't understand why the doctors were being so slow about putting him right. He had a great deal more life inside him and a dozen unfinished projects. He wanted to go to America, for instance, and we were always planning to meet there. We could never decide whether to go by sea or to fly. We had adolescent fantasies about both kinds of travel. If we didn't go this year, then it would be next. Though we mightn't be able to go together, quite certainly we would meet in Manhattan at the Fifth Avenue Hotel, which was nice and old-fashioned and not too expensive. I was sure that in one of those upper rooms with the air conditioner buzzing in the window, we'd at last have the real conversation we'd always awaited—the kind that adolescents do have about sex, death, God, and the stars.

Looking just this little way back to my birthday and his death I see that this "real conversation" I was always expecting had to be preceded by a journey or the prospect of one—a journey to New York or a journey to death. The journey would make us young enough to be incautious, incautious enough to talk. It occurred to me that caution grows with age and is as hard to defeat as the tremulous footstep, the fear of telegrams and unexpected staircases. I don't think the young realize how frightened the old may be. A poet I know wrote that Blake's tiger, "burning bright in the forests of the night" was really "tremulous with fright." It must have been an old tiger. On the other hand, Thomas Traherne wrote: "O what venerable and reverend creatures did the aged seem! Immortal Cherubims!"

WHAT CHILDREN SEE

But how few people, after loud, didactic middle age, feel themselves as wise and sure as angels. How nervous they are of the deposit that has accumulated deep inside them; the experience of dangerous chance, the knowledge that accidents do happen and that in other, younger people malice and pride may swarm like bees in a hive. This is why the old are surprised to be still alive and acceptable, why they may bore us with references to their years as if longevity were a medal pinned on their thin chests entitling them to our praise. They seem to say, "If you can admire me for nothing else, then you must do homage to my years." We fall into the trap that their humility has laid. With them we avoid the issues. We put them under glass in the museum they've claimed for themselves. Only when it's forced on us do we stumble on old age in a particular person with all the surprise and delight we usually feel for a child.

Children relish the aged. There's a stage in their lives where they are far more interested in them than in other children. I remember mourning my grandmother when I was twelve. I was up a sycamore with my sister when the telegram came and my father stood at the bottom of the tree and told us that, three hundred miles away, back in our old home, she had died. In a void of forgetfulness of most of that stage of my life, I can remember our talking about it up amongst the leaves. She had no age for us at all. She was a lay figure, an authority, passing up the stairs, seen in the garden—a face with bright eyes and a blue brooch beneath. We mourned her like this, by interest and recollection. We both certainly knew in the sycamore that something great had happened to us. When we came down we had seen death as close as the clouds above the tree.

My grandfather kept going long after her death because he was twelve years younger and, in a robust way, wicked. He set fire to his bedclothes smoking Hignett's Cavalier Mixture in a Welsh boardinghouse. He accepted the drama such a death invited and died with ceremony like a Christian or a Jew, as a religious man should. As his burned body weakened and he found it harder to get Invalid Stout to his lips, he became ever more wry and portentous. To my brothers and me he would recite nineteenth-century limericks of a cautionary kind. To my mother he would talk differently—with bulging eyes and every appearance of brave remorse, he would tell her how glad he was that God had allowed him to burn a little in this world to shorten his incineration in the next.

I never got to know either of them of course, neither my grandfather nor my grandmother. (There wasn't enough time for a proper overlap. They are left as stone figures in my mind, like Henry Moore's King and Queen, gazing out over the landscape of my youth.) But it is through the memory of them that I reach other old people, that perhaps I shall reach my own self in age if it comes.

Old people do not wear out evenly. Just as something goes first in the body—the arteries, the sight, or the hearing—so do things lapse and collapse in the character. Other qualities remain, may even be strengthened by time like the natural buttresses on a cliff face. Jung said there should be education in middle age for the second half of life. Its requirements, he suggested, are so different from those of the first half. After middle age people can get lost. They don't know what to do with the youngness that remains in them nor what they want. I've seen white-haired maniacs in expensive sports cars, old men talking of yachts and high life in the Mediterranean, the desperate sixties rushing off in search of an adolescent playground that they no longer really want. Strangely, I've heard other aging men in pubs talking longingly of pills and hormones and virility regained.

THE LIBIDO WHISPERS

I knew a chemist once who dosed himself with pills and married again, at sixty-five, a bride of twenty-five. He was a very obliging man and when I was with him talking in the shop after hours and people came knocking on the glass doors he would say, "Knock! Knock! Knock! It's always the same. When I'm dead they'll come knocking on my grave."

His hormones wore him out. Instead of peaceful evenings over the shop or a game of bowls up the road, I saw him springing about in roadhouses and seaside resorts with his young wife petulantly at his side. He moved to the South Coast and died of a heart attack while reaching for a bottle of gargle.

My Uncle Doggo was different. He had a slow cancer of the tongue and came to stay with us and die when he was over eighty. Poverty had kept him alive, the excitement of outwitting it—stealing a free ride on the underground, finding an unexpected present in the post or a long cigarette end in an ashtray. Because he had a Victorian faith in eternity and his own place in it, he was happy to go on living as long as possible in the real, eighty-year-old present.

When he first arrived he was dimmed with a headful of hospital tranquilizers. There was no definition in his day and, until we took him off the drugs, no seemly senile confusion at night. We locked the gate at the top of the stairs and left on the landing light. He pattered about in his dressing gown, revisiting the past as an old man should when his brain oxygen runs low in the small hours. His fantasies did him no harm and he was all the brisker for them in the mornings. Sometimes if he disturbed us too often in the night, we took a few of his tranquilizers ourselves.

Jung said that in the first half of life all one's energy is directed toward growth. In the second, he said, the libido whispers ever more audibly of death. I don't see why one should not listen to this voice. With the death of every friend and enemy, every contemporary, the bell tolls. The aged live in a landscape loud with bells. They are reminded. If they turn away back to the active pursuit of youth as opposed to the placid contemplation of it, they may be driven mad. But if the music of death is listened to, the slow tocsins become a carillon. There are possibilities of sweetness and we do not have to say each summer, "Another May and June gone forever."

The purely physiological attack on senility is not enough. I'm all for the props: a little digitalis to make steady the fluttering heart, anything that will safely relieve pain, and antibiotics to control chronic infection. But I don't want pills to control my moods and I don't want grafts. I don't want to borrow a young motorcyclist's liver or testicles. I want if possible to grow old evenly, as comfortably as may be with a good pair of glasses, snug false teeth, and my rupture, if I have one, repaired or controlled. Far from regretting the decline of some appetites I would like to have them sped on their way so that having done with them, others, neglected until now, might take their place. I'm not averse to climbing trees because I have that kind of feet and legs, but I can see that other people mightn't wish at fifty to climb and hang and feel their muscles stretching and cracking. Only Charlie Chaplin was meant to be Charlie Chaplin. Some other old man might take his pleasure in fine bindings and silence.

STAGGERING PROMISES

In the second half of my life I'd love to be able to be in the presence of beautiful women without hunger and pain. I'd like to become less acquisitive altogether, to be able to see some exquisite piece of porcelain in some other man's house and be wholly glad that it was there and not mine. I dream sometimes about something I read about a Mexican household with each generation fulfilling its function in a house large enough to contain all. In such a house my wife and I share our section of the roof and courtyard. Our children have married sympathetically. There's enough tension for a little anger but not so much as will keep us smarting all night with the reproaches and comparisons we made when we were first married. Our grandchildren are happily or foolishly living their lives about us, making us nostalgic at one moment and sad at the next. It's not a question of our being wanted, it's a question of our being there, like trees, like wisdom, and like death within whose shadow the children play.

I want, as Bergson did, the second half of my life to be rich in the supernatural. I would like to search out the possibility of God and take to myself, if I could, the hopeless, the staggering promises of religion. Nobody, when I was young, needed to convince me of the promises and joys of money or sex. When I was even younger, the things I was told about heaven and angels fell with equal simplicity into my mind. They dropped like smooth pebbles into a pool and I accepted them so readily that before I was five I'd forgotten them. But now I would like to unearth them, to clean them as precisely as an archaeologist finding jewels in the conduits of an ancient city.

Above all, I'd like to become braver, what the boring psychiatrists call more "integrated." Out of integration comes courage. If age has made a man whole there should be few areas in himself that he's afraid to enter. He becomes more truthful. He knows that he cannot give offense because his opinions are unequivocally held, their roots are in the clean secrets of himself. Already I'm tired of dodging myself socially and morally. I'm sick of the compromises I'm always making with my desires. In old age I want to be so sure of myself, of the structure I'm standing on, that I can afford to forget it forever. Yeats wrote:

> What shall I do with this absurdity—
> O heart, O troubled heart—this caricature,
> Decrepit age that has been tied to me
> As to a dog's tail?

He was thinking and seeing as Shakespeare thought and saw; as we still mistakenly do, he was looking upon old age as a progressive subtraction from life—*sans* teeth, *sans* eyes, *sans* everything.

We shall have to change our approach. Without senility or decrepitude, with unimpaired faculties, more and more of us are going to live longer. Medicine will give us an old age without hardened arteries or softened brains. As research into genetics and the stress and virus diseases progresses, there will be fewer easy ways out for ourselves or for the society which has to cater for our healthy dotage.

But there are some things which medicine can't provide: detachment, ardor, and goodness. There's still the risk of appalling boredom, of an endless impatience with the repetitiveness of life as it unwinds like an out-of-date film—all the worse for being seen without a cataract. For these reasons I think that only a minority of old people may be said to be graduates in old age, to be delightful to know, to have made an addition out of life instead of a subtraction. The secret they possess is that in middle age they plowed youth in. They went back beyond it to their childhood, interested not so much in the answers to life as in the questions they had once asked and then forgotten.

I believe that it is in these questions—the kind I so longed to discuss with my dying friend—that the old may be splendid. It is when they have long spoken to themselves of love, God, death, and the stars, that they are ageless and that society is the richer for them.

THE DISTINCTIVE

Individuals in a Mob

THE SCHOLAR AND THE "ALIENATED GENERATION"

A. Craig Baird

A professor of communications discusses the plight of the academician in a world of tremendous technological advancement.

THE SCHOLAR AND THE AGE

May I begin by reminding you of our orbiting American universe? What of this world that we octogenarians of the lost generation dimly understand but try to discuss?

First, this is the age of widely expanded communication. Quantitatively at least our voices and words have recently multiplied beyond all calculation. No previous age or people has used without interruption so many words—and perhaps alas, so many empty words. People everywhere—in workshops, service clubs, political campaigns, street corners, back alleys—are informing, persuading, inspiring, or denouncing those within reach. I refer here also to our new radio-television universe, to worldwide loudspeakers, films, to Telstar and Early Bird, and to the greater broadcasting wonders of tomorrow.

What of this communicative age and your generation? Fifteen years ago we writers and speakers aptly labeled the oncomers on campuses and elsewhere as the "silent generation." Soon after 1945 the national climate seemed to breed orthodoxy and platitudes. McCarthyism, for example, looked under every bed for radicals and tried to muzzle any who were caught. We faulty do-gooders of 1950 exhorted our students to hold their ground and speak up. We urged them to heed well Churchill's "iron curtain" speech at Fulton, Missouri, March 5, 1946. We also wanted these students to harken to the birth cries of the United Nations after 1945. Now that silent generation is no more. Those students of 1945 or 1950, with cap and gown, moved into what they regarded as hostile world. You and your fellows also take your place in a world you never made. Yet you move ahead free from economic or social lockstep. Perhaps you are more callous and cynical. At least you walk stalwart and clear-eyed.

About us are the laydowns, the sit-ins, the teach-ins, the campus manifestoes. With us are placards and marchers who gang around administrators' buildings and block downtown traffic. These rebellions are different from the usual spring uprisings that some of us long ago shared on college or university campuses. Irving Kristol, in his recent article "What's Bugging the Students?" analyzed these campus so-called rebels, and their speeches and writings. He concluded that this movement is a sign of the underlying momentum of cultural shift. It is apparently not ideological or idealistic. It is not chiefly leftist or antimilitary, or anti-American. Nor is it dominated by far-out professionals. According to him and others, the activity seems to be basically a reaction against the ideas, principles, and patterns hardly adapted to this new age.

Lewis Feuer, former professor of philosophy at the University of California, describes the movement as a revival of the concept of "alienation." States he, "It is evidence among America's younger generation as a search for a deeper philosophy than the academics provide." Curiously, this word "alienated," according to him, "has become the philosophical slogan of many of the oncoming generation."

This new age of multiplied communication, may I add, is also the Atomic Age. Dr. Margaret Mead sums it up thus:

> Within a single decade, human beings were asked to learn that all the assurance that had been based on scientific knowledge had been shattered by the very knowledge in which they trusted. They had to learn that there is no assurance of continuity.

Thus is our age of thermonuclear bombs, push-button operations, electronic brains. As you have often been told, we have seen more technological change in the past twenty years than in all the previous history.

May I here add one more historic note. On October 4,

1957, you and I officially left behind the old-fashioned industrial age. On that day and night, the Soviet Sputnik whirled about the earth in an eliptical orbit, 18,000 miles an hour with a complete circuit every ninety-six minutes. Six hundred or more miles above us were the lethal Van Allen radiation bands. In the nearer space we sent into orbit our manned and unmanned space vehicles.

Thus overnight ended our world of dominating earth-bound E and H and U bombs, our secure leadership of sixty or a hundred small and large nations, our commanding influence in the United Nations, our secure NATO and other alliances, the complacent pursuit of more and more gadgets, our hopes of balanced national debt, and our familiar ways of scientific and humanistic learning. Our sights are now on the moon.

Where stands the scholar in this age of universal communication, this new order of science and technology, this atomic power, and space exploration?

THE SCHOLAR AND DECISION-MAKING

The scholar's role, as always, has been that of decision-making. Responsibility by those who know and think and care, as always, in this world where ignorance clashes with ignorance through the night, is to do. Obsolete is the Ivy Tower.

The mission of the university still is to produce scholars who act. Its aim is much the same as those of the original Athenian Academy and Lyceum. Its aim is still to encourage free and full discussion, dialectic, and decision-making.

Why this greater emphasis today in higher education on decision-making? Because more than ever time is of the essence. The revolutionary and quick changes, the greater risks involved as each important issue demands answers—all discourage indecisive deliberations. As Ralph Perry of Harvard put it:

> For each new problem comes a moment of decision. The choice must be made before it is too late. Otherwise life is meaningless.

After Perry spoke came the Atomic and Space Age, with more insistent questions demanding early answers. In the face of these new pressures, some of those who protested, like some existentialists, have viewed their stark and limited span of life, have described existence as meaningless, and have said, "What's the use?"

In contrast to some shortsighted educators who still make mere knowledge a fetish, Thomas Huxley, in one of his lectures a century ago, on scientific education, declared that "the end of life is not knowledge, but action." Emerson, too, in the 1837 Phi Beta Kappa address at Harvard, declared that "action with the scholar is subordinate, but it is essential. Without it he is not a man. Without it thought can never ripen into truth." Thinking and doing are not dichotomies. For the scholar they are a continuum from initiation to the completed action.

THE SCHOLAR AND INTELLECTUAL JUDGMENTS

Thus decision-making, to be worthwhile, must express reason rather than impulsive reaction. Your grappling with private and public problems must represent reflection and discrimination. Dependable decisions must stem from facts and must frame and settle the choices. Such at least is the theory of our higher education. But many intelligent members of the present and oncoming generation look askance at this concept of thinking. To them it is narrow and without proper account of human behavior. These disparagers of severe logic compose the considerable body of anti-intellectuals. They belittle nationalism as artificial, limited, obsolete. According to many of them, thinking must be freed from the outworn syllogistic formalism. It must be explained as social and not purely mental functioning. Life, to these anti-rational philosophers and their lay followers, is not settled by resort to mental equivalents of filing systems or other logical machinery.

These irrationalists do not bypass thinking. They merely question whether Rodin's thinker was not merely a normal man rather than a classical deductionist. They do concern themselves with the total man, his complicated conditioning and behavior. According to them, he is a creature of drives, motives, sentiments, habits. His thought processes are intermittent and inconsistent. Man, they say, exists prior to essence; that is, man is himself and prior to his ideas. He is finite, marked by his limited beginning and end. According to George Santayana, "Importance springs from the stress of nature, from the cry of life, and not from reason and its pale prescription."

Those who question the reign of reason even cite Woodrow Wilson, who in his Phi Beta Kappa address at Yale in 1908 said:

> Life is essentially illogical. The world is governed by a tumultuous sea of commonalities made up of the passions, and we can only hope that the good passions outweigh the bad ones.

What is my reply to this anti-intellectualism? We grant that man is irrational. We adjust our curricula and philosophy to the needs, interests, and personalities of the learners. Although many of us are humanists and pay homage to literature and the fine arts, we are also at home with the psychologists, political scientists, sociologists, and experimental scientists.

We of this latest biological and physical universe insist, nevertheless, that reason—call this intellectual quality what you will—is the one way to satisfactory deliberation and action. Thought, as John Dewey and other liberal philosophers have expounded, is man's chief reliance in the face of his perplexities. Lester Ward, American pioneer sociologist, in his *Dynamics of Sociology,* in 1882, stated:

> The advent with man of the thinking, knowing, foreseeing, calculating, designing; investing, and constructing faculty, repealed the law of nature and enacted in its stead the psychological law,—the law of the mind.

We reason badly. Yet by what other means can our problems be solved? Systematic thinking, as we have often said, is recent in the ascent of man. Aristotle in the fourth century B.C.—conscious as he was of the fickleness of the Athenians—well insisted on the supremacy of intellectual proofs. Graham Wallas, of our time, concluded:

> Thought may be late in evolution. It may be deplorably weak in driving power. But without its guidance no man or organization can find a safe path amid the

vast impersonal complexities of the universe as we have learned.

THE SCHOLAR AND SOCIAL JUDGMENT

How does our scholar implement these marks of mental acuity and common sense? He does so through his social intelligence. Reason, feeling, and will we long have learned to understand as a combined reaction system. This psychological monism means that logic is conditioned by the social climate in which it is shaped.

Here the scholar, confronting always humanity in the aggregate, faces the continued dilemmas and the need for the difficult choices. Shall he succumb to the crowd and become a new kind of robot? Or shall he try to closet his private personality? How far is he to conform to the mass mind, about which we hear so much? Out of Madison Avenue, Wall Street, and every other center of communication and influence comes the summons, justified or not, to standardize.

What are the predictive results for those who join the group? If we believe the prophets of doom, this crowd is a heterogeneous mass. It has no direction. It deteriorates and finally is of Toynbee's lost society. These risks for the scholar either way are great, but they have always been so with him. Emerson warned the Harvard faculty and students from becoming victims of society. Said he, "Society is everywhere in conspiracy against its members." And he added, "In the degenerate state, when victim of society, the scholar tends to become a mere thinker, or worse still, the parrot of other people's thinking." Is there a golden mean between metaphysical freedom and determinism? Experimental studies will hardly give the answers. But the decisions by the socially-minded scholars will continue to assure both individual growth and those movements toward social betterment!

THE SCHOLAR AND VALUE JUDGMENTS

Finally the scholar with his intellectual and social conditioning is ethically committed. His logical and social practices and decisions turn out to be moral and value judgments. The line between sound social decisions and those of morality and ethics is so thin as to disappear.

How can these practical policies have justification unless they are linked with the best interests of the people involved? How can any programs deserve scholarly support unless they express commitment to human values?

The role of the educated is always one of committal to value systems. As somebody said, scholars are those who care. They not only conceive what is desired but what ought to be desired. They visualize justice, right, liberty, freedom, quality, intellectual and social integrity, and character. These intangible but basic concepts become the scholar's assumptions, hypotheses and tenets. These values pervade the content and details of his communication. And these communications in turn, so he hopes, will contribute to a better world. Such is the place of value judgments in the wisdom of the scholar.

Today, as often in the past, we hear much of the moral decay of the West. Richard M. Weaver of the University of Chicago wrote not long ago of our approaching a condition "in which we shall be amoral without capacity to perceive it and degraded without means to measure our descent." Raymond Aron writes about the *The Opium of the Intellectuals*, and Dr. Thomas Molnar analyzes the *Decline of the Intellectual*.

We are not cynical about the decline or death of intellectualism—as we Americans use that word. The scholar who has concern for human values is on his way to becoming a genuine scholar. An article in *The New York Times* not long ago proclaimed the death of philosophy. Not only is it alive, but it is every learned man's mature possession—or should be. As Chauncey Goodrich of Yale, more than a hundred years ago, described the scholarly mind of young Edmund Burke of Trinity College, Dublin:

> He looked upon a subject like a man standing upon an eminence, taking a large and rounded view of it on every side, contemplating each of its parts under a vast variety of relations, and these relations often complex and remote.

If my understanding here of the scholar is sound, his mind is philosophical and his practical activity is to give effective support to "truth," however we use that word.

Adlai Stevenson, at Salt Lake City, on October 20, 1952, said, "We are marked men, we Americans. We have been tapped by fate—for which we should forever give thanks, not laments." Stevenson was obviously thinking of the problems of war and peace, finances, trade—the issues discussed by Aristotle and all thinkers since.

And Stevenson added with confidence, "What a day to live in."

MUST WRITERS HATE THE UNIVERSE?

Joseph Wood Krutch

A perceptive essayist-critic complains about the literary avant-garde's contempt for man.

There are not many nations so indefatigably given to honoring men of letters that a cabinet minister would preside over a ceremony in which the principal speaker eulogized a *poet maudit* upon whose newly erected monument was inscribed the poet's own clarion call to his fellows: "We have set out as pilgrims whose destination is perdition . . . across streets, across countries, and across reason itself." Simultaneously, and in accordance with a French custom which always reminds me of the monkish habit of digging up old bones to make way for new ones, the name of the street was changed from that of a forgotten worthy to Rue Guillaume Apollinaire.

The cabinet minister involved was André Malraux; the sculptor of the monument was Picasso; the honored poet, Guillaume Apollinaire, was that champion of, successively, Cubism, Dada, and Surrealism, among whose own best-known works are the volume of poems called *Hard Liquor (Alcools)*, the novel *The Assassinated Poet*, and the play *The Breasts of Tiresias*. One of his more notable pronouncements was the prediction that the dominant influence upon the twentieth century might well be that of the Marquis de Sade —a prophecy which, incidentally, seems in the course of being fulfilled.

Even if we had in this country a Minister of Arts, we cannot quite imagine him officially honoring a poet who urged painters as well as men of letters to set out resolutely on a road leading to that pit of hell, the descent into which—so an elder poet said—is easier than the road back again. No, one can't imagine an American Minister of Culture doing that. In fact, the proponents of government support to the arts are most likely to fear that we would be, officially at least, oppressively pure, genteel, and middlebrow.

But if we are not yet quite up to the French in this respect, there is no doubt that the avant-garde, even when perverse and sadistic, is no longer without honor even in rather surprising quarters, and that mass-circulation magazines give frequent and extensive treatment to movies, plays, novels, and poems which in one way or another—extravagant concern with usually abnormal sexuality, violence, cruelty, or at least the nihilism of the absurd—seem to be headed along the road which Apollinaire bid them take.

In March 1966, Cyril Connolly, a leading English critic, was commissioned by the ultrarespectable *Sunday Times* of London to make a list of the hundred literary works which best presented various aspects of modernism in intellectual literature. He headed his list with that same Guillaume Apollinaire whom the French Minister of Culture was so eager to honor, and though it is true that his list does include certain works which are neither beatnik, sadistic, existential, nor sexually perverse, at least a half—and perhaps two-thirds—of them might, I think, be classified as guideposts to perdition.

Among them—and remember these are not offered merely as striking works of literature but as typical of the modern spirit—are *Nadja (Nothing)* by the surrealist André Breton; *Journey to the End of the Night* by the pro-Nazi and violently anti-Semitic Céline; *The Immoralist* by Gide; *Là Bas* by Huysmans; *Cruel Stories* by Villiers de L'Isle-Adam; *Les Illuminations* by Rimbaud; and many others more or less in the same spirit of world-weariness, world-hatred, or perverse indulgence. And he finds the quintessence of modernity in Baudelaire as translated by Robert Lowell:

Only when we drink poison are we well—
We want, this fire so burns our brain tissue,
To drown in the abyss—heaven or hell.
Who cares? Through the unknown we'll find the new.

Readers curious enough to consult the full text with Connolly's own comments on individual works will find that he calls Baudelaire's poetry "a beam of light glowing for posterity," even though, it would seem, the poet himself declares that he does not care whether it points the way to a heaven or a hell. Connolly also states that Breton, one of his heroes, proposed to "wring the neck of literature" and quotes with apparent approval the following sentence, of which it is said "nothing more surrealist has even been written": "Beautiful as the chance encounter on a dissecting table of an umbrella and a sewing machine."

Commenting on the list and Connolly's explanatory notes, *Time* (which certainly does not appeal to merely minority interests) remarks that, though the list will seem perverse to many, it is, nevertheless, "an achievement in taste and learning."

I do not believe that more than a very small fraction of *Time*'s readers really share the convictions or admire the enterprises of such writers. Yet they are obviously much interested in them and they are timid about expressing any doubts. When they give deserved praise to, say, Tennessee Williams for his theatrical skill, they are half afraid of not taking seriously enough the implications of his extraordinary notions concerning sexual abnormality and are half convinced that their own normality needs to be apologized for. If a whole school of novelists (now a bit *démodé*) defines its conception of the good life as driving a stolen automobile at ninety miles an hour after a revivifying shot of heroin, almost nobody says merely, "Pooh," or, "Don't be silly."

Those of us who read such highbrow (or is it middlebrow?) weeklies as *The Nation* or *The New Leader* have come to expect a curious contrast between the front and the back of the book. Though the opening pages are full of schemes for improving the condition of this or that, the section devoted to the arts is occupied frequently by reviews of books, movies, paintings, and musical compositions which are bitterly cynical, pessimistic, and, by old-fashioned standards, obscene. This seems to reflect truly a similar contrast between the tastes and preoccupations of two different groups of "intellectuals." Most of them are either do-gooders, on the one hand or, on the other, ready to entertain at least the possibility that the road to perdition is the wise one to take. If you are not a potential member of the Peace Corps, you are almost certainly a devotee of the absurd. You want either to rescue the underdeveloped countries or to explore once more the meaninglessness of the universe or the depravity of some version of the *dolce vita*. When *Time*, as it recently did, puts Sartre and Genet on its "best reading list" for a single week, neither of these writers can be said to be, by now, attractive to only a few.

Do I exaggerate either the violence, perversity, or nihilism of most of the most discussed modern writers or the tendency of even the mass magazines to select their works as the best or, sometimes, as only the most newsworthy books?

Let us look at a few excerpts from two or three publications which illustrate what I am driving at. Look first at a review in *The New Leader*. It concerned James Baldwin's so-called novel, *Another Country*, and it was written by the magazine's staff critic, Stanley Edgar Hyman, who, though far from approving of the book, described it as follows:

> The protagonist of *Another Country*, a young Negro jazz drummer named Rufus Scott, kills himself on page 88, and the rest of the book is taken up with the adventures and misadventures, mostly sexual, of the half-dozen people who had been close to him. Of the important characters, only Rufus and his sister Ida are Negro, but almost everything in the book that is powerful and convincing deals with Negro consciousness.
>
> That consciousness, as the novel shows it, seethes with bitterness and race hate. "Let the liberal white bastards squirm" is Rufus's most charitable feeling towards Vivaldo, his best friend; his less charitable feeling is a passionate desire for the extinction of the white race by nuclear bombs. Ida is even fiercer. She regularly affirms, in language not quotable in this family magazine, the total sexual inadequacy of whites, as well as their moral sickness and physical repulsiveness. . . . The other Negroes in the book share this bitterness and hatred without exception. A big Negro pimp who lives by beating up and robbing the white customers of his Negro whore clearly does it out of principle; before robbing Vivaldo he stares at him "with a calm steady hatred, as remote and unanswerable as madness." The Silenski boys are beaten up by Negro boys unknown to them out of simple racial hostility and Richard, their father, automatically comments: "Little black bastards." Rufus's father, seeing his son's mangled corpse, remarks

only: "They don't leave a man much, do they?" A musician who had been Rufus's friend, finding Ida out with a white man, calls her "black white man's whore" and threatens to mutilate her genitals twice, once for himself and once for Rufus.

Though *The New Leader*'s critic was by no means favorably impressed, the jacket of *Another Country* is able to cite the even better known and academically very respectable critic Mark Shorer, who called *Another Country* "powerful." Is that the adjective he would have chosen if this almost insane outburst of racism had been the work of some Southern Ku Klux Klanner—as it might easily be made to seem by reading "white" where Baldwin says "black" and "black" where he says "white"? Why is black racism "powerful," white disgusting?

Now for a movie, as admiringly described in *Time*:

> The *Naked Prey* spills more beauty, blood, and savagery upon the screen than any African adventure drama since *Trader Horn*. Squeamish viewers will head for home in the first twenty minutes or so, when producer-director-star Cornell Wilde swiftly dooms three last-century white hunters and a file of blacks, attacked and captured by a horde of warriors from a tribe they have insulted. One victim is basted with clay and turned over a spit, another is staked out as a victim of a cobra.
>
> The only survivor is Wilde. In a primitive sporting gesture, the natives free the courageous white man without clothes, weapons, or water—and with ten stalwart young spearsmen poised to track him down. Hunted now, the hunter begins to run, and *Prey* gathers fierce momentum as a classic, singleminded epic of survival with no time out for faint-hearted blondes or false heroines.

It used to be said that the theater was often more searching, more bitter, and more "adult" than the movies ever dared to be. Today it can hardly keep up with them but it tries, as witnessed by this account of the latest play by a man widely regarded as Britain's leading playwright:

> *A Bond Honoured,* British playwright John Osborne's adaptation of an atrocious horror show by seventeenth-century Spaniard Lope de Vega, has a hero who commits rape, murder, treason, multiple incest, and matricide, and blinds his father—after which he is crucified in precise imitation of Christ. London's critics cast one look at the tasteless mayhem at the Old Vic and held their noses. Whereupon Osborne, thirty-six, flipped his Angry Aging Man's lid, firing off telegrams to the London papers. Osborne declared an end to his "gentleman's agreement to ignore puny theater critics as bourgeois conventions. After ten years it is now war, open and frontal war, that will be as public as I and other men of earned reputations have the considerable power to make it."

The account is again from *Time* but its pooh-poohing of this masterpiece got an angry reply from Kenneth Tynan, the drama critic who was for a time the regular reviewer for *The New Yorker*:

> Of the twelve newspaper critics, at least four held their breath. Herald Hobson in the *Sunday Times* said of Osborne: "He is not only our most important dramatist; he is also our chief prophet." According to Randall Bryden of the *Observer,* "The effect of *A Bond Honoured* in performance is marvelously theatrical." Allen Brien of the *Sunday Telegraph* thought it "a serious, ambitious, and valuable play which matures in the memory and fertilizes the imagination," while for Milton Shulman in the *Evening Standard* it was "a stunning parable with a magnificent theatrical impact."

Having glanced at the conspicuous American novel, a conspicuous movie, and a conspicuous play, let's look now at two serious American critics, taking first Leslie Fiedler. His well-known contention is that the best American fiction from *Huckleberry Finn* to Hemingway and Faulkner is always concerned with a repressed homosexuality. In his most recent book he comes up with the following opinions:

> [On the death of Ernest Hemingway] . . . One quarry was left him only, the single beast worthy of

him; himself. And he took his shotgun in hand, probably renewing his lapsed allegiance to death and silence. With a single shot he redeemed his best work from his worst, his art from himself.

> [Of President Kennedy and the arts] . . . John F. Kennedy, as Louis XV, seemed up to the moment of his assassination the true symbol of cultural blight; not only our first sexually viable President in a century, after a depressing series of uncle, grandfather, and grandmother figures, but the very embodiment of middlebrow culture climbing.

I have been leaning heavily on *Time* because it seems to me to be the publication which best gauges the interests, if not necessarily the opinions, of the largest number of literate Americans. But for a second critic—and, incidentally, an excellent example of the schizophrenia of the liberal weeklies—I will choose an essay by Susan Sontag, the most "in" of contemporary "far-out" critics. It was, paradoxically, published in *The Nation,* which has been for long the very paradigm of do-goodism. The article takes off from a discussion of Jack Smith's film *Flaming Creatures,* which is described thus:

> A couple of women and a much larger number of men . . . frolic about, pose, posture, and dance with one another; enact various scenes of voluptuousness, sexual frenzy, romantic love, and vampirism . . . to the accompaniment of a sound track which includes . . . the chorale of flutish shrieks and screams which accompany the group rape of a bosomy woman, rape happily converting itself into an orgy . . . shots of masturbation and oral sensuality. . . . *Flaming Creatures* is outrageous and it intends to be. But it is a beautiful film . . . a triumphant example of an esthetic vision of the world and such a vision is perhaps always, at its core, epicene.

Just why an esthetic vision of the world is perhaps always, at its core, homosexual is not explained and suggests the same reply which Chesterton made to the estheticism of the nineties. The art of those who professed it, so they claimed, was morally neutral, but, said Chesterton, if it really were neutral it would often find itself dealing sympathetically with respectability, virtue, piety, and conventional behavior. The fact that it never did treat any of these things in even a neutral manner was sufficient proof that the art of its practitioners was not morally neutral but actually—to come back to Apollinaire again—an invitation to take the road to perdition.

If Miss Sontag does not explain why an esthetic vision must be epicene, she does undertake to explain why modern art must be "outrageous": "Art is always the sphere of freedom. In those difficult works of art we now call avant-garde, the artist consciously exercises his freedom." This argument is obviously parallel with that favorite of the Sartrian existentialists, namely, the contentions that: (1) the unmotivated act is the only positive assertion of freedom; and (2) the best unmotivated act is one of arbitrary cruelty. Why this should be so I have never understood, nor do I understand why the freedom of the artist can be demonstrated only by the outrageous. In the atmosphere of the present moment, the boldest position a creative or critical writer could take would be one championing not only morality but gentility and bourgeois respectability. Even the article which I am writing at this moment will probably be more contemptuously or even vituperatively dismissed than it would be if I were defending sadism, homosexuality, and nihilism.

Look at how "square" and "fuddy-duddy" the American Telephone & Telegraph Company can be, as demonstrated by recent full-page advertisements which answer the question posed in headline type: "WHAT CAN YOU DO ABOUT OBSCENE, HARASSING, OR THREATENING TELEPHONE CALLS?" Doesn't AT&T know that one of the simplest beginner's techniques for achieving existential freedom in a splendidly unmotivated act is to make an obscene telephone call? From that one can easily work up to the various vandalisms so popular with teenagers and, finally, to unmotivated murder. What can so triumphantly demonstrate an existential freedom as torturing and killing for kicks? Didn't Apollinaire himself say that de Sade was the freest man who ever lived?

What, precisely, is the road—or are the roads—which have led to the state of mind illustrated by the quotations in this article? I do not think that any analysis ending in a satisfactory answer to that question has ever been made. Someone with the stomach for it might undertake a study as nearly classic as Mario Praz's *The Romantic Agony*, which traces so brilliantly the origin and destination of 1890 decadence to which modernism is more closely parallel than is usually admitted, and of which it is, perhaps, only another phase. Cyril Connolly has this to say:

> [It] began as a revolt against the bourgeois in France, the Victorians in England, the Puritanism and materialism of America. The modern spirit was a combination of certain intellectual qualities inherited from the Enlightenment: lucidity, irony, skepticism, intellectual curiosity, combined with the impassioned intensity and enhanced sensibility of the Romantic, their rebellion and sense of technical experiment, their awareness of living in a tragic age.

All that is true enough and familiar enough but it doesn't go far enough. It does not explain why the most obvious and unique characteristics of the current avant-garde are not any of the characteristics of the Enlightenment or of any romanticism except that commonly called "decadent." How, for instance, do lucidity, irony, skepticism, or even intellectual curiosity become preludes to "the century of de Sade"? How did an assualt on Victorian complacency and hypocrisy end by practicing a sort of unmotivated vandalism? In London a recent city-wide series of "happenings" in which forty "artists" from ten nations took part was publicized as a reminder that "society will ignore the manifestations of destruction in art at its peril." Perhaps, as we say, the publicist had something there. Were certain members of the public justified when they objected to the performance of Juan Hidalgo, the representative from Spain, whose specialty, it seems, is cutting off the heads of chickens and flinging them at the audience?

I suppose that anyone who undertook to trace the development of modernism would have to begin by asking whether or not there is a single dominating characteristic of this latest development, any one which, at least by its frequent emphasis, seems to distinguish contemporary modernism from the movement out of which it is said to have grown. True, this modernism does indeed seem to be compounded of many simplicities and not all who represent it include all of them in their mixtures. Thus one distinguishing characteristic

THE NEWSMAN: SOCIETY'S LONESOME END

Wes Gallagher

The general manager of Associated Press reviews the confusing role of professional journalists in an age of instant communication.

Several years ago the Army football coach, Col. Earl "Red" Blaik, devised a new offense in which one end stayed at the far side of the field and sometimes didn't even come to the huddle between plays. Sportswriters dubbed this player "the lonesome end." He was part of the team but remote from it; he was part of the action but divorced from it.

The first lonesome end was Cadet Bill Carpenter. He played his position perfectly and followed through in later life—recently he was decorated with the nation's second highest award for bravery. As a captain in Vietnam, he called down fire on his own position when it looked as though it would be overrun by the Vietcong. The image of the lonesome end in football was criticized—particularly in the middle of the week, when the sportswriters don't have anything else to write about. But Carpenter didn't worry about his image at West Point or in Vietnam.

There are some parallels between the lonesome end and the journalist. Today, it is the newsman, the reporter, the editor that stand alone, separated from society but a vital part of it—divorced from the action but a recorder of it.

If the reporter writes about drug addiction, he is charged with making it attractive to nonusers; if he doesn't, he is suppressing the news. If he writes about Negro nationalists, he is accused of writing about a tiny minority; if he doesn't, he is told he is not reporting the true militancy of the Negro. If he writes of the military victory in Vietnam, he is attacked by the doves; if he writes of the failure of the Vietnamese to clear their house of corruption, he is attacked by the hawks. If he reports that the rapist was a six-foot-four-inch Negro, he is charged with stirring racial hatred; if he doesn't, he is accused of misrepresenting the crime. If he reports that the Mets are strictly a dismal bunch of stumblebums, he is against the new team in town; if he doesn't, he is a publicity agent. And so it goes.

The newsman is the lonely end of society. From his position he looks at a strife-torn, controversial world which seems bent on its own destruction. He is in constant danger of losing his reportorial aplomb. But the world has frequently seemed like this. For example:

> It was the best of times, it was the worst of times, it was the age of wisdom, it was the age of foolishness. . . . It was the season of light, it was the season of darkness, it was the spring of hope, it was the winter of despair.

Does this reflect our times? Possibly, but it was written by Charles Dickens about the French Revolution. And consider these views:

> We are unsettled to the fiery roots of our being. There isn't a human relation, whether of parent and child, husband and wife, worker and employer, that doesn't move in a strange situation. We are not used to this complicated civilization and don't know how to behave when personal contact and eternal authority have disappeared. There are no precedents to guide us, no wisdom that wasn't meant for a simpler age. We have changed our environment more quickly than we knew how to change ourselves.

Our good friend Walter Lippmann wrote this in 1914. It is little wonder that, after making this Cassandra-like prediction of the future fifty-four years ago, Mr. Lippmann is hard-pressed for adjectives to describe our present situation.

Then there is youth—that much-maligned group:

> We live in a decadent age. Young people no longer respect their parents. They are rude and impatient. They inhabit taverns and have no self-control.

This evaluation was made 6,000 years ago; it is the inscription on an Egyptian tomb. Incidentally, those youth who think that today's hippie philosophy of love and disdain for materialistic society is new might ponder this:

> It is not love but booty this Iron Age applauds.

Cicero made that observation in 56 B.C. And, not long ago, former White House Press Secretary Bill Moyers provided this report of a Cabinet meeting:

> The President was much inflamed and got into one of those passions when he cannot command himself, ran on much on the personal abuse which has been bestowed on him, defied any man on earth to produce one single act of his since he has been in government which was not done on the purest motives, that by God he had rather be on his farm than to be made emperor of the world—and yet they were charging him with wanting to be king. That rascal, the newspaper editor, had even sent him three of his papers every day as if he thought he could become the distributor of his papers. He could see in this nothing but an impudent design to insult him.

Mr. Moyers was not referring to President Lyndon Johnson, but was quoting Thomas Jefferson on George Washington. When Moyers quoted this in a recent speech, he added that he believed that the government and the press worry too much about their relationship to each other. To that I can only say amen. He also said that news is made by the press against government, just as fire is made by flint striking against rocks—which is as good a description as any.

We are beset today with the problem of rioting in our cities, multiple crises growing out of segregation and integration, or black nationalism, or the never-ending war in Vietnam, or the lightning war in the Middle East. But it is well for the journalist to remember that civilizations of the past faced similar problems which they felt were fully as important. It is also well to remember that some of these ancient problems were never settled in any black-and-white way, but simply lapsed into a state of tolerability. Many of our problems today will never be solved, but simply will be accepted by generations in the future as undesirable but tolerable.

The difference between this age and others is that instant communications have spread the effect of problems over vast multitudes of people. And these people differ in color, history, and civilization. These differences, in turn, multiply the effect of common problems, making their solution difficult and sometimes impossible.

It is the journalist—the newsman—who is the master of these new communications. It is his responsibility to see that these scientific miracles serve mankind to bridge gaps, not create them. This is a tremendous responsibility.

The concept of objectivity in the news and the reporter being a noncombatant and an observer rather than a partisan is relatively new in journalism. It is this striving for objectivity that places the journalist apart from society today; it is this struggle for objectivity that keeps him awake at night as he wrestles with the facts; it is this concept of nonpartisanship that makes him fair game for the partisans.

There is a simple solution for some journalists. It is a guaranteed tranquilizer. If he wants to, he can become a partisan spokesman in one of the controversies of the day—for or against the war in Vietnam, for or against integration, for or against Israel or the Arabs. In one of these secure positions he will at least have some friends and he can flail away at his enemies with gusto. He can fit the facts to his prejudices. He can be a professional liberal or a professional conservative.

But to the true newsman partisanship is the original sin—the apple in the journalistic Eden. It is easy to eat but hard to digest, because a journalist deals in facts, and they continually come back to haunt him—because facts are often contradictory. And the journalist, knowing this, cannot seize the easy partisan solution without a crisis of conscience.

We have recently been deluged in controversy over free

press and fair trial. The subject is likely to be talked to death—and perhaps this wouldn't be a bad solution. The American Bar Association has shed rivers of tears about sensational crime coverage, but there are more sensation-seeking lawyers than sensation-seeking reporters. It wasn't a newspaper reporter who tossed an artificial limb into a jury box in an accident case; it was lawyer Melvin Belli. If the bar wants less sensationalism, let it first clean its own house. Let it act against the lawyers who turn courtrooms into theaters. Until it does, the Bar Association does not come before the court of public opinion with clean hands.

Critics seldom let logic confuse their thinking. And the critics will have much to say this year, for 1968 is likely to be the most controversial year since the Civil War; all of us will need to keep a firm grip on our reportorial calm.

The political cancers that have eaten into the roots of American society—Vietnam, segregation-integration, rioting in the cities—will be present in their most malignant form. They will feed on the fiery oratory and illogic of a Presidential year. As the candidates crisscross the country, it is hard to envision a city that will not be wracked with dissension, protests, and, possibly, rioting. The supporters of the liberals, conservatives, blacks, whites, war advocates, antiwar exponents will be highly vocal. They will be long on expression but short on listening. There will be much talk but no communication. It will be the task of the journalist to bring some sense to this.

To cope with this emotional news of our age there has been much talk of codes for the journalist. In fact, the talk of codes reached a peak a short time ago when Representative William L. Hungate of Missouri reported that he had conducted a private poll of Congress, and the majority of Senators and Representatives answering said that they favored a code for newsmen who cover the House and Senate. The idea of Congress, which has been loath to adopt a code of ethics for itself, writing a code for reporters has a curious ring to it.

The public will not be served nor problems solved by the adoption of unenforceable press codes, news blackouts, news time lapses, or similar restrictions. The public has serious doubts about many facets of the news now, without having its confidence further undermined by the adoption of vague generalities which infer that there is something in the news too distasteful for them to know or—even more insulting—too difficult for them to understand. Restrictions foster rumors which are far worse than the truth. The Detroit *News* and *Free Press* have spent weeks and literally thousands of hours of reporters' time running down every possible rumor as to what took place during the rioting there. They printed the truth as they found it, but they would be the first to admit that many readers in Detroit undoubtedly still feel something is being hidden. Of course, the same feeling exists about Vietnam—despite the millions of words printed and spoken.

There is a credibility problem, and not only on the part of government. The newsman must establish his credibility. He must convince the public he is truly detached from the causes of the day; convince them by his skills as a reporter that he has no cause to serve except to get the truth; convince them by his honesty he is truly the public's eyes and ears, their trusted representative at complex or distant events; convince them he will not succumb to the red dogs of the lobbyists; convince them that he is motivated only by pride in his profession. And he must convince the public that he is willing to call down the fire of the partisans on his own head, as Captain Carpenter did, if it becomes necessary—and it will become necessary.

If he does these things, he will be believed; not loved, but respected, which is all he can ask. His constant difficult task will be to put the news in perspective. When he writes about the draft protests, he should point out that this phenomenon is not new. In fact, during the Civil War draft riots in New York City, between four hundred and five hundred rioters were killed. In addition, the rioters killed ninety-eight federal registrars in the North. These figures make even the rioting in Detroit look small. When writing about Vietnam he should constantly point out to the reader that no one—hawk or dove—has produced a viable solution. When examining race relations, he should emphasize that the black community is divided among the black nationalists who want to establish their own black society and those who want an integrated society with the whites; that the white society is also divided between those who favor integration as the solution and those who would keep an all-black society separate. Despite this, there is no common ground even for a sensible dialogue.

Perspective is the indispensable key for the reporter in this age, as I have tried to point out by citing quotations to show that our problems are neither new nor unique. I emphasize again that the difference between this age and others is that instant communications have given the journalist an immense audience; thus his work can have a tremendous impact on our civilization.

The work of the journalist is just as necessary to our society as that of the scientist, doctor, or the highest public official. In these times it may be even more important. Journalism offers young men and women today the greatest of challenges to make a worthwhile contribution to mankind. And for a job well done it will offer the greatest of personal satisfactions, even though one will constantly find himself to be society's "lonesome end."

BREAKTHROUGH:
THE SAGA OF JONAS SALK

Richard Carter

A biographer describes the frustrations of a doctor-scientist who loses his anonymity and engenders the animosity of his whole profession.

On April 12, 1955, the world learned that a vaccine developed by Jonas Edward Salk, M.D., could be relied upon to prevent paralytic poliomyelitis. This news consummated the most extraordinary undertaking in the history of science, a huge research project led by a Wall Street lawyer and financed by the American people through hundreds of millions of small donations. More than a scientific achievement, the vaccine was a folk victory, an occasion for pride and jubilation. A contagion of love swept the world. People observed moments of silence, rang bells, honked horns, blew factory whistles, fired salutes, kept their traffic lights red in brief periods of tribute, took the rest of the day off, closed their schools or convoked fervid assemblies therein, drank toasts, hugged children, attended church, smiled at strangers, forgave enemies.

Delighted journalists stoked the fires. It seemed that this Salk, a somewhat withdrawn and indistinct figure during the months of excitement that preceded the announcement of his success, was not really an ivory-tower type at all. Behind the studious reserve, it seemed, was a warm, even saintly human being. He had worked seven days a week, sometimes for twenty-four hours at a stretch, it was reported, lest the vaccine be delayed for one needless minute and one child be crippled for lack of it. Yet he had not allowed his humanitarian feelings to stampede him. He was too much the man of science to compromise the rigid discipline of his calling: No medical experiments had ever been carried out with more laborious care than his. Moreover, he had a sunny smile. He was only forty. He and his attractive wife had produced three lively boys. He liked good music and long walks. He was charmingly bashful about personal publicity. He had been raised on the verge of poverty and had accumulated no wealth of his own, but was not seeking to enrich himself with his discovery (as the vaccine was so often described). Indeed, he had not patented it, would get no royalties from its sale, and had insisted that all qualified manufacturing laboratories everywhere enjoy free and equal access to the formula.

The ardent people named schools, streets, hospitals, and newborn infants after him. They sent him checks, cash, money orders, stamps, scrolls, certificates, pressed flowers, snapshots, candy, baked goods, religious medals, rabbits' feet and other talismans, and uncounted thousands of letters and telegrams, both individual and round-robin, describing their heartfelt gratitude and admiration. They offered him free automobiles, agricultural equipment, clothing, vacations, lucrative jobs in government and industry, and several hundred opportunities to get rich quick. Their legislatures and parliaments passed resolutions, and their heads of state issued proclamations. Their universities tendered honorary degrees. He was nominated for the Nobel prize, which he did not get, and a Congressional medal, which he got, and membership in the National Academy of Sciences, which turned him down. He was mentioned for several dozen lesser awards of national or local or purely promotional character, most of which *he turned down.*

Not all of this happened on April 12, 1955, but much of it did. Salk awakened that morning as a moderately prominent research professor on the faculty of the University of Pittsburgh School of Medicine. He ended the day as the most beloved medical scientist on earth. Worshipful humanity had borne him far beyond mere fame and had enthroned him among the immortals, where he sat gasping in a paroxysm of embarrassed discomfort, wondering whether he would ever be able to extricate himself from this, the latest and most horrendous pickle of an eventful career.

Jonas Salk saw calamity in his triumph because he knew perfectly well that his colleagues in biological science were offended by the uproar and would hold him accountable for it. Nine years later the pain was still fresh: "The worst tragedy that could have befallen me was my success. I knew right away that I was through—cast out."

The need to be admired by professional colleagues is more noticeable among scientists than among other men. An author may repel his peers with sentences that do not parse, but if the public buys his books, the attitude of other authors will cause him only brief regret. Other creative types comparable to scientists, such as poets, painters, actors, and musicians, can also extract a measure of gratification from the praise of an inexpert laity. But the scientist is trapped. However pleasantly the occasional cheers of the multitude may resound in his ears, he depends for lasting professional and emotional security on the respect accorded him by other scientists. Charles Darwin was candid about it when he wrote that his love of science had "been much aided by the ambition to be esteemed by my fellow naturalists." Max Planck observed that the scientist's joy is "the certainty that every result he finds will be appreciated by specialists throughout the world."

This spiritual dependence on the opinion of the scientific community arises from the nature of scientific work and is but incidentally related to the hungers of vanity. After all, scientists alone are able to appreciate fully what a Darwin or Salk talks about. They alone can evaluate his work by subjecting it to confirmatory tests. They alone can give the word that opens or closes the door to larger opportunity. They alone can award the professional honors that signify accomplishment.

Salk was painfully aware that his colleagues did not agree with the laity that he was a new Pasteur or even that he had "discovered" anything. They would not fail to notice that the press was exaggerating the significance of his contribution to what had been a prolonged, cumulative effort by many distinguished workers. Had he not allowed the vaccine to be named after him? Was this not in itself a betrayal of those on whose work his own had depended—a usurpation of credit?

They had been annoyed for years by his unconcealed desire for professional independence and recognition. All of them had been propelled by the same ambition and many had satisfied it, but few had ever seemed as inexorable about it as Salk. They were uneasy about the self-assurance with which he tackled major problems, the speed with which he offered his solutions, the glibness with which he defended them, the stubbornness with which he refused to be deflected from whatever course he had mapped for himself, the nimbleness with which he altered course when ready. They did not know that he had only lately stopped quaking in their presence. They thought him cold as ice.

One of their most imperative traditions required them to protect their freedom of thought and inquiry against the political power and financial blandishments of nonscientists. But the age of the multimillion-dollar scientific crash program had arrived, and they had already begun to breach the tradition, measuring each other now in terms of the monetary grants they were able to obtain from nonscientists. Salk's prowess was confirmed and his unpopularity consolidated when he emerged, practically overnight, as the most lavishly supported biological scientist in history, having vaulted over the heads of older, better-established, equally ambitious workers. His virus laboratory in Pittsburgh was, in the words of one critic, "the smoothest, biggest, damnedest thing you ever saw, like a big, damned industrial plant except it was in a medical school."

No discussion of Salk's spectacular detour from the professional pecking order was complete without cynical reference to his close friendship with Basil O'Connor, high-flying president of the National Foundation for Infantile Paralysis. As head of the organization through which the public fought polio, the celebrated lawyer was by far the most influential layman in American medical research. Scientists clucked their tongues at the flamboyant aggressiveness with which he promoted the polio menace, the ease with which he raised more money for his cause than was collected for cancer, heart disease, or mental illness. But his organization dispensed grants of unprecedented generosity; scientists who deplored O'Connor's methods fell all over themselves to court the foundation's favor. O'Connor knew this and kept himself unreachable, scrupulously making no scientific move without the approval of his advisory committees of hard-boiled senior scientists; unreachable, the gossip suggested, until he met Salk and found in him a friend as close as a son.

Salk had already begun to lap his field before he attracted O'Connor's personal interest, but this was either unknown or ignored. Virologists unable to reconcile themselves to Salk's high-pressure performance decided that he had traded this scientific freedom to O'Connor in exchange for undeserved, unseemly stardom.

The events of April 12 seemed to confirm such gossip. Among the offenses commited that day against the totems and taboos of the scientific community was the raucous manner in which the big news was announced. Scientists who came (by invitation) to the University of Michigan at Ann Arbor to hear whether the vaccine had actually prevented paralytic polio found the place overrun with reporters and television camera crews. The atmosphere was as febrile as that of a political convention or a sex trial, more conducive to press agentry than to academic deliberation. And if this were not enough to illuminate the primrose path down which Salk allegedly was traveling, somebody noted that the day was the tenth anniversary of the death of Franklin D. Roosevelt, founder of the National Foundation for Infantile Paralysis. Basil O'Connor had been Roosevelt's law partner and crony. The choice of April 12 was seen, therefore, as a promotional vulgarity intended to fill the coffers of the National Foundation. Thus was supplied one more controversial note to the proceedings, one more affront to Salk's exasperated peers, one more embarrassment to Salk himself.

As a social thinker whose interest in the ways of mankind antedated his interest in medical science, Jonas Salk felt that the matters of form to which his detractors gave so much uncomplimentary attention were not quite the heart of the problem. The basic difficulty, he believed, was far more serious: His vaccine was actually a development of epochal importance. If it turned out to be as lastingly efficacious as he claimed it might be, one of the older and more comfortable tenets of orthodox virology would be annulled. History demonstrates, as Salk well knew, that he who undermines dogma undermines its champions and earns their wrath.

His original intention had not been to find fame as developer of a polio vaccine. As a basic scientist, he merely had sought to test the traditional notion that only natural infection or an infectious vaccine made of living disease organisms could offer durable protection against a viral disease. According to that hallowed theory, a vaccine compounded of killed, noninfectious viruses simply would not do. Salk suspected that this was nonsense. For one thing, it was unverified lore received from the past. For another, it conflicted with realities observed in the prevention of other kinds of infectious disease. For yet another, it had about it the stink of the shaman, the medicine man, the magician—as if the effectiveness of a vaccine depended not on chemistry but on some occult life force. In other words, Salk saw his challenge to orthodoxy as not only experimental but ideological.

It certainly was. The professional controversies that obstructed the development and testing of his unconventional killed-virus vaccine were waged with the intensity that man usually reserves for his holy wars. The brilliant, articulate Dr. Albert Sabin attacked Salk's work and defended orthodoxy on the front page of every important newspaper in the United States—not once but often. Despite these polemics, Sabin retained the respect of most virologists, demonstrating that there are, after all, circumstances wherein a scientist can obtain publicity without provoking hostility among his colleagues.

There were, of course, no scrimmages of that sort on April 12, the day of announcement and celebration. When the eminent Dr. Thomas Francis, Jr., declared that his studies had proved the vaccine safe and effective, Sabin and other antagonists of the Salk position participated in the general applause. And when Salk himself took the podium, they all rose from their chairs to award him the standing ovation demanded by a public occasion of that kind.

But if anyone actually intended an armistice, this sentiment was never conveyed to Jonas Salk. "I felt like a drowning man," he says. Before April 12 he had dared hope that the success of his vaccine would give him the beginning of a foothold on the professional esteem he needed so badly. He had hoped that the success, if it came, might at last direct close attention to some of his beautiful experiments, the revolutionary implication of which had for so long been overlooked, minimized, or misconstrued. Instead, he felt more than ever an object of scientific scorn.

Worse difficulty lay ahead. So did greater triumph.

MY OWN PRIVATE
VIEW OF MYSELF

Marilyn Monroe,
as Told to Richard Meryman

A movie star—sex symbol—tells how fame brought loneliness rather than love and acceptance.

Sometimes wearing a scarf and a polo coat and no makeup and with a certain attitude of walking, I go shopping—or just looking at people living. But then you know, there will be a few teenagers who are kind of sharp and they'll say, "Hey, just a minute—you know who I think that is?" And then they'll start tailing me. And I don't mind. I realize some people want to see if you're real. The teenagers, the little kids, their faces light up—they say "gee" and they can't wait to tell their friends. And old people come up and say, "Wait till I tell my wife." You've changed their whole day.

In the morning the garbage men that go by 57th Street when I come out the door say, "Marilyn, hi! How do you feel this morning?" To me it's an honor, and I love them for it. The workingmen—I'll go by and they'll whistle. At first they whistle because they think, oh, it's a girl, she's got blond hair and she's not out of shape, and then they say, "Gosh, it's Marilyn Monroe!" And that has its—you know, those are the times it's nice, people knowing who you are and all of that, and feeling that you've meant something to them.

I don't know quite why, but somehow I feel they know that I mean what I do—both when I'm acting on the screen or when if I see them in person and greet them —that I really always do mean hello and how are you? In their fantasies they feel—Gee, it can happen to me!

But when you're famous you kind of run into human

nature in a raw kind of way. It stirs up envy, fame does. People you run into feel that, well, who is she—who does she think she is, Marilyn Monroe? They feel fame gives them some kind of privilege to walk up to you and say anything to you, you know, of any kind of nature—and it won't hurt your feelings—like it's happening to your clothing. One time here I am looking for a home to buy and I stopped at this place. A man came out and was very pleasant, very cheerful, and said, "Oh, just a moment, I want my wife to meet you." Well, she came out and said, "Will you please get off the premises?"

You're always running into people's unconscious. Let's take some actors—or directors. Usually they don't say it to me, they say it to the newspapers because that's a bigger play. You know, if they're only insulting me to my face that doesn't make a big enough play because all I have to do is say, "See you around, like never." But if it's the newspapers, it's coast to coast and on around the world. I don't understand why people aren't a little more generous with each other. I don't like to say this, but I'm afraid there is a lot of envy in this business. The only thing I can do is I stop and think, "I'm all right but I'm not so sure about *them!*"

For instance, you've read there was some actor that once said about me that kissing me was like kissing Hitler. Well, I think that's *his* problem. If I have to do intimate love scenes with somebody who really has these kind of feelings toward me, then my fantasy can come into play. In other words, out with him, in with my fantasy. He was never there.

But one thing about fame is the bigger the people are or the simpler the people are, the more they are not awed by you! They don't feel they have to be offensive, they don't feel they have to insult you. You can meet Carl Sandburg and he is so pleased to meet you. He wants to know about you and you want to know about him. Not in any way has he ever let me down. Or else you can meet working people who want to know what is it like. You try to explain to them. I don't like to disillusion them and tell them it's sometimes nearly impossible. They kind of look toward you for something that's away from their everyday life. I guess you call that entertainment, a world to escape into, a fantasy.

Sometimes it makes you a little bit sad because you'd like to meet somebody kind of on face value. It's nice to be included in people's fantasies but you also like to be accepted for your own sake.

I don't look at myself as a commodity, but I'm sure a lot of people have. Including, well, one corporation in particular which shall be nameless. If I'm sounding picked on or something, I think I am. I'll think I have a few wonderful friends and all of a sudden, oooh, here it comes. They do a lot of things—they talk about you to the press, to their friends, tell stories, and you know, it's disappointing. These are the ones you aren't interested in seeing every day of your life.

Of course, it *does* depend on the people, but sometimes I'm invited places to kind of brighten up a dinner table—like a musician who'll play the piano after dinner, and I know you're not really invited for yourself. You're just an ornament.

When I was five—I think that's when I started wanting to be an actress—I loved to play. I didn't like the world around me because it was kind of grim—but I loved to play house and it was like you could make your own boundaries. It goes beyond house—you could make your own situations and you could pretend and even if the other kids were a little slow on the imagining part you could say, "Hey, what about if you were such and such and I were such and such—wouldn't that be fun?" And they'd say, "Oh, yes," and then I'd say, "Well, that will be a horse and this will be—" It was play, playfulness. When I heard that this was acting, I said that's what I want to be—you can play. But then you grow up and find out about playing, that they make playing very difficult for you.

Some of my foster families used to send me to the movies to get me out of the house and there I'd sit all day and way into the night—up in front, there with the screen so big, a little kid all alone, and I loved it. I loved anything that moved up there and I didn't miss anything that happened—and there was no popcorn either.

When I was eleven the whole world which was always closed to me—I just felt like I was on the outside of the world—suddenly, everything opened up. Even the girls paid a little attention to me just because they thought, "Hmmm, she's to be dealt with!" And I had this long walk to school—2½ miles to school, 2½ miles back—it was just sheer pleasure. Every fellow honked his horn—you know, workers driving to work, waving, you know, and I'd wave back. The world became friendly.

All the newspaper boys when they delivered the paper would come around to where I lived, and I used to hang from a limb of a tree, and I had sort of a sweatshirt on— I didn't realize the value of a sweatshirt in those days—and then I was sort of beginning to catch on, but I didn't quite get it because I couldn't really afford sweaters. But here they'd come with their bicycles, you know, and I'd get these free papers and the family liked that, and they'd all pull their bicycles up around the tree and then I'd be hanging, looking kind of like a monkey, I guess. I was a little shy to come down. I did get down to the curb, kinda kicking the curb and kicking the leaves and talking, but mostly listening.

And sometimes the families used to worry because I used to laugh so loud and so gay; I guess they felt it was hysterical. It was just this sudden freedom because I would ask the boys, "Can I ride your bike now?" And they'd say, "Sure." Then I'd go zooming, laughing in the wind, riding down the block, laughing, and they'd all stand around and wait till I came back, but I loved the wind. It caressed me.

But it was kind of a double-edged thing. I did find, too, when the world opened up that people took a lot for granted, like not only could they be friendly, but they could get suddenly overly friendly and expect an awful lot for very little.

When I was older, I used to go to Grauman's Chinese Theatre and try to fit my foot in the prints in the cement there. And I'd say, "Oh, oh, my foot's too big, I guess, that's out." I did have a funny feeling later when I finally put my foot down into that wet cement. I sure knew what it really meant to me—anything's possible, almost.

It was the creative part that kept me going—trying to be an actress. I enjoy acting when you really hit it right. And I guess I've always had too much fantasy to be only a housewife. Well, also, I had to eat. I was never kept, to be blunt about it. I always kept myself. I have always had a pride in the fact that I was on my own. And Los Angeles was my home, too, so when they said, "Go home!" I said, "I *am* home."

The time when I sort of began to think I was famous I was driving somebody to the airport and as I came back there was this movie house and I saw my name in lights. I pulled the car up at a distance down the street—it was too much to take up close, you know—all of a sudden. And I said, "God, somebody's made a mistake." But there it was, in lights. And I sat there and said, "So that's the way it looks," and it was all very strange to me, and yet at the studio they had said, "Remember you're not a star." Yet there it is up in lights.

I really got the idea I must be a star, or *something*, from the newspapermen—I'm saying men, not the women—who would interview me and they would be warm and friendly. By the way, that part of the press, you know, the men of the press, unless they have their own personal quirks against me, they were always very warm and friendly and they'd say, "You know, you're the only star," and I'd say, "Star?" and they'd look at me as if I were nuts. I think they, in their own kind of way, made me realize I was famous.

I remember when I got the part in *Gentlemen Prefer Blondes*. Jane Russell—she was the brunette in it and I was the blonde—she got 200,000 dollars for it and I got my five hundred dollars a week, but that to me was, you know, considerable. She, by the way, was quite wonderful to me. The only thing was I couldn't get a dressing room. I said, finally —I really got to this kind of level—I said, "Look, after all, I am the blonde and it is *Gentlemen Prefer Blondes!*" Because still they always kept saying "Remember, you're not a star." I said, "Well, whatever I am, I *am* the blonde!"

And I want to say that the people—if I am a star—the people made me a star—no studio, no person, but the people did. There was a reaction that came to the studio, the fan mail, or when I went to a premiere, or the exhibitors wanted to meet me. I didn't know why. When they all rushed toward me, I looked behind me to see who was there and I said, "My heavens!" I was scared to death. I used to get the feeling, and sometimes I still get it, that sometimes I was fooling somebody. I don't know who or what—maybe myself.

I've always felt toward the slightest scene—even if all I had to do in a scene was just to come in and say, "Hi,"—that the people ought to get their money's worth and that this is an obligation of mine, to give them the best you can get from me. I do have feelings some days when there are some scenes with a lot of responsibility toward the meaning, and I'll wish, gee, if only I would have been a cleaning woman. On the way to the studio I would see somebody cleaning and I'd say, "That's what I'd like to be. That's my ambition in

MY OWN PRIVATE VIEW OF MYSELF

life." But I think all actors go through this. We not only *want* to be good; we have to be.

You know, when they talk about nervousness—my teacher, Lee Strasberg—when I said to him, "I don't know what's wrong with me but I'm a little nervous," he said, "When you're not, give up, because nervousness indicates sensitivity."

Also, a struggle with shyness is in every actor more than anyone can imagine. There is a censor inside us that says to what degree do we let go, like a child playing. I guess people think we just go out there, and you know, that's all we do—just do it. But it's a real struggle. I'm one of the world's most self-conscious people. I really have to struggle.

An actor is not a machine, no matter how much they want to say you are. Creativity has got to start with humanity and when you're a human being, you feel, you suffer—you're gay, you're sick, you're nervous or whatever. Like any creative human being, I *would* like a bit more control so that it would be a little easier for me when the director says, "One tear, right now," that one tear would pop out. But once there came two tears because I thought, "How dare he?"

Goethe said, "Talent is developed in privacy," you know? And it's really true. There is a need for aloneness which I don't think most people realize for an actor. It's almost having certain kinds of secrets for yourself that you'll let the whole world in on only for a moment, when you're acting.

But everybody is always tugging at you. They'd all like sort of a chunk of you. They kind of like take pieces out of you. I don't think they realize it, but it's like "rrrr do this, rrrr do that." But you do want to stay intact—intact and on two feet.

I think that when you are famous every weakness is exaggerated. This industry should behave like a mother whose child has just run out in front of a car. But instead of clasping the child to them, they start punishing the child. Like you don't dare get a cold—how dare you get a cold! I mean, the executives can get colds and stay home forever and phone it in, but how dare you, the actor, get a cold or a virus. You know, no one feels worse than the one who's sick. I sometimes wish, gee, I wish they had to act a comedy with a temperature and a virus infection. I am not an actress who appears at a studio just for the purpose of discipline. This doesn't have anything at all to do with art. I myself would like to become more disciplined within my work. But I'm there to give a performance and not to be disciplined by a studio! After all, I'm not in a military school. This is supposed to be an art form, not just a manufacturing establishment.

The sensitivity that helps me to act, you see, also makes me react. An actor is supposed to be a sensitive instrument. Isaac Stern takes good care of his violin. What if everybody jumped on his violin?

If you've noticed in Hollywood where millions and billions of dollars have been made, there aren't really any kind of monuments or museums, and I don't call putting your footprint in Grauman's Chinese a monument—all right, this did mean a lot to sentimental-ballyhoo me at the time. Gee, nobody left anything behind, they took it, they grabbed it and they ran—the ones who made the billions of dollars, never the workers.

You know a lot of people have, oh gee, real quirky problems that they wouldn't dare have anyone know. But one of my problems happens to show—I'm late. I guess people think that why I'm late is some kind of arrogance and I think it is the opposite of arrogance. I also feel that I'm not in this big American rush—you know, you got to go and you got to go fast but for no good reason. The main thing is, I do want to be prepared when I get there to give a good performance or whatever to the best of my ability.

A lot of people can be there on time and do nothing, which I have seen them do, and you know, all sit around and sort of chit-chatting and talking trivia about their social life. Gable said about me, "When she's there, she's there. All of her is there! She's there to work."

I was honored when they asked me to appear at the President's birthday rally in Madison Square Garden. There was like a hush over the whole place when I came on to sing "Happy Birthday"—like if I had been wearing a slip I would have thought it was showing, or something. I thought, "Oh, my gosh, what if no sound comes out!"

A hush like that from the people warms me. It's sort of like an embrace. Then you think, by God, I'll sing this song if it's the last thing I ever do. And for all the people. Because I remember when I turned to the microphone I looked all the way up and back and I thought, "That's where I'd be—way up there under one of those rafters, close to the ceiling, after I paid my two dollars to come into the place."

Afterwards they had some sort of a reception. I was with my former father-in-law, Isadore Miller, so I think I did something wrong when I met the President. Instead of saying, "How do you do?" I just said, "This is my former father-in-law, Isadore Miller." He came here an immigrant and I thought this would be one of the biggest things in his life—he's about seventy-five or eighty years old and I thought this would be something that he would be telling his grandchildren about and all that. I should have said, "How do you do, Mr. President," but I had already done the singing, so well you know. I guess nobody noticed it.

Fame has a special burden, which I might as well state here and now. I don't mind being burdened with being glamorous and sexual. But what goes with it can be a burden—like the man was going to show me around but the woman said, "Off the premises." I feel that beauty and femininity are ageless and can't be contrived, and glamor—although the manufacturers won't like this—cannot be manufactured. Not real glamor, it's based on femininity. I think that sexuality is only attractive when it's natural and spontaneous. This is where a lot of them miss the boat. And then something I'd just like to spout off on. We are all born sexual creatures, thank God, but it's a pity so many people despise and crush this natural gift. Art, real art, comes from it—everything.

I never quite understood it—this sex symbol—I always thought symbols were those things you clash together! That's the trouble, a sex symbol becomes a thing. I just hate to be a thing. But if I'm going to be a symbol of something I'd rather have it sex than some other things they've got symbols of! These girls who try to be me— I guess the studios put them up to it, or they get the ideas themselves. But gee, they haven't—you can make a lot of gags about it—like they haven't got the foreground or else they haven't the background. But I mean the middle, where you live.

All my stepchildren carried the burden of my fame. Sometimes they would read terrible things about me and I'd worry about whether it would hurt them. I would tell them, "Don't hide these things from me. I'd rather you ask me these things straight out and I'll answer all your questions. Don't be afraid to ask anything. After all, I have come up from way down."

I wanted them to know of lives other than their own. I used to tell them, for instance, that I worked for five cents a month and I washed one hundred dishes, and my stepkids would say, "One hundred dishes!" and I said, "Not only that, I scraped and cleaned them before I washed them. I washed them and rinsed them and put them in the draining place, but," I said, "thank God I didn't have to dry them." Kids are different from grownups —you know when you get grown up you can get kind of sour, I mean that's the way it can go, but kids accept you the way you are.

I always tell them. "Don't admire somebody because they are grown up or because they say certain things—kind of observe them a little bit." I think probably that is the best advice I have given them. Just observe people for a while and then make up your own mind. And I used to tell them that about myself. I said, "See if I'm worth being a friend. That's up to you, and you figure it out after a while."

Fame to me certainly is only a temporary and a partial happiness—even for a waif and I was brought up a waif. But fame is not really for a daily diet, that's not what fulfills you. It warms you a bit but the warming is temporary. It's like caviar, you know—it's good to have caviar but not when you have to have it every meal and every day.

I was never used to being happy, so that wasn't something I ever took for granted. I did sort of think, you know, marriage did that. You see, I was brought up differently from the average American child because the average child is brought up expecting to be happy—that's it, successful, happy, and on time. Yet because of fame I was able to meet and marry two of the nicest men I'd ever met up to that time.

I don't think people will turn against me, at least not by themselves. I like people. The "public" scares me but people I trust. Maybe they can be impressed by the press or when a studio starts sending out all kinds of stories. But I think when people go to see a movie, they judge for themselves. We human beings are strange creatures and still reserve the right to think for ourselves.

Once I was supposed to be finished—that was the end of me. When Mr. Miller was on trial for contempt of Congress, a certain corporation executive said either he named names and I got him to name names, or I was finished. I said, "I'm proud of my husband's position and I stand behind him all the way," and the court did too. "Finished," they said. "You'll never be heard of."

It might be kind of a relief to be finished. It's sort of like I don't know what kind of a yard dash you're running, but then you're at the finish line and you sort of sigh —you've made it! But you never have—you have to start all over again. But I believe you're always as good as your potential.

I now live in my work and in a few relationships with the few people I can really count on. Fame will go by and, so long, I've had you, fame. If it goes by, I've always known it was fickle. So at least it's something I experienced, but that's not where I live.

COMPLEX QUERY:
WHAT MAKES A GOOD SPY?

Arthur T. Hadley

A World War II intelligence officer and playwright-journalist surveys the secret agent's hostile world.

The world of the secret agent is a solitary world. His is the aloneness of the infantryman proceeding up a deserted enemy street. The hostile world stretches out infinitely in all directions around him with the tension of a high note held too long. Within this world he has no friend. He and his fear exist alone.

Just so was Francis Gary Powers alone on his U-2 spyplane mission when he was brought down 1,200 miles within the Soviet borders.

I remember sitting in a quiet Georgetown garden with an old friend. It was a soft, mint-julep afternoon in the spring of one of those fat, contented years shortly after the Korean war's end. My friend and I maintain the fiction that I don't know what he does. It's easier. That afternoon he was obviously on the rack. So much so, and this was so unusual, that I broke our rule and said, gesturing at the soft green peace of the garden to indicate the apparent peace of the world, "It must be even rougher, now."

"It is," he answered. And then, after an instant: "I blew a nasty one last week. Killed a few people. Must have set the cold war back months."

He should not have come out of his world apart and said that to me. But in his own world of secret intelligence there was no one he could talk to. His superiors would have regarded his depression as a dangerous sign of weakness. Intelligence security is so rigid his colleagues couldn't know what he was doing. So he sat alone in his separate world, while the peaceful world of the garden went on happily, not understanding.

The official bureaucratic designation for a man who takes on this demanding work is "agent, intelligence, covert." In the argot of his trade he is "opps black"—a "black operator." "White operators," or "agents, intelligence, overt," are those who analyze foreign technical journals, listen to Russian broadcasts, interview refugees. Their work may be secret, but they do not pretend to be something they are not. Theirs is not the extreme isolation and danger. They are not "in black." Agents like Powers, who both pretend to be something they are not and penetrate the Curtain, Bamboo or Iron, are "in deep black."

What mental and psychological qualities make up the ideal black agent? Different nations set different standards. Nevertheless, intelligence agents themselves are in general agreement about the necessary attributes. The man they describe is a far remove from the all-American boy or the pip-pip-and-all-that British colonel of spy fiction. These agents outline their ideal with such observations as:

"Lonely, complicated jobs take lonely, complicated guys."

"The quiet, bookish type, without bravado, sticks longest."

"Team players who don't need the coach or the team."

"The thinking fanatic."

Obviously, the ideal black agent on either side of the cold war must have extreme technical competence. The Soviet Union is a well-guarded, closed society. Those who snoop in or around it cannot be amateurs. The West, while not so secretive, has effective counterespionage, too. There is a legendary story in intelligence about a British colonel in World War II who, at great hazard, broke into a supersecret German torpedo factory and blew up the coffee urn. Being a tea drinker, he didn't recognize that piece of equipment. Those days, one hopes, are past.

Many black agents now are electronics specialists. Parabolic microphones and transistorized radio transmitters the size of a book of matches have changed agents' methods of operation. So has the aqualung, the inflatable airplane, high-speed aerial photography, infrared and radar detection devices, and the electronic processing of data.

Beneath the armor of technical competence lie the essential basic traits. Intelligence is an absolute must—not quiz-show glibness, but the ability to sit down with a sheet of paper and solve complex, original problems.

Much of the time, the agent has no "book" to go by. The situation he confronts is unique. There is no one to turn to for guidance, no committee to render a considered opinion, no staff to brief him on the big picture. On his decision rests not merely the future of some company, but that awesome entity, the national security.

His intelligence should be imaginative. He must outthink, not outfight, the enemy. Then, there are certain tough basic questions to which the ideal agent has worked out his answers. For example: "Since almost all men talk under torture in time (and women, too, though their psychology enables them to hold out longer), how long should I hold out? And why?" Or: "Since the enemy will stoop as low as necessary to gain his ends, how far should we stoop?"

The ideal agent must have faced up to the possible necessity of suicide. Actually, the dividing line between suicide and other hazards does not appear so great to those inside the black area. There is a macabre joke well known in intelligence circles about a secret agent going off alone on a particularly dangerous job inside an enemy country. The last words of his chief are: "Hold out, and keep reporting to the last man."

The agent has one overriding security rule: if he knows certain types of information he is to kill himself rather than fall into enemy hands, and he is issued the necessary equipment to do so. Other situations are left to his judgment.

The ideal agent must be a psychologically well-balanced individual—not ordinary, but so well-balanced as to appear normal. He needs the same deep, introspective knowledge of himself that the ideal psychiatrist needs. He should have looked perceptively at himself and the world around him and come up with his own philosophy.

His balance must be self-sustaining, an internal gyroscope. The man who needs praise, fellowship, coaching or even understanding cannot maintain the pace. Nor will the shibboleths of conventional wisdom sustain the agent in his dark hour. Conventional wisdom does not recognize the occasional necessity of murder or suicide.

The introspective intelligence necessary in the ideal agent shows up in the postwar published writings of British black operators about their work. A mystic quality permeates *Hugh Dormar's Diaries*. Both W. Stanley Moss' *Ill Met by Moonlight* and Fitzroy Maclean's *Eastern Approaches* are ripe with scholarship.

French resistance leaders had the same intellectual quality. Albert Camus is remembered as a philosopher, not as an agent. The man who called himself Colonel Remy wrote in *How a Resistance Dies*—perhaps the most agonizing tale ever told of an agent's work—an excellent antidote for anyone bemused by the glamour of working in black.

Ideal agents are hard to come by. Defectors from the Soviet Union indicate that even Russia has trouble finding them. The West must not only find them, but persuade them to volunteer. Inevitably, many of any country's agents are foreign nationals.

Since good agents are so hard to find, their superiors are likely to condone eccentricities in their off-duty behavior—which, to be frank, is often very odd. Two highly successful American black agents spring to mind. One used to borrow suits of armor from a museum and ride through the countryside looking for someone to joust with. (He found people who would, too.) The other would put on a ragged suit of clothes about once every two months and, going to the toughest part of a rather tough town, start a barroom brawl. He didn't always win, but he claimed it kept him in shape and worked off his tensions.

The tensions are constant. The presence of danger not only creates its own anxiety, but heightens the anxiety-producing factors in the agent's other problems.

One is schizophrenia—never letting on in one life what is being done in the other. Several Soviet agents have defected to the West because their "Western" personalities finally became dominant. One American, whose job is recruiting new agents, greets his friends with the mocking question: "Met any well-balanced schizophrenics lately?"

The secrecy of the work produces tensions in another way. An agent knows only his small portion of the job, not where he fits into the whole. He must be able to accept the necessity of performing morally despicable actions in situations of extreme danger over prolonged periods of time without knowing why.

The moral horror of certain actions he must take contributes to his psychological malaise. For example: You are a secret agent who has been leading a twenty-man resistance group in a hostile country for two years. You have shared desperate and intimate hardships with your men and have their complete trust. You are now ordered to betray your resistance group into ambush and to make certain none of them survives.

The example is not farfetched. In the middle of July 1944, when it became obvious to the Russians that the war in Europe was won, secret orders went out to Communist agents working with resistance groups in France, Yugoslavia, Poland and Greece to liquidate non-Communist resistance groups. From the French Alps to Mount Olympus, Red agents betrayed their closest comrades to the Germans. In liberated France, it was easier to murder, and explain to the Americans that the murdered were really collaborators.

The black operator does not face decisions every day as tough as the example. But even in the easiest, difficult moral choices are there. For some agents, after a time, the decisions become impossible. They break down. Every government in the business maintains special hospital rooms, plus doctors and nurses with security clearances, to handle the emotional problems of agents whom the work has pushed too far.

A more subtle form of breakdown that faces the Western agent in particular comes when the decisions all begin to seem easy. The agent has become either brutalized or so fanatical about his cause that his human values have disappeared. As Arthur Koestler has pointed out (and Koestler and George Orwell will be found among the black agents' most quoted authors) the yogi and the commissar, in the end, show the same image to the mirror.

COMPLEX QUERY: WHAT MAKES A GOOD SPY?

Quite a few years ago, I talked to one of America's most famous intelligence agents—famous, that is, within the small circle where such fame is possible. I had sought him out because I had heard that he had accurately forecast what the enemy was going to do before one of America's bitterest military disasters. His warning had been rejected and, after the débâcle, his reports had been destroyed and he had been relieved for having been right.

I asked him about the incident. He answered that his superiors were absolutely right to destroy his reports and relieve him. Faith in the national leadership was essential for the war effort and he and his reports jeopardized that faith.

I was younger then, and I looked at the man closely for signs of irony or bitterness as he made that statement. I saw none. I concluded that the poor man had been beaten down by the magnitude of his job. I felt, as many reading this may feel, that he needed a good psychiatrist or a tonic to buck him up and help him regain his lost confidence.

I now realize the man had that final ingredient of the ideal intelligence agent: a fanatical devotion to duty. He had been absolutely right. His warnings had not been misunderstood or disregarded, but deliberately set aside. The result had been a major American disaster. For the country's future, his retirement had become a necessity. It is not always wise to prove the boss wrong in industry, either.

However, when a man has been removed for such reasons, we in America and throughout the West feel he has been treated badly. The ideal agent must feel he has been treated in the only way possible. In Koestler's novel *Darkness At Noon*, the hero, Rubishov, confesses to things he has not done rather than embarrass the regime. He knows his voluntary confession will mean his death.

This necessity for fanaticism makes the role of the Westerner-turned-agent particularly difficult. The agent himself, like the criteria by which he is selected, is in large part the product of his environment. We in the West consider many of the actions an agent must take morally reprehensible. People who do such things, or order them done, or even those who write about the agent's problem with sympathy, are considered ogres or worse. Yet for national survival our agents are ordered to—and do—perform such actions.

But, and the but is crucial, the Western agent cannot just perform the action and forget it. He must, in his "worst" moments, retain his respect for life and human dignity. He is under orders not to become the mirror image of the enemy.

The rack on which the Western agent is stretched is well-described in Shakespeare's *Henry V*. King Henry wanders in disguise among his soldiers, conversing with them, just before the battle of Agincourt. The soldiers are debating how they will fight on the morrow. One of them wonders what will happen to his soul if the cause for which he dies "be not good."

"If the King's cause be wrong," replies another soldier, "our obedience to the King wipes the crime of it out of us."

"Not so," answers Henry. "Every subject's duty is the King. But every subject's soul is his own."

Our Western philosophy of freedom and moral responsibility splits the Western-reared agent in two. In societies where the subject's duty and soul both belong to the King, agents don't have the same problems—nor citizens the same freedoms.

The lack of complete fanaticism, the holding to moral values, puts an agent brought up in a free society under a much greater strain than his opposite number elsewhere. As a result, the West will lose rounds in the cold war. The strains and losses are unavoidable.

To combine the West's humanistic heritage of the individual's responsibility and freedom with the need for obedience and service to the state is not easy today. Deciding the proper mix of freedom and responsibility is a problem we all face. The secret agent, the black operator, merely faces the problem in its most acute form. He is our frontiersman in more ways than we realize.

THE DISTRESSED

Agitated Man

A YOUNG PSYCHIATRIST LOOKS AT HIS PROFESSION

Robert Coles

A much-published writer-psychiatrist deals with the detachment required of members of his profession and the problems it causes.

Recently, in the emergency ward of the Children's Hospital in Boston, an eight-year-old girl walked in and asked to talk to a psychiatrist about her "worries." I was called to the ward, and when we ended our conversation I was awake with sorrow and hope for this young girl, but also astonished at her coming. As a child psychiatrist, I was certainly accustomed to the troubled mother who brings her child to a hospital for any one of a wide variety of emotional problems. It was the child's initiative in coming which surprised me. I recalled a story my wife had told me. She was teaching a ninth-grade English class, and they were starting to read the Sophoclean tragedy of *Oedipus*. A worldly thirteen-year-old asked the first question: "What is an Oedipus complex?" Somehow, in our time, psychiatrists have become the heirs of those who hear the worried and see the curious. I wondered, then, what other children in other times did with their troubles and how they talked of the Greeks. I wondered, too, about my own profession, its position and its problems, and about the answers we might have for ourselves as psychiatrists.

We appear in cartoons, on television serials, and in the movies. We are "applied" by Madison Avenue, and we "influence" writers. Acting techniques, even schools of painting, are supposed to be derived from our insights, and Freud has become what Auden calls "a whole climate of opinion." Since children respond so fully to what is most at hand in the adult world, there should have been no reason for my surprise in that emergency ward. But this quick acceptance of us by children and adults alike is ironic, tells us something about this world, and is dangerous.

The irony is that we no longer resemble the small band of outcasts upon whom epithets were hurled for years. One forgets today just how rebellious Freud and his contemporaries were. They studied archaeology and mythology, were versed in the ancient languages, wrote well, and were a bit fiery, a bit eccentric, a bit troublesome, even for one another. Opinionated, determined, oblivious of easy welcome, they were fighters for their beliefs, and their ideas fought much of what the world then thought.

This is a different world. People today are frightened by the memory of concentration camps, by the possibility of atomic war, by the breakdown of old empires and old ways of living and believing. Each person shares the hopes and terrors peculiar to this age, not an age of reason or of enlightenment but an age of fear and trembling. Every year brings problems undreamed of only a decade ago in New York or Vienna. Cultures change radically, values are different, even diseases change. For instance, cases of hysteria, so beautifully described by Freud, are rarely found today. A kind of innocence is lost; people now are less suggestible, less naïve, more devious. They look for help from many sources, and chief among them, psychiatrists. Erich Fromm, in honor of Paul Tillich's seventy-fifth birthday, remarked:

> Modern man is lonely, frightened, and hardly capable of love. He wants to be close to his neighbor, and yet he is too unrelated and distant to be able to be close. . . . In search for closeness he craves knowledge; and in search for knowledge he finds psychology. Psychology becomes a substitute for love, for intimacy.

Now Freud and his knights are dead. Their long fight has won acclaim and increasing protection from a once reluctant society, and perhaps we should expect this ebb tide. Our very acclaim makes us more rigid and querulous. We are rent by rivalries, and early angers or stubborn idiosyncrasies have hardened into a variety of schools with conflicting ideas. We use proper names of early psychiatrists—Jung, Rank, Horney—to describe the slightest differences of emphasis or theory. The public is interested, but understandably confused. If it is any comfort to the public, so are psychiatrists, at times. Most of us can recall our moments of arrogance, only thinly disguised by words which daily become more like shibboleths, sound hollow, and are almost cant.

Ideas need the backing of institutions and firm social approval if they are to result in practical application. Yet I see pharisaic temples being built everywhere in psychiatry; pick up our journals and you will see meetings listed almost every week of the year and pages filled with the abstracts of papers presented at them. These demand precious time in attendance and reading, and such time is squandered all too readily these days. Who of us, even scanting sleep, can keep up with this monthly tidal wave of minute or repetitive studies? And who among us doesn't smile or shrug as he skims the pages, and suddenly leap with hunger at the lonely monograph that really says something? As psychiatrists we need to be in touch not only with our patients but with the entire range of human activity. We need time to see a play or read a poem, yet daily we sit tied to our chairs, listening and talking for hours on end. While this is surely a problem for all professions, it is particularly deadening for one which deals so intimately with people and which requires that its members themselves be alive and alert.

It seems to me that psychiatric institutions and societies too soon become bureaucracies, emphasizing form, detail, and compliance. They also breed the idea that legislation or grants of money for expansion of laboratories and buildings will provide answers where true knowledge is lacking. Whereas we desperately need more money for facilities and training for treatment programs, there can be a vicious circle of more dollars for more specialized projects producing more articles about less and less, and it may be that some projects are contrived to attract money and expand institutions rather than to form any spontaneous intellectual drive. We argue longer and harder about incidentals, such as whether our patients should sit up or lie down; whether we should accept or reject their gifts or answer their letters; how our offices should be decorated; or how we should talk to patients when they arrive or leave. We debate for hours about the difference between psychoanalysis and psychotherapy; about the advantages of seeing a person twice a week or three times a week; about whether we should give medications to people, and if so, in what way. For the plain fact is that as we draw near the bureaucratic and institutionalized, we draw near quibbling. Maybe it is too late, and much of this cannot be stopped. But it may be pleasantly nostalgic, if not instructive, to recall Darwin sailing on the *Beagle,* or Freud writing spirited letters of discovery to a close friend, or Sir Alexander Fleming stumbling upon a mold of penicillin in his laboratory—all in so simple and creative a fashion, and all with so little red tape and money.

If some of psychiatry's problems come from its position in the kind of society we have, other troubles are rooted in the very nature of our job. We labor with people who have troubled thoughts and feelings, who go awry in bed or in the office or with friends. Though we talk a great deal about our scientific interests, man's thoughts and feelings cannot be so easily understood or manipulated as atoms. The brain is where we think and receive impressions of the world, and it is in some ultimate sense an aggregate of atoms and molecules. In time we will know more about how to control and transform all cellular life, and at some point the cells of the brain will be known in all their intricate functions. What we now call "ego" or "unconscious" will be understood in terms of cellular action or biochemical and biophysical activity. The logic of the nature of all matter predicts that someday we will be able to arrange and rearrange ideas and feelings. Among the greatest mysteries before us are the unmarked pathways running from the peripheral nervous system to the thinking areas in the brain. The future is even now heralded by machines which think and by drugs which stimulate emotional states or affect specific moods, like depressions. Until these roads are thoroughly surveyed and the brain is completely understood, psychiatry will be as pragmatic or empirical as medicine.

Social scientists have taught us a great deal about how men think and how they get along with one another and develop from infancy to full age. We have learned ways of reaching people with certain problems and can offer much help to some of them. Often we can understand illnesses that we cannot so readily treat. With medicines, we can soften the lacerations of nervousness and fear, producing no solutions, but affording some peace and allowing the mind to seek further aid. Some hospitals now offer carefully planned communities where new friendships can arise, refuges where the unhappy receive individual medical and psychiatric attention. Clinics, though harried by the inadequate size of their staffs and by increasing requests, offer daily help for a variety of mental illnesses. Children come to centers devoted to the study and treatment of early emotional difficulties. If the etiologies are still elusive, the results of treatment are often considerable. Failures are glaring, but the thousands of desperate people who are helped are sometimes overlooked because of their very recovery. Indeed, it is possible that our present problems may give way to worse ones as we get to know more. The enormous difficulties of finding out about the neurophysiology of emotional life may ultimately yield to the Orwellian dilemma of a society in which physicists of the mind can change thoughts and control feelings at their will.

However, right now I think our most pressing concern is less the matter of our work than the manner of ourselves. For the individual psychiatrist, the institutional rigidities affect his thoughts and attitudes, taint his words and feelings, and thereby his ability to treat patients. We become victims of what we most dread; our sensibilities die, and we no longer care or notice. We dread death of the heart—any heart under any moon. Yet I see organization men in psychiatry, with all the problems of death-like conformity. Independent thinking by the adventurous has declined; psychiatric training has become more formal, more preoccupied with certificates and diplomas, more hierarchical. Some of the finest people in early dynamic psychiatry were artists, like Erik Erikson, schoolteachers, like August Eichhorn, or those, like Anna Freud, who had no formal training or occupation but motivations as personal as those of a brilliant and loyal daughter. Today we are obsessed with accreditation, recognition, levels of training, with status as scientists. These are the preoccupations of young psychiatrists. There are more lectures, more supervision, more examinations for specialty status, and thus the profession soon attracts people who take to these practices. Once there were the curious and bold; now there are the carefully well-adjusted and certified.

When the heart dies, we slip into wordy and doctrinaire caricatures of life. Our journals, our habits of talk become cluttered with jargon or the trivial. There are negative cathects, libido quanta, "presymbiotic, normal-autistic phases of mother-infant unity," and "a hierarchically stratified, firmly cathected organization of self-representations." Such dross is excused as a short cut to understanding a complicated message by those versed in the trade; its practitioners call on the authority of symbolic communication in the sciences. But the real test is whether we best understand by this strange proliferation of language the worries, fears, or loves in individual people. As the words grow longer and the concepts more intricate and tedious, human sorrows and temptations disappear, loves move away, envies and jealousies, revenge and terror dissolve. Gone are strong, sensible words with good meaning and the flavor of the real. Freud called Dostoevsky the greatest psychologist of all time, and long ago Euripedes described in *Medea* the hurt of the mentally ill. Perhaps we cannot expect to describe our patients with the touching accuracy and poetry used for Lady Macbeth or Hamlet or King Lear, but surely there are sparks to be kindled, cries to be heard, from people who are individuals.

If we become cold, and our language frosty, then our estrangement is complete. Living in an unreliable world, often lonely, and for this reason attracted to psychiatry as a job with human contacts, we embrace icy reasoning and abstractions, a desperate shadow of the real friendships which we once desired. Estrangement may, indeed, thread through the entire fabric of our professional lives in America. Cartoons show us preempted by the wealthy. The New Haven community study by A. B. Hollingshead and F. C. Redlich, *Social Class and Mental Illness,* shows how few people are reached by psychiatrists, how much a part of the class and caste system in America we are. Separated from us are all the troubled people in villages and farms from Winesburg to Yoknapatawpha. Away from us are the wretched drunks and the youthful gangs in the wilderness of our cities. Removed from us are most of the poor, the criminal, the drug addicts. Though there are some low-cost clinics, their waiting lists are long, and we are all too easily and too often available to the select few of certain streets and certain neighborhoods.

Whereas in Europe the theologian or artist shares intimately with psychiatrists, we stand apart from them, afraid to recognize our common heritage. European psychiatry mingles with philosophers; produces Karl Jaspers, a psychiatrist who is a theologian, or Jean-Paul Sartre, a novelist and philosopher who writes freely and profoundly about psychiatry. After four years of psychiatric training in a not uncultured city, I begin to wonder whether young psychiatrists in America are becoming isolated by an arbitrary definition of what is, in fact, our work. Our work is the human condition and we might do well to talk with Reinhold Niebuhr about the "nature and density of man," or with J. D. Salinger about our Holden Caulfields. Perhaps we are too frightened and too insecure to recognize our very brothers. This is a symptom of the estranged.

In some way our hearts must live. If we truly live, we will talk clearly and avoid the solitary trek. In some way we must manage to blend poetic insight with a craft and unite intimately the rational and the intuitive, the aloof stance of the scholar with the passion and affection of the friend who cares and is moved. It seems to me that this is the oldest summons in the history of Western civilization. We can answer this request only with some capacity for risk, dare, and whim. Thwarting us at every turn of life is the ageless fear of uncertainty; it is hard to risk the unknown. If we see a patient who puzzles us, we can avoid the mystery and challenge of the unique through readily available diagnostic categories. There is no end to classifications and terminologies, but the real end for us may be the soul of man, lost in these words: "Name it and it's so, or call it and it's real." This is the language of children faced with a confusion of the real and unreal, and it is ironic, if human, to see so much of this same habit still among psychiatrists.

Perhaps, if we dared to be free, more would be revealed than we care to admit. I sometimes wonder why we do not have a journal in our profession which publishes anonymous contributions. We might then hear and feel more of the real give and take in all those closed offices, get a fuller flavor of the encounter between the two people, patient and psychiatrist, who are in and of themselves what we call "psychotherapy." The answer to the skeptic who questions the worth of psychotherapy is neither the withdrawn posture of the adherent of a closed system who dismisses all inquiry as suspect nor an eruption of pseudoscientific verbal pyrotechnics. Problems will not be solved by professional arrogance or more guilds and rituals. For it is more by being than by doing that the meaningful and deeply felt communion between us and our patients will emerge. This demands as much honesty and freedom from us as it does from our patients, and as much trust on our part as we would someday hope to receive from them.

If the patient brings problems that may be understood as similar to those in many others, that may be conceptualized and abstracted, he is still in the midst of a life which is in some ways different from all others. We bring only ourselves; and so each meeting in our long working day is different, and our methods of treatment will differ in many subtle ways from those of all our colleagues. When so much of the world faces the anthill of totalitarian living, it is important for us to affirm proudly the preciously individual in each human being and in ourselves as doctors. When we see patients, the knowledge and wisdom of many intellectual ancestors are in our brains, and hopefully, some life and affection in our hearts. The heart must carry the reasoning across those inches or feet of office room. The psychiatrist, too, has his life and loves, his sorrows and angers. We know that we receive from our patients much of the irrational, misplaced, distorted thoughts and feelings once directed at parents, teachers, brothers, and sisters. We also know that our patients attempt to elicit from us any of the attitudes and responses of these earlier figures. But we must strive for some neutrality, particularly in the beginning of treatment, so that our patients may be offered, through us and their already charged feelings toward us, some idea of past passions presently lived. Yet so often this neutrality becomes our signal for complete anonymity. We try to hide behind our couches, hide ourselves from our patients. In so doing we prolong the very isolation often responsible for our patients' troubles, and if we persist, they will derive from the experience many interpretations but little warmth and trust.

I think that our own lives and problems are part of the therapeutic process. Our feelings, our own disorders and early sorrows are for us in some fashion what the surgeon's skilled hands are for his work. His hands are the trained instruments of knowledge, lectures, traditions. Yet they are, even in surgery, responsive to the artistry, the creative and sensitive intuition of the surgeon as a man. The psychiatrist's hands are himself, his life. We are educated and prepared, able to see and interpret. But we see, talk, and listen through our minds, our memories, our persons. It is through our emotions that the hands of our healing flex and function, reach out, and finally touch.

We cannot solve many problems, and there are the world and the stars to dwarf us and give us some humor about ourselves. But we can hope that, with some of the feeling of what Martin Buber calls "I-Thou" quietly and lovingly nurtured in some of our patients, there may be more friendliness about us. This would be no small happening, and it is for this that we must work. Alert against dryness and the stale, smiling with others and occasionally at ourselves, we can read and study, but maybe wince, shout, cry, and love, too. Really, there is much less to say than to affirm by living. I would hope that we would dare to accept ourselves fully and offer ourselves freely to a quizzical and apprehensive time and to uneasy and restless people.

THE REJECTION OF THE INSANE

Greer Williams

A medical consultant talks about society's inability to meet the problems of the mentally disturbed in a realistic way.

The way society handles its psychotics, by putting them away in human dumps, has been the subject of repeated public scandal. Surely the American press, whatever its failures, has lived up to its responsibility in this instance. It has published millions of words about inhuman care of the mentally sick since Nellie Bly wrote "Ten Days in a Madhouse" for the New York *World* in 1888. Most of this writing has been predicated on the assumption that if the plight—the shameful, subhuman condition—of the chronically sick of mind who populate the back wards of state hospitals were well exposed, the public would rise up in moral indignation and bring about reform. But the public remains unmoved, or, when it does move, does not move far enough. The thing that appears to be missing is public and professional action commensurate with the size of the mental-illness problem.

One of the most revealing disclosures in *Action for Mental Health*, the final report of the Joint Commission on Mental Illness and Health, published in 1961 by Basic Books, is that comparatively few of 277 state hospitals—probably no more than twenty percent—have actively participated in the modern therapeutic trend toward humane, healing hospitals and clinics of easy access and easy exit, instead of locked, barred, prisonlike depositories of alienated and rejected human beings.

It is true, of course, that these institutions never have been quite the end of the road that has become fixed in the public's mind. Actually, the number of patients now discharged annually from mental hospitals exceeds the annual number of first admissions. Including in the total figure the accumulated load of old patients who remain stubbornly psychotic, the average state hospital discharges thirty percent of its patients each year. The worst mental hospitals return to the community forty to fifty percent of the patients they treat for schizophrenia, the most serious of major mental illnesses; the best hospitals discharge seventy-five to eighty-five percent.

But the typical state hospital, through the accumulation of its chronically ill patients and its tendency to make many patients worse instead of better, remains substantially what it was a hundred years ago, an asylum for the "incurably insane." As such, it is characterized by rigidly authoritarian control, solemn vigilance, and covert despair. It does a good job of keeping patients physically alive and mentally sick. If a patient will not eat, he may be force-fed; if he will not talk—well, he is less trouble that way. And as for the tranquilizing drugs, they make agitated patients friendlier and more cooperative, and therefore make the lives of attendants and nurses more tolerable. Thus, the drugs have introduced enthusiasm where there was none.

There has been some increase in hospital staffs. The average hospital has one employee (including psychiatrists) for every three patients; this compares with two or more employees per patient (not counting attending physicians) in the average community general hospital. But, with the exceptions indicated, the state hospital system of caring for the mentally ill—nearly a million patients every year—has shown an amazing resistance to change for the better.

What is wrong here? Why, in the care of the mentally ill, do we lag, in the achievement of both our humanitarian and scientific goals, behind the public demand for mental-health services—especially in clinics, where the waiting lists run on for months, and even years—and behind other major public-health programs?

The reason of longest standing, perhaps, is that people do not recognize the insane, or psychotic, simply as sick human beings in need of help. Instead, people see the psychotic's behavior, the symptoms of illness, as immoral or illegal, and therefore deserving of punishment rather than pity. We frequently go to great lengths to explain our friend's clearly irrational and uncontrolled behavior simply as "the way he is"; that is, we put up with him until he does something that brings him a mental patient or psycho label. After that, we do not quite trust him, whatever he does.

Publicly recorded insanity, like convicted crime, tends to produce a stigma that cuts the bonds of human fellowship. Many other dread diseases—tuberculosis, syphilis, cancer—have in their time and their way branded their victims as unfit for human society. In modern times, however, the horror and shame of diseases recognized to be psysically caused and highly lethal have tended to disappear—or, at any rate, to be offset—as they came under public scrutiny and attack. The person who goes to the hospital with cancer or heart disease and recovers is accepted back into the community in a way that the mental patient almost never is.

The stigma question leads us to the feeling of helplessness and hopelessness that the insane produce in us. If we only knew what to do with a mentally ill person, how to manage him, where to take him, how to get him well again, we would not feel so confused. Even the family doctor, let alone the psychiatrist, is hard to reach these days. At best, the mentally ill are a great nuisance; at worst, we are scared to death of them. In either case, they embarrass us.

In a broad sense, what we are saying is that, if we only had more scientific knowledge of diagnosis and treatment or preventive techniques at our disposal, then we could conquer mental illness, including our feelings about it. There is a mixture of truth and fallacy here. In the first place, the mentally ill on the whole are not so dangerous as most people believe. Those disposed to physical violence are the exception rather than the rule, although, as with airliners, we read more about the few crashes than all the safe landings. When attacked by a person bent on destruction, one must defend himself or flee. But often psychotics are enraged by an impetuous or treacherous use of force against them that would equally anger a normal person.

Second, mental illness is not categorically a one-way street. Nobody is totally insane, any more than he is totally infected with a germ or totally cancerous. Some get well without treatment; others improve greatly if treated well; some recover and have later relapses; a few never recover. It only misleads, therefore, to say that lack of an adequate technology, or a good scientific tool kit, is the main reason why the public fails to attack mental illness with vigor proportionate to the size of the problem.

Medical science is still searching for the cause and cure of cancer and of the major forms of heart disease, but the lack of better methods of treatment or prevention has not resulted in inhuman, substandard care for patients. In reality, the schizophrenic has a far better chance for recovery and a useful life than the victim of any of several major physical illnesses. There is an important economic difference, of course: in lung cancer or coronary thrombosis, death removes treatment failures from the scene, whereas chronic schizophrenics do not get well and do not die; they accumulate in public institutions.

Some would say that this is the big obstacle—so many patients with major mental illness live on and become indigent. Long hospitalization and psychiatric treatment impose costs the average family cannot afford. Thus, the burden of mental-patient care, a good four-fifths of it, falls on the state. State hospitals spend from two to six dollars per patient per day, compared with upward of thirty dollars a day in community general hospitals and leading private mental hospitals.

It is customary, at least among Republicans, automatically to regard state medicine as bad medicine, because it imposes a tax burden and involves politics. These make for a poor quality of medical care, it is argued. The generalization is a weak one, however. County tuberculosis hospitals have done a generally creditable job of long-term care for tuberculous patients at taxpayers' expense, at an average of thirteen dollars per patient per day. Many did so even before modern advances in surgical and drug treatment. Of course, the patient load has been smaller for tuberculosis than for mental illness.

The Veterans' Administration psychiatric hospitals, themselves well within the snake-pit range of description until after the war, now provide an acceptable quality of tax-paid mental-patient care at an average cost per patient of twelve dollars per day. It is easy to document this observation. The hospitals' national standard-setting agency, the Joint Commission on Accreditation of Hospitals, has approved only thirty percent of state hospitals, contrasted with one hundred percent of V.A. psychiatric hospitals. Why can't state hospitals do as well? One answer seems to be that the federal government has far greater financial resources than the states have, and, above all, veterans have influence through a well-organized pressure group.

We now approach the nub of the matter. The insane sick are friendless, unless their families have money or a mental-health worker unexpectedly befriends them. It is a truism in voluntary health organizations that people are prone to work for a cause which they can identify with personally. But an organization which seeds itself with workers who have been mentally ill accepts a considerable handicap. And how many others are prepared to identify themselves with insanity in the family? One psychiatrist, Dr. J. Sandbourne Bockoven of Framingham, Massachusetts, pinpoints these issues:

> The very essence of mental illness is an incapacity to get along with other people, hence organization behind a leader is impossible. The friends or relatives of the mentally ill are equally immobilized through fear of stigmatizing themselves.

Quite a number of groups of former mental patients have come into being and then languished; none has flourished as, for example, Alcoholics Anonymous has. The difference seems to be that alcoholics, basically neurotic, are usually successful persons while sober. In any event, their "cure," refusing a drink, is only slightly stigmatizing.

A psychosis is essentially a social disorder, or, as defined by the late Dr. Harry Stack Sullivan, founder of the Washington School of Psychiatry, one involving interpersonal relationships. The normal person will do whatever he has to do to get along in his group; the psychotic will not. He suffers from a sort of mental arthritis that turns individualism into a disease.

The person with an acute psychosis sooner or later disturbs or offends other people and is likely to be treated as a disturber and offender. He does not fit our conception of a sick person in need of help; often he does not recognize himself as sick. It has been observed countless times that the sight or even the thought of a person "out of his mind" stimulates fear in us; fear of what the irrational person might do, fear of what we ourselves might do in response to this threat, fear arising from the power of suggestion that "I, too, will go crazy." For many of us, self-control is a lifelong problem. The insane person has somehow lost control. We feel sorry for him, but not nearly as sorry as relieved to have him out of the way. We have some of the same feelings about a physically sick person, too, but he gives us little reason to lose faith in him. We can see that he is sick. If conscious, he knows he is sick. He behaves predictably.

If we spent our lives among psychotics rather than encountering them rarely, we would realize that a calm alertness is desirable, but fearfulness and distrust are not necessary. You hear of patients killing themselves, but did you ever hear of a patient killing his psychiatrists or nurse? It is extremely rare. It was known more than one hundred and fifty years ago by the French physician Philippe Pinel and the Quaker layman William Tuke that figuratively turning the other cheek is not only a humane but a healing approach to the insane if pursued with friendly firmness and the sane recognition that the first problem is breaking the vicious circle of provocation and retaliation. Of course, it takes a good deal more brotherly love and physical courage than many of us have to find this out.

The mental-hygiene, or mental-health, movement was born out of the need to relieve medical and social guilt over the unloving and often brutally punishing way mental-hospital workers used to treat the uncooperative insane. Not a physician but a young layman, a manic-depressive college graduate named Clifford Beers, while still in a straightjacket and padded cell, swore he would get out and crusade against the evils he saw in mental institutions. Beers succeeded; his *A Mind That Found Itself* was published in 1908.

Perhaps today Beers would receive a place on the future-appointments book of a good psychiatrist, work out his hostility and aggressions on the couch, and pay the fee out of his Book-of-the-Month Club and Hollywood royalties. Happily, he won the support of three great doctors who gave him a hearing rather than a diagnosis: William James, the psychologist; Adolf Meyer, the psychiatrist, and William H. Welch, the pathologist. They, with others, founded the National Committee for Mental Hygiene and made Beers its executive secretary.

Almost from the outset the movement was enthralled with the vision of doing away with mental illness entirely.

One of the original circle, probably Meyer, told Beers that his own illness could have been prevented. Was not that the better approach? It turned out to be wishful thinking, but the mental hygienists had their heads turned by the microbe hunters, who were having impressive successes in disease prevention through sanitation and immunization. Eugenics and progressive education were also in the air. The larger goal became "building healthy minds in healthy bodies," but instead of a simple remedy such as chlorine in drinking water or a vaccine to be scratched into the arm, there were complicated concepts of mental-health education and child guidance. Yet raising a child for a mentally healthy maturity is still a matter of theory, not scientific predictability, a half century later, even when we add the interpretations and zeal of psychoanalysis. There is little scientific evidence today that mental-hygiene education does in fact prevent mental illness, although we certainly believe it promotes human understanding and reduces stress. Furthermore, as our knowledge of genetic chemistry and the mathematical certainty of accidents of chromosome linkage has advanced, there is little cause of optimism about the production of healthy minds to order.

There are many persons in the mental-health field, including some staff members of the National Institute of Mental Health, who still pursue the will-o'-the-wisp of positive mental health in preference to trying to love the mentally ill. Ironically, Beers himself provided some substance for their attitudes. His crusade did not come off well, in either its original or acquired objectives. As is characteristic of one with his disorder, he had his ups and downs, eventually dying in a mental hospital in 1943.

The medical profession is as remiss as the public itself in grappling with the mental-illness problem. It is common knowledge, confirmed by surveys, that the average physician as well as the average layman has unfavorable, sometimes openly antagonistic attitudes toward persons with psychological disturbances and toward psychiatrists themselves. The ordinary doctor's training and experience is not slanted toward an appreciation of emotions and their implications, and many doctors have only one approach to mental illness: they try to get the patients out of their offices as quickly as possible.

Surprisingly enough, when we narrow the circle of rejection to the private practice of psychiatry, we find somewhat the same situation as far as psychotics are concerned. I have heard psychiatrists say they were interested in neurotics but wanted no part of psychotics. Their logic was indisputable: they could help the former but not the latter, they said; besides, their only possible basis for successful psychotherapy is that the patient wants help and will pay for it. Psychiatrists who work in mental hospitals or clinics with psychotics do not share these opinions; they frankly concede the limitations of psychiatric knowledge, but know and can see that persons with major mental illness can be helped, whether they pay or not. These psychiatrists are vastly in the minority.

Not long ago a young psychiatrist clarified for me the pivotal difficulty in the care of psychotics. I have the general impression that he had witnessed major mental illness in his own family, and therefore had the strongest of motives for wanting to help its victims—a personal one.

"Even before I went to medical school," he told me, "I wanted to go into psychiatry and I wanted to treat psychotics. This was the real challenge. So I came to Boston to train in a hospital under three men who had the same objective. When I finished, I received a teaching and research appointment in this hospital, but the salary was low and I had the privilege of doing part-time private practice if I wished.

"So I started seeing patients privately, and again decided to concentrate on psychotics. I reached a point where I was treating six, in intensive psychotherapy, and felt that I was rebuilding their characters. There is a great satisfaction in it, but I found that I simply could not take them—not continuously. These are the most trying, tiring people on earth. So I cut down to three psychotics and filled in the open time with neurotics and mild character disorders."

I felt a little sad, but also vastly relieved. Psychiatrists and their public-relations spokesmen long have remonstrated with the public for turning its back on the mentally ill. "Mental illness is no different from any other illness. The mentally ill should be treated the same way as any other sick people." These are expressions of good intentions. The public gives them some lip service, and a few sensitive and compassionate persons succeed in living by these principles, but our actions show that most of us really don't agree with them, and for good reason. Psychotics are hard to take. Even the most conscientious of psychiatrists may find them so.

A study made at Washington University, St. Louis, of criminal psychopaths confirms the pervasiveness of this rejection mechanism. Among social scientists studying the antisocial character of these persons, there was reported to be an active but not readily admitted effort to escape working with them. Likewise, a study of chronic schizophrenic patients under experimental treatment with a certain hormone at McLean Hospital in Boston bears out our thesis. A scientific analysis indicated that the treated patients were having more normal social relationships with other patients than those receiving a placebo. Further analysis showed that the treated group was not initiating these friendly approaches, but that the other patients were approaching them. It is of interest that the apparent effect of the drug was to make its users somewhat more receptive.

The psychotic's lack of appeal strikes me as a satisfactory explanation of why, in the last analysis, the fight against mental illness never seems to get anywhere at the level of social action. It is safe to say that in our culture nobody gets anywhere without a positive appeal of some kind. However, upon further reflection, I would agree that the explanation is not a satisfactory one at the intellectual level. Why do we have so much difficulty in understanding psychological problems and solving them in the first place?

The great difficulty is that many people have trouble in recognizing psychological sickness as sickness, or in seeing sickness as having psychological forms. Unless the mind is educated to think in psychological as well as physical terms from a fairly early age, it may experience great difficulty in later life in thinking about itself and about other minds in relation to itself. The difficulty can be overcome, but against some odds, for the mind seems to resist the process, as if, in the varied universe of knowing, it were the one constant—fixed, dependable, *sane*. Most of us, in sum, are psychologically handicapped persons mentally blind to our physical bias.

The mental-health movement is engaged in an uphill pull against intellectual resistance to psychological insight. The nature of the psychotic's trouble impels him to reject social order and, heeding the ancient law of retaliation, we repay him in kind.

There is some evidence that the process has begun to

reverse itself among younger, better educated people, since we have had a two-generation exposure to psychological and psychoanalytic information. Therapeutic techniques have evolved that break the circle of rejection and defeat it. Evaluations of the psychosocial approaches, proving old truths scientifically, show that some psychiatrists get amazingly good results from psychotherapy with schizophrenics. They also show that other persons, working individually or in groups in hospitals and clinics—social workers, psychologists, nurses, occupational therapists, attendants, enlightened volunteers—can do as much for the psychotic in their way as the psychiatrist can in his (it may be in the same way). In all cases, some kind of as yet ill-defined personal relationship develops between the therapist and patient. In most cases, the secret of reducing the fears, frustrations, and fatigues that beset those who try to work with psychotics is close moral support, given regularly or as needed by the therapist's superiors or peers.

We know that insanity presents a quite different problem from a broken leg or gallbladder attack. We also know that the line between abnormal and normal behavior is so blurred that anyone may step across it at one time or another. The psychotic, like the normal person, has good days as well as bad. The difference between mental illness and mental health is not as zero to a hundred, but, to press a fictitious measurement, it may perhaps be as little as forty-nine to fifty-one.

Consequently, with a fuller awareness of what people understand and believe, the mental-health educators are going to have to revise their mental-hygiene copybooks. Mental health is different from other health problems. Because it is different, we have to solve it differently. This new approach remains to be tested and proved, of course. Nevertheless, the older one has left so much to be desired, as studies of public attitudes have abundantly shown, that we have nothing to lose through a sharper public focus on our resistance to thinking about mental illness and on our rejection of its victims. We can hardly hope to hit a target unless we can locate it and aim at it.

DEPOSITION: TESTIMONY CONCERNING A SICKNESS

William Burroughs

A former addict turned author paints a vivid word picture of the nightmare world of narcotics.

I awoke from The Sickness at the age of forty-five, calm and sane, and in reasonably good health except for a weakened liver and the look of borrowed flesh common to all who survive The Sickness. . . . Most survivors do not remember the delirium in detail. I apparently took detailed notes on sickness and delirium. I have no precise memory of writing the notes which have now been published under the title *Naked Lunch*. The title was suggested by Jack Kerouac. I did not understand what the title meant until my recent recovery. The title means exactly what the words say: NAKED Lunch—a frozen moment when everyone sees what is on the end of every fork.

The Sickness is drug addiction and I was an addict for fifteen years. When I say addict I mean an addict to *junk* (generic term for opium and/or derivatives including all synthetics from demerol to palfium.) I have used junk in many forms: morphine, heroin, dilaudid, eukodal, pantapon, diocodid, diosane, opium, demerol, dolophine, palfium. I have smoked junk, eaten it, sniffed it, injected it in vein-skin-muscle, inserted it in rectal suppositories. The needle is not important. Whether you sniff it smoke it eat it or shove it up your ass the result is the same: addiction. When I speak of drug addiction I do not refer to keif, marijuana or any preparation of hashish, mescaline, Bannisteria Caapi, LSD6, Sacred Mushrooms or any other drug of the hallucinogen group. . . . There is no evidence that the use of any hallucinogen results in physical dependence. The action of these drugs is physiologically opposite to the action of junk. A lamentable confusion between the two classes of drugs has arisen owing to the zeal of the U. S. and other narcotic departments.

I have seen the exact manner in which the junk virus operates through fifteen years of addiction. The pyramid of junk, one level eating the level below (it is no accident that junk higher-ups are always fat and the addict in the street is always thin) right up to the top or tops since there are many junk pyramids feeding on peoples of the world and all built on basic principles of monopoly:

1—Never give anything away for nothing.
2—Never give more than you have to give (always catch the buyer hungry and always make him wait).
3—Always take everything back if you possibly can.

The Pusher always gets it all back. The addict needs more and more junk to maintain a human form . . . buy off the Monkey.

Junk is the mold of monopoly and possession. The addict stands by while his junk legs carry him straight in on the junk beam to relapse. Junk is quantitative and accurately measurable. The more junk you use the less you have and the more you have the more you use. All the hallucinogen drugs are considered sacred by those who use them—there are Peyote Cults and Bannisteria Cults, Hashish Cults and Mushroom Cults—"the Sacred Mushrooms of Mexico enable a man to see God"—but no one ever suggested that junk is sacred. There are no opium cults. Opium is profane and quantitative like money. I have heard that there was once a beneficent non-habit-forming junk in India. It was called *soma* and is pictured as a beautiful blue tide. If *soma* ever existed the Pusher was there to bottle it and monopolize it and sell it and it turned into plain old time JUNK.

Junk is the ideal product . . . the ultimate merchandise. No sales talk necessary. The client will crawl through a sewer and beg to buy. . . . The junk merchant does not sell his product to the consumer, he sells the consumer to his product. He does not improve and simplify his merchandise. He degrades and simplifies the client. He pays his staff in junk.

Junk yields a basic formula of "evil" virus: *The Algebra*

of Need. The face of "evil" is always the face of total need. A dope fiend is a man in total need of dope. Beyond a certain frequency need knows absolutely no limit or control. In the words of total need: *"Wouldn't you?"* Yes you would. You would lie, cheat, inform on your friends, steal, do *anything* to satisfy total need. Because you would be in a state of total sickness, total possession, and not in a position to act in any other way. Dope fiends are sick people who cannot act other than they do. A rabid dog cannot choose but bite. Assuming a self-righteous position is nothing to the purpose unless your purpose be to keep the junk virus in operation. And junk is a big industry. I recall talking to an American who worked for the Aftosa Commission in Mexico. Six hundred a month plus expense account:

"How long will the epidemic last?" I inquired.

"As long as we can keep it going. . . . And yes . . . maybe the aftosa will break out in South America," he said dreamily.

If you wish to alter or annihilate a pyramid of numbers in a serial relation, you alter or remove the bottom number. If we wish to annihilate the junk pyramid, we must start with the bottom of the pyramid: *the Addict in the Street,* and stop tilting quixotically for the "higher ups" so called, all of whom are immediately replaceable. *The addict in the street who must have junk to live is the one irreplaceable factor in the junk equation.* When there are no more addicts to buy junk there will be no junk traffic. As long as junk need exists, someone will service it.

Addicts can be cured or quarantined—that is allowed a morphine ration under minimal supervision like typhoid carriers. When this is done, junk pyramids of the world will collapse. So far as I know, England is the only country to apply this method to the junk problem. They have about five hundred quarantined addicts in the U.K. In another generation when the quarantined addicts die off and pain killers operating on a non-junk principle are discovered, the junk virus will be like smallpox, a closed chapter—a medical curiosity.

The vaccine that can relegate the junk virus to a landlocked past is in existence. This vaccine is the Apomorphine. Treatment discovered by an English doctor whose name I must withhold pending his permission to use it and to quote from his book covering thirty years of apomorphine treatment

DEPOSITION: TESTIMONY CONCERNING A SICKNESS

of addicts and alcoholics. The compound apomorphine is formed by boiling morphine with hydrocloric acid. It was discovered years before it was used to treat addicts. For many years the only use for apomorphine which has no narcotic or pain-killing properties was as an emetic to induce vomiting in cases of poisoning. It acts directly on the vomiting center in the back brain.

I found this vaccine at the end of the junk line. I lived in one room in the Native Quarter of Tangier. I had not taken a bath in a year nor changed my clothes or removed them except to stick a needle every hour in the fibrous gray wooden flesh of terminal addiction. I never cleaned or dusted the room. Empty ampule boxes and garbage piled to the ceiling. Light and water long since turned off for non-payment. I did absolutely nothing. I could look at the end of my shoe for eight hours. I was only roused to action when the hourglass of junk ran out. If a friend came to visit—and they rarely did since who or what was left to visit—I sat there not caring that he had entered my field of vision—a gray screen always blanker and fainter—and not caring when he walked out of it. If he had died on the spot I would have sat there looking at my shoe waiting to go through his pockets. Wouldn't you? Because I never had enough junk—no one ever does. Thirty grains of morphine a day and it still was not enough. And long waits in front of the drugstore. Delay is a rule in the junk business. The Man is never on time. This is no accident. There are no accidents in the junk world. The addict is taught again and again exactly what will happen if he does not score for his junk ration. Get up that money or else. And suddenly my habit began to jump and jump. Forty, sixty grains a day. And it still was not enough. And I could not pay.

I stood there with my last check in my hand and realized that it was my last check. I took the next plane for London.

The doctor explained to me that apomorphine acts on the back brain to regulate the metabolism and normalize the blood stream in such a way that the enzyme system of addiction is destroyed over a period of four or five days. Once the back brain is regulated apomorphine can be discontinued and only used in case of relapse. (No one would take apomorphine for kicks. *Not one case of addiction to apomorphine has ever been recorded.*) I agreed to undergo treatment and entered a nursing home. For the first twenty-four hours I was literally insane and paranoid as many addicts are in severe withdrawal. This delirium was dispersed by twenty-four hours of intensive apomorphine treatment. The doctor showed me the chart. I had received minute amounts of morphine that could not possibly account for my lack of the more severe withdrawal symptoms such as leg and stomach cramps, fever and my own special symptom, The Cold Burn, like a vast hive covering the body and rubbed with menthol. Every addict has his own special symptom that cracks all control. There was a missing factor in the withdrawal equation—that factor could only be apomorphine.

I saw the apomorphine treatment really work. Eight days later I left the nursing home eating and sleeping normally. I remained completely off junk for two full years—a twelve-year record. I did relapse for some months as a result of pain and illness. Another apomorphine cure has kept me off junk through this writing.

The apomorphine cure is qualitatively different from other methods of cure. I have tried them all. Short reduction, slow reduction, cortisone, antihistamines, tranquilizers, sleeping cures, tolserol, reserpine. None of these cures lasted beyond the first opportunity to relapse. I can say definitely that I was never *metabolically* cured until I took the apomorphine cure. The overwhelming relapse statistics from the Lexington Narcotic Hospital have led many doctors to say that addiction is not curable. They use a dolophine reduction cure at Lexington and have never tried apomorphine so far as I know. In fact, this method of treatment has been largely neglected. No research has been done with variations of the apomorphine formula or with synthetics. No doubt substances fifty times stronger than apomorphine could be developed and the side effect of vomiting eliminated.

Apomorphine is a metabolic and psychic regulator that can be discontinued as soon as it has done its work. The world is deluged with tranquilizers and energizers but this unique regulator has not received attention. No research has been done by any of the large pharmaceutical companies. I suggest that research with variations of apomorphine and synthesis of it will open a new medical frontier extending far beyond the problem of addiction.

The smallpox vaccine was opposed by a vociferous lunatic group of anti-vaccinationists. No doubt a scream of protest will go up from interested or unbalanced individuals as the junk virus is shot out from under them. Junk is big business; there are always cranks and operators. They must not be allowed to interfere with the essential work of inoculation treatment and quarantine. *The junk virus is public health problem number one of the world today.*

Since *Naked Lunch* treats this health problem, it is necessarily brutal, obscene and disgusting. Sickness is often repulsive details not for weak stomachs.

Certain passages in the book that have been called pornographic were written as a tract against Capital Punishment in the manner of Jonathan Swift's *Modest Proposal.* These sections are intended to reveal capital punishment as the obscene, barbaric and disgusting anachronism that it is. As always the lunch is naked. If civilized countries want to return to Druid Hanging Rites in the Sacred Grove or to drink blood with the Aztecs and feed their Gods with blood of human sacrifice, let them see what they actually eat and drink. Let them see what is on the end of that long newspaper spoon.

I have almost completed a sequel to *Naked Lunch*. A mathematical extension of the Algebra of Need beyond the junk virus. Because there are many forms of addiction I think that they all obey basic laws. In the words of Heiderberg: "This may not be the best of all possible universes but it may well prove to be one of the simplest." If man can *see.*

POST SCRIPT .... WOULDN'T YOU?

And speaking *Personally* and if a man speaks any other way we might as well start looking for his Protoplasm Daddy or Mother Cell .... *I Don't Want To Hear Any More Tired Old Junk Talk And Junk Con.* ... The same things said a million times and more and there is no point in saying anything because *NOTHING Ever Happens* in the junk world.

Only excuse for this tired death route is THE KICK when the junk circuit is cut off for the non-payment and the junk-skin dies of junk-lack and overdose of time and the Old Skin has forgotten the skin game simplifying a way under the junk cover the way skins will. .... A condition of total exposure is precipitated when the Kicking Addict cannot choose but see smell and listen. . . . Watch out for the cars. . . .

It is clear that junk is a Round-the-World-Push-an-Opium Pellet-with-Your-Nose-Route. Strictly for Scarabs—stumble bum junk heap. And as such report to disposal. Tired of seeing it around.

Junkies always beef about *The Cold* as they call it, turning up their black coat collars and clutching their withered necks . . . pure junk con. A junky does not want to be warm, he wants to be Cool-Cooler-COLD. But he wants The Cold like he wants His Junk—NOT OUTSIDE where it does him no good but INSIDE so he can sit around with a spine like a frozen hydraulic jack . . . his metabolism approaching Absolute ZERO. TERMINAL addicts often go two months without a bowel move and the intestines make with sit-down-adhesions—Wouldn't you?—requiring the intervention of an apple corer or its surgical equivalent. . . . Such is life in The Old Ice House. Why move around and waste TIME?

Room for One More Inside, Sir.

Some entities are on thermodynamic kicks. They invented thermodynamics. . . . Wouldn't you?

And some of us are on Different Kicks and that's a thing out in the open the way I like to see what I eat and visa versa mutatis mutandis as the case may be. *Bill's Naked Lunch Room.* . . . Step right up. . . . Good for young and old, man and bestial. Nothing like a little snake oil to grease the wheels and get a show on the track Jack. Which side are you on? Fro-Zen Hydraulic? Or you want to take a look around with Honest Bill?

So that's the World Health Problem I was talking about back in The Article. The Prospect Before Us Friends of MINE. Do I hear muttering about a personal razor and some bush league short con artist who is known to have invented The Bill? Wouldn't You? The razor belonged to a man named Occam and he was not a scar collector. Ludwig Wittgenstein *Tractatus Logico-Philosophicus:* "If a proposition is NOT NECESSARY it is MEANINGLESS and approaching MEANING ZERO."

"And what is More UNNECESSARY than junk if You Don't NEED it?"

Answer: "Junkies, if you are not ON JUNK."

I tell you boys, I've heard some tired conversation but no

other OCCUPATION GROUP can approximate that old thermodynamic junk Slow-DOWN. Now your heroin addict does not say hardly anything and that I can stand. But your Opium "Smoker" is more active since he still has a tent and a Lamp . . . and maybe 7-9-10 lying up in there like hibernating reptiles keep the temperature up to Talking Level: How low the other junkies are whereas We—WE have this tent and this lamp and this tent and this lamp and this tent and nice and warm in here nice and warm nice and IN HERE and nice and OUTSIDE ITS COLD. . . . ITS COLD OUTSIDE where the dross eaters and the needle boys won't last two years not six months hardly won't last stumble bum around and there is no class in them. . . . But WE SIT HERE and never increase the DOSE . . . never—never increase the dose never except TONIGHT is a SPECIAL OCCASION with all the dross eaters and needle boys out there in the cold. . . . And we never eat it never never never eat it. . . . Excuse please while I take a trip to The Source Of Living Drops they all have in pocket and opium pellets shoved up the ass in a finger stall with the Family Jewels and the other shit.

Room for one more inside, Sir.

Well when that record starts around for the billionth light year and never the tape shall change us non-junkies take drastic action and the men separate out from the Junk boys.

Only way to protect yourself against this horrid peril is come over HERE and shack up with Charybdis. . . . Treat you right kid. . . . Candy and cigarettes.

I am after fifteen years in that tent. In and out in and out in and OUT. *Over* and *Out.* So listen to Old Uncle Bill Burroughs who invented the Burroughs Adding Machine Regulator Gimmick on the Hydraulic Jack Principle no matter how you jerk the handle result is always the same for given coordinates. Got my training early . . . wouldn't you?

Paregoric Babies of the World Unite. We have nothing to lose but Our Pushers. And THEY are NOT NECESSARY.

Look down LOOK DOWN along that junk road before you travel there and get in with the Wrong Mob. . . .

STEP RIGHT UP. . . . Only a three Dollar Bill to use BILL'S telescope.

A word to the wise guy.

THE CRIMINAL AND THE COMMUNITY

Gus Tyler

An executive of the International Ladies' Garment Worker's Union challenges Americans to make room for reformed lawbreakers.

The community has a far greater role in the process of correction than it knows. The attitude of the community conditions the attitude of the entire correctional system. The funds the community is prepared to commit to correction determine the quantity and the quality of the service. The relationship of the community to the offender affects the return of the outcast to the society. This many-sided give and take between the community and the criminal is a basic fact in all cultures. It is especially so in a democratic society where governmental agencies, such as the correctional system, are responsive to the voice of the voter.

Regrettably, the community does not generally realize that it is called upon to involve itself in the correctional system. The ordinary citizen prefers to turn this matter over to the police and penal institutions who are charged with "taking care" of the delinquents in the human family. The caretakers are viewed as a necessary evil, carrying on an unpleasant work of little prestige. Hence, the society pays little heed to the "system," appropriates little money and makes few demands for quality performance.

To the extent that the community has, historically, become involved with the correctional system it has been due to the outcry of sensitive souls who rebelled against the brutalizing impact of an insensitive penal process. The actual process of reform has fallen to a handful of dedicated professionals who have sought to impart a modern philosophy of correction. On either side of this small body of humanitarians and sophisticated technicians stand the great mass of inert citizens and a large legion of uninspired hirelings. The fact that the correctional system has incorporated some of the insights of sociology, psychology and business efficiency into its techniques is a tribute to the persistence and skill of a dedicated cadre. They need the backing of an awakened public that is informed, involved and inspired in the crusade to make the criminal "out" a societal "in." With such community participation our correctional system can become a valuable reservoir of untapped and creative social energy instead of a stagnant swamp that willy-nilly converts once hopeful humans into hopeless pests of the social order.

The failure of our present system is patently revealed in the figures on recidivism—a professional term applied to the repeater who makes entrances and exists into and out of "correction" a way of life. Having been disowned by the society, he disowns the society, building his social order around the jail.

"Records furnish insistent testimony to the fact that these repeated offenders constitute the hard core of the crime problem," reported the President's Commission on Law Enforcement and Administration of Justice in 1967. A Massachusetts study showed that thirty-two percent of the men who could be followed in a long-range study over fifteen years repeatedly committed serious crimes during this period and that additional ones did so on a now-and-then basis. A California study showed that of parolees released between 1946 and 1949, forty-three percent were reimprisoned by 1952. A summary review of state and federal prison records reveals that about one out of every three released from prison will be back in five years. To this high figure must be added all those who commit crimes without arrest or conviction.

The rate of recidivism is most tragically revealed in the fate of a juvenile offender. In the words of the President's Commission:

> The earlier a juvenile is arrested or brought to court for an offense, the more likely he is to carry on criminal activity into adult life; the more serious the first offense for which a juvenile is arrested, the more likely he is to continue to commit serious crimes, especially in the case of major crimes against property; the more fre-

quently and extensively a juvenile is processed by the police, court, and correctional system, the more likely he is to be arrested, charged, convicted and imprisoned as an adult.

Whatever it is that the present system of correction does, it appears that it does little to correct. It may punish; it may remove; but it reforms only a minority—a minority that might very well have reformed itself without the "system."

The basic reason that the correctional system fails is that the community has no clear, consistent and comprehensive philosophy as to how the offender should be treated. The public attitude is a mixture of three levels of behavior: primitive, pragmatic and progressive. The primitive, arising as a "gut" reaction, calls for punishment; the pragmatic, in self-defense, calls for removal of the offender; while the progressive calls for reformation of the offender, the community or both.

In practice, though not in theory, the primitive tends to predominate. There is still the feeling that, when an offender is incarcerated, he is not only rendered momentarily harmless but that his punishment will also teach him to behave. The ancient thirst for revenge against the violator of the tribal mores conditions the basic community attitude toward the criminal. Because community attitude is more intestinal than rational, the offender is looked upon as an "outsider," a member of that class of nonpeople, the criminals. As such, he—like most strangers—becomes faceless, treated as a number rather than a name, as a collective noun rather than as an individual soul. Contrary as this primitive behavior is both to our Judeo-Christian ethic and our democratic ethos, it is the unstated premise of our correctional system.

The end result is the high rate of recidivism—or worse. For many, the system of correction becomes the place of corruption, where the soft become tough, where the amateur becomes a professional, and where the accidental becomes permanent.

REQUIREMENTS FOR CHANGE

An overdue revolution in correction requires basic changes in: (*a*) principles; (*b*) practice; (*c*) personnel.

The basic change in principle must assert that the object of correction is to correct. This is only possible if the individual offender is treated as an individual case, in the same way that a doctor treats each patient for his or her specific ailment. To use punishment as a nostrum does not cure the criminal or protect the society.

A second basic principle is community participation in the rehabilitative process, by easing the road back for the offender and by opening opportunities for the returnee. This means more than offering some jobs; it means participation in the rehabilitation, involvement in the "system," use of noninstitutional arrangements for offenders, and changes in the community itself to prevent further breeding of criminals.

What do these principles mean in practice?

The first responsibility of the community begins with crime prevention, the structuring of the social order to minimize criminality. Although violators of the law come from every economic and social category in the nation, the statistical evidence continues to prove that the overwhelming percentage of those who are tried and convicted come from lower-income groups. Once again, in the words of the President's Commission:

> The common serious crimes that worry people most —murder, forcible rape, robbery, aggravated assault, and burglary—happen most often in the slums of large cities. . . . The offenses, the victims and the offenders are found most frequently in the poorest and most deteriorated and socially disorganized areas of cities. [These areas are characterized by] low income, physical deterioration, dependency, racial and ethnic concentrations, broken homes, working mothers, low levels of education and vocational skill, high unemployment, high proportions of single males, overcrowded and substandard housing, high rates of tuberculosis and infant mortality, low rates of home ownership or single-family dwellings, mixed land use, and high population density.

These are the areas that compose the "other America," standing outside the affluent society and hungrily looking in. Denied the delights of economic and social democracy, this "other" and "under" world breeds its marauders who turn to crime to redistribute the wealth, to voice their frustrations and to express the mores of the disinherited, distressed and disturbed.

Crime is a function of economics—but it is also a function of ethics. The proof lies in the vast numbers of slum dwellers who never commit a crime and in the increasing number of affluent suburban dwellers who do commit crimes. "What appears to be happening throughout the country, in the cities and in the suburbs, among the poor and among the well-to-do," reports the President's Commission, "is that parental, and especially paternal authority over young people is becoming weaker." The traditional root of ethical conduct —the home—seems to be rotting, either because it is under- or overnourished. Whatever the reason, this is a circumstance that cannot be corrected by cops, courts, or confinement. The revitalization of a vigorous ethic is the responsibility of the community, beginning with each in his own community. Crime prevention—like charity—begins at home!

THE PROBLEMS OF DETENTION

A crucial corner of the total social environment with which the community must concern itself is the sad home away from home, the house of detention. It is here that the offender, or the accused, or the stray, is often first expelled from the accepted society and propelled into the world of crime. Because the community lacks facilities to house a variety of souls who are momentarily the charges of the police or the courts—to sort them out and to assign them to the most appropriate surroundings—the "system" dumps them all indiscriminately into a barrel full of rotten apples. "Detention" too often becomes a way of mass-producing criminals, especially among juveniles.

In a scathing indictment of detention practices, the special report of the National Council on Crime and Delinquency concludes that

> confusion and misuse pervade detention. It has come to be used by police and probation officers as a disposition; judges use it for punishment, protection, storage, and lack of other facilities. More than in any other phase of the correctional process, the use of detention is colored by rationalization, duplicity, and double-talk,

generally unchallenged because the law is either defective or not enforced and because it is always easy to make a case for detaining on the grounds of the child's offenses or demands of the public as interpreted by the police or the press.

Who may be caught up in this detention? A child removed from the home to protect him against his parents; a pregnant girl awaiting placement; a youth with a brain injury; a material witness; a youngster in need of lodging until a foster home is found; a truant; a retarded child waiting for an opening in an institution; an adolescent who is being punished to shock him into good behavior; a gang leader who, at an early age, is a professional.

The haphazard nonsystem of detention leads to overcrowded facilities and to prolonged stays. Under pressure from communities to "do something" and to "do it now" to protect the public from the offender, judges tend to respond by committing the offending child to the "training school," once called a "reformatory." The result is that the evils of detention are now institutionalized. Into these new surroundings, most appropriate for fairly hardened types, are tossed the motley elements to be found in detention. The offender, who was initiated into the penal world through detention, now begins to learn the more advanced rites of the "other" world in the training school. From the rate of recidivism—one out of two will return—it is not irrelevent to ask, "For which world are they being trained?"

In the "school," the juvenile or even adult is not simply exposed to contact with people of bad habits. He is moved into a "society"—the penal society—run by its own ruling class. Within any such institution, there are "governors," risen from the penal "colony," who establish the rules and the rulers. Those to be "ruled" are often the innocents, armed with none of the tough weapons of counteroffense for the general community or for the incarcerated community. In sum, the "school," like a jail or a maximum-safety prison, is a structured society governed by the toughest and best organized in the criminal world, indoctrinating inmates in the *Weltanschauung* and techniques of the antisocial.

How can the community break through this vicious circle?

Detention must become a selective process. The local jail should not be a dumping ground. The National Council on

Crime and Delinquency (NCCD) proposes some major reforms to be handled through bureaus of probation and detention set up in the separate states. These would emphasize case and group work with children and parents; establish standards for both the physical facilities and nature of care in detention; prohibit use of common jails for detaining children; set up a diagnostic service; secure treatment where necessary; develop special foster homes for those who need care outside their own homes.

NCCD maintains that if detention were placed on a selective, supervised, and scientific basis—with the necessary facilities and personnel to back it up—

> relatively little juvenile detention will be necessary; where used, it will be the diagnostic door to the most disturbed child's correctional treatment.

CRIMINAL THERAPY

The role played by a sophisticated detention system in handling juveniles can, likewise, be played by a knowledgeable presentencing procedure in the correction of adults. In criminal therapy, this is the equivalent of the patient's history in medical therapy. It allows the judge to know the offender as well as the offense, and thereby to make the cure fit the judged and not just make the punishment fit the crime. "This role," notes the NCCD report,

> has recently been expanded so that information that helps differentiate one offender from another is offered not only at presentence stage but also in other decisional situations—the prearraignment, pre-pleading, and pretrial stages of the court process.

This work is normally turned over to probation agencies, which are also charged with the responsibility for surveillance, service and counseling. The probation agency is an active link between the offender and the community. In the event the offender is put in a noninstitutional environment for correction, he is under the eye of probation. In the case of the juvenile offender, probation directs the client to appropriate services that may help him in his problems. The offender, and often the family, need counseling so that they may develop some insight into their unfortunate circumstance and thus be motivated to take steps—both alone and with outside help.

In the NCCD report, it is recommended that probation go beyond these traditional functions, to play a creative role in the community, to open opportunities. "Probation is in the community," it notes,

> and must, therefore, be concerned with the community's conditions and circumstances that foster deviant behavior and with the resources and opportunities required by offenders for responsible conduct. For example, it must not ignore the problem of unemployment of youth —disadvantaged youth especially—whose proportion in the labor market is rising. Successful integration of probationers depends to a large measure on employment opportunity; it must be undertaken as a community-wide endeavor, with the probation agency in the forefront of the effort. Seeking jobs for probationers individually is no longer enough to deal with the problem.

Although the basic concept of probation is to use the community as the proper place for rehabilitation, there is a growing interest in specialized environments, in halfway houses that are neither penal institutions nor the open community *per se*. This is especially signicant when applied to misdemeanant behavior.

Drunkenness is the most common misdemeanant behavior. Of the 2.5 million misdemeanant offenses in the United States in 1964, reported by the Department of Justice in its *Uniform Crime Reports,* more than 1,400,000 were for drunkenness. In response, a number of innovative programs have been developed for alcoholics, ranging from group therapy and hospital care to the use of special medication.

In the same vein, homeless men are referred to "shelters" or are involved in antipoverty programs. In Seattle, Washington, the Office of Economic Opportunity recruits ex-probationers as correctional aides, thereby providing meaningful work, extending a useful service, and offering new tools for coping with the misdemeanant. Other communities are using volunteer workers to assist misdemeanants, claiming a "success rate of ninety-four percent."

A new kind of headstart program in a number of cities screens the case before criminal proceedings are initiated. The object is to avoid bringing the matter to trial and to substitute a variety of community agencies to solve the individual's problem.

In any such program, there is always the need for public education so that innovation will not be resisted out of fear of the "criminal" elements. Halfway houses are viewed with alarm in many communities, where residents prefer to have offenders—especially ex-convicts and narcotics users—both out of sight and out of mind.

All these are approaches to maximize the offender's continuing relations with the community on the principle that the ultimate purpose of correction is to make the offender or potential offender an "inner" rather than an "outer." The same kind of innovative approaches are required for the convict who is institutionalized. For that reason, many institutions have been giving increased attention to vocational and academic training, to the counseling of inmates, and to bridges with the community.

Job training has been spurred by the increasing realization that job openings are not meaningful to men without job skills. This is especially true in a society that demands fewer common laborers and more people with education and specialized training. An added spur for such training is the recent availability of funds for a variety of manpower training programs.

Inmate counseling serves to prepare the individual to relate to himself and to the community. Whereas this was originally a highly formalized relationship—like a patient with his analyst—the current trend is to put the counseling on a more informal basis, right in the cell block or dormitory. To reach out to as many as possible in this way, the one-time specialist trains other workers in the institution to carry on the service.

Finally, the community can play a major part in breaking up what the NCCD report calls "the abysmal isolation of the correctional institution." Listed among the kinds of community groups that carry on this work are Alcoholics Anonymous, Narcotics Anonymous, the Jaycees, the Bad Check Associates, Synanon, Opportunities, Inc., community theaters, athletic clubs. These groups are avenues through which the community can permeate the prison wall, starting the convict on the early road back.

All of the aforementioned are but a few of the ways that an awakened and aroused community can use its voice and its presence to correct correction. They are but a selection of proposals contained in the historic report of the National Council on Crime and Delinquency to which this essay has repeatedly referred. Its standards for correctional institutions run to sixteen pages. Its recommendations for immediate reform run into the dozens. This essay is, at best, but a synopsis of and footnote to this monumental document, which has been reinforced by the findings and recommendations of the President's Commission report.

THE OBSTACLE OF COST

Between all these positive proposals and their realization there stand two obstacles. We referred to the first in our opening comments on the public attitude. The second is cost.

To streamline the correctional system and move it into the last quarter of the twentieth century requires proper personnel. Present personnel is overworked, undertrained, undifferentiated and underpaid. It makes little difference as to what sector of the personnel we refer, whether it is a probation officer, a jailer, a social worker, a psychiatrist, a counselor, or a maximum-security guard. The work load is totally unrealistic and allows the responsible officer only enough time to go through the motions of relating to an offender, convict or parolee. The job definitions are gross, making demands on the same person for a variety of special skills, each one of which would demand considerable training and supervision. The educational requirements are far below what is needed for sophisticated application of modern insights and techniques. Because the pay scale is so low it is unable to attract people with the needed educational background or specialized schooling.

To develop a proper personnel for the correctional system will demand greater expenditures; to develop proper facilities will require still greater expenditures. But against the cost of cure must be weighed the current costs of the prolonged malady. The total levy assessed by crime against society is beyond measurement, for after the economic costs are totaled, there still remain the huge losses in wasted manpower, in social decay, in violence. Much of our present system is devoted to handling the same people over and over again, unwittingly creating a hard core of criminals who overload the police, the courts and the penal system. It is against these mountainous social costs, that the community must measure its expenditures to create a modern system of correction.

What is called for, then, is a larger societal input in correction to get a greater social output. The total sum is only the first step. Budgeting of that expenditure in well-thought-out ways is the second step. Taken together, the end cost may be less than America pays today for crime in our culture.

Retentionists, if they are to be consistent, must argue that it is better for a thousand murderers to be executed (even though they can be safely released) than for the lives of half a dozen innocent persons to be sacrificed. Abolitionists find this unacceptable.

CONCLUSION

The argument against capital punishment and in favor of abolition is by no means conclusively established. Not only capital punishment but all criminal justice is liable to the complaint that it is riddled with inequities. It seems a moral certainty, furthermore, that sometimes at least the death penalty must have served to deter crime where life imprisonment would have failed. Nor can anyone claim, finally, that life imprisonment (which, of course, does not mean "life" at all) offers complete protection to society. Yet the trends in public opinion, the views of government spokesmen, the unmistakable decline in executions and the piecemeal abolition of death penalties across the nation—all these are clear signs that whatever the facts and the consequences, the death penalty is now in the twilight of its historical role as a mode of social defense against crime in America.

SUICIDE IN DENMARK

Herbert Hendin

A noted psychoanalyst questions the high incidence of self-destruction in a country which supposedly offers its citizens every reason for living.

The Danish suicide rate is 22 in 100,000. It is twice that of the United States or England, over three times that of Holland, and there is evidence that it has been higher than that of most of the rest of Europe for the last hundred years. Although it is at present equaled by the suicide rates in Switzerland, West Germany, Austria, and Japan, one can say that, excepting the Japanese, the Danish suicide rate is the most publicized. Certainly it is only in Denmark that visitors on the tourist buses are told by their guides about silverware, Tuborg and Carlsberg beer—and the high local suicide rate.

The problem of suicide in Denmark had long been caught up in arguments pro and con about the social-welfare measures that obtain in Denmark. Certainly suicide is a measure of social tension within a given society, and studying the motivations of suicidal patients in that society will throw a good deal of light on the sources of those tensions. But suicide is only one barometer of social tension. Crime, alcoholism, homosexuality and neurosis are equally such barometers. One cannot consult one such index without reference to all the others. For example, the Danish homicide rate is strikingly low. While their suicide rate is twice that of the United States, the United States' homicide rate is ten times that of Denmark.

Other questions about Danish suicide are of equal or greater interest than simply the question of its frequency. What motivates a Dane to suicide? Are his reasons different from those of an American or a German? What light do his reasons throw on the particular pressures and tensions within his country? The purpose of studying the motivations of individual Danish suicidal patients is also to answer questions like these. This leads to a consideration of what might be called national character and national psychosocial conflicts. Such study is an outgrowth of the work pioneered by Columbia's Abram Kardiner, who has for many years been concerned with correlating social institutions with individual character. My own research with suicidal patients in the United States brought me to this line of inquiry some time ago, and, when it came to studying the Danes, gave me a good basis for making comparisons. For the present purpose, I think it is possible to demonstrate that suicide is at least the likely form of expression that certain social tensions would take in Denmark, given the particular Danish character and circumstances.

Denmark lends itself well to a study of national character and institutions. Although the rural areas of Jutland and Zealand are as different from Copenhagen as rural Iowa is from New York City, nevertheless Denmark is homogeneous in her traditions, institutions and attitudes in comparison to the hybrid and diverse population of the United States. It was fortunate for this study that an extremely high percentage of the Danish people, including those of relatively little general education, speak English fluently, English being a compulsory language from the beginning of school in Denmark. It was additionally fortunate because my interviewing technique was for the most part psychoanalytic in nature; that is, it relied as much on what the patient unwittingly revealed as on what he actually said. And perhaps my own relative unfamiliarity with the institutions and attitudes of the country turned out to be more of an advantage than a disadvantage. Every day I would be struck by attitudes on the part of my patients remarkably different from attitudes common in the United States but which I would have taken for granted and overlooked had I spent my life in Denmark.

For example, one afternoon I heard a young Danish soldier at the Copenhagen Military Hospital, who had made a suicide attempt, threatening his Danish psychiatrist with a successful attempt if he were returned to camp. The doctor replied that he didn't believe the boy would actually kill himself. The boy in turn said that the doctor couldn't in fact be certain, and that if he did kill himself it would be on the doctor's conscience. Such incidents are extremely common in Denmark, and threatening suicide is perhaps the commonest way that a Danish boy will try to get out of the army. How different from the behavior of American servicemen. Not that our boys want to get out of the service any the less, but how different is the means they are likely to employ—vague psychosomatic complaints or difficult-to-diagnose syndromes (including, for instance, the famous low back pain), are probably the most common. Suicide threats are relatively infrequent. The American boy feels that the threat of suicide is futile for he has little expectation that those around him are going to take him at all seriously; and in a large measure he is right. The Danish boy, on the other hand, can be quite certain that such threats will arouse immediate concern and anxiety among his comrades and superiors. In the United States, one finds that suicide threats occur less among the military than among civilians. To be effective, a threat must have a receiver, and among Americans such threats are usually directed at mothers, fathers, wives and husbands. The American sergeant is none of these.

On another afternoon, while a rather sick Danish girl was telling me about her life and childhood, she stopped and said that she could go no further because to do so would only make me feel guilty. Why should it make me feel guilt? Well, she said, because I probably had had a happier childhood and I would feel guilty on that account. I assured her that, since I did not feel responsible for her unhappy childhood, I would not feel guilty—that, at most, I might only feel fortunate to have escaped whatever she had gone through. She was then able to continue. But what was this girl doing? She obviously *wished* to make me feel guilty, and then felt guilty herself for wanting to make me feel so. What a refined, sophisticated and complex psychology of guilt! The behavior of this girl and the Danish soldier could be reiterated in a number of similar illustrations and was indicative of a particular and extraordinary knowledge of, use of, and ability to arouse guilt in others through one's own suffering or misfortune, and the expectation of being able to do so has important bearing on the whole question of suicide.

It also raises the question of where this is learned. Does the Danish mother use the arousal of guilt as a disciplinary technique and, if so, how much? It is one of many kinds of discipline that can be used with children. It is in fact used by many subcultures within the United States, and no one can say for certain how effective it is compared with other forms of discipline. But from interviews with Danish patients and talks with Danish mothers and Danish psychiatrists, particularly those working with children, it is evident that this is the principal form of discipline used in Denmark. The mother simply lets the child know how hurt she is and how badly she feels at his or her misbehavior. The child is thereby disciplined—and at the same time gets a lesson in the technique of arousing guilt which he can later put to his own uses.

Discussion of the problem of guilt leads naturally enough to the whole question of aggression and how it is handled, expressed or controlled. In general, far less overt destructiveness or violence is evident among Danish patients than will be seen among American patients. Even in the United States, patients of Scandinavian origin in a "disturbed ward" are more apt to be mute than actively enraged and throwing things. A disturbed ward in a Danish hospital is altogether a far quieter place than a similar ward in one of our hospitals. The strikingly low Danish homicide rate, in comparison with the American, is also relevant here. In a recent year there were only twenty-eight homicides in the entire country, thirteen of which were children killed in connection with their parents' suicides.

This control of aggression begins, of course, in childhood. The Danish child, while indulged in many ways, is not permitted anything like the aggressiveness toward his parents and siblings that is tolerated in an American child. Consequently, Danish children appear to Americans exceedingly well-disciplined and well-behaved, while American children often seem like monsters to the Danes.

If there is, by the way, a socially acceptable outlet for aggression among the Danes, it is their sense of humor. They are very fond of teasing and are proud of their wit. Their humor will often cloak aggressive barbs in such a manner as to get the point across without actually provoking open friction.

Now certainly a great deal has been written, with regard to suicide, about the importance of aggression turned inward. Yet, it is far from the whole story about suicide in general and very far from the whole story about suicide in Denmark. The English, for example, curb aggression in their children and have a low homicide rate without the high Danish suicide rate.

It is rather the forms of dependence in Denmark that are unique, in my observation, and equally important and fundamental to the whole Danish vulnerability to depression and suicide. As one Danish psychiatrist put it to me, you can, in a way, divide Denmark into two groups: those who are looking for someone to take care of them and those who are looking for someone to take care of. There is a good deal of truth in this epigram.

Here, too, it is best to begin with the child. The Danish child's dependence on his mother is encouraged far more than that of the American child. Danish mothers are most apt to boast of how well their children look, how well they eat, and how much they weigh—and far less likely to boast of those activities or qualities of the child that in any way tend to separate him from the mother: how fast the child can walk or talk or do things by himself. The child is fondled, coddled and hugged more often, and probably to a later age, than is general in the United States. The American mother may not curb her child's aggressiveness—out of the fear that she may damage his initiative. The Danish mother is much less ruled by this concern and the child's aggressiveness is strictly checked—is, in a sense, part of the price he pays for his dependence. Of course, the very checking of the child's aggressiveness serves, in turn, to increase and foster this dependence. Such behavior appears to make the separation from the mother, when it does come, all the harder to bear. Many seek a return to the maternal relationship either directly or through a mother-substitute, while others achieve this kind of gratification vicariously—through attending to the needs of the first group.

Of course, mixtures and alternations are common. Characteristic was the attitude of one twenty-two-year-old Danish girl who was unable to manage her own life in Copenhagen and who yearned to return to her parents' farm in north Zealand and to be taken care of by her mother. In the next breath she expressed the idea that perhaps the solution to her problem was to go to England and live with a young artist she had met while there on a visit, since he was totally helpless and needed her.

The search for this dependence results in greater need of the sexes for each other, and more moving of the sexes toward each other, with less fear and more ease than is usual in the United States. Mutual attraction is not impeded, either, by the extensive competition between the sexes that is so common in the United States. Of course, these expectations of dependent gratification from the opposite sex are often disappointed and are a major cause for the ending of relationships and a major factor in Danish divorces.

The Danish husband is very often rather like a privileged eldest child. He usually has little to do with the discipline of the children. Resentment on the part of fathers at the birth of children is quite common and is most strikingly evident in the widespread loss of potency or loss of sexual interest on the part of the husband after the birth of the first child.

On the other hand, frigidity among Danish women appears to be as widespread as it is in the United States. This, despite their very feminine manner, their noncompetitiveness with men, and the fact that they are permitted somewhat more sexual freedom during adolescence than Americans are, though no more during childhood. (The attitude of Danish mothers toward sexual activity in their children is generally to prohibit it and at the same time to deny its existence—very much as American mothers do.) Yet female frigidity does not appear to be of the guilt-ridden sort common in the United States thirty years ago, or of the competitive sort common today. Rather it seems to be caused by the woman's dependent longings and by her image of herself as a little girl rather than a grown woman.

It is only this dependency concern that can explain the Danes' extreme vulnerability to depression and suicide following the ending of relationships. Both the protector and the protected will be vulnerable in such a situation. Typical was the attitude of one man who made a serious suicide attempt when his wife left him after twenty years of marriage. He had not been happy with her and in many ways he had precipitated her leaving; but three months later he said he had no desire to live because there was no one to take care of his apartment, to prepare his meals, and to attend to his needs.

I have spoken of the manipulation of guilt, the control of aggression, and the forms of dependency. My last observation on the subject of dependency is perhaps the most interesting. Related to the whole question of dependency but important in its own right, are the Danish attitudes toward death and afterlife and suicide itself.

In working with suicidal patients in the United States, it is not unusual for one to encounter fantasies of reunion after death with a lost loved one. But in Denmark such fantasies are so much more common as to be almost the rule. This, despite the fact that most of the Danes I interviewed tended to stress their "not being religious," with an overtone of pride. Yet, the Lutheran version of an afterlife is universally taught in the schools and the child often picks up the idea of reunion after death from his parents even before school. Even if formal religion ceases to be of interest in later life, the idea of afterlife and a reunion with loved ones after death remains. Such fantasies are not only more common among the Danes, they are more openly expressed; with American patients they generally have to be ascertained from dreams. Certainly the hold of such ideas is consistent with the dependency constellation of which I have already spoken.

I saw one Danish patient with such a fantasy following a serious suicide attempt in which he had turned on the gas. He was a fifty-six-year-old man who had been separated for several months from his wife. When questioned, he expressed the idea that after death he expected to be reunited with his mother, who had died eight years before—and eventually, following his wife's death, with his wife. He felt that he and his wife would not have the difficulties between them in an afterlife that they had had on earth. He recalled having held such a conception of an afterlife from his earliest school years, and perhaps before. When asked if he had not also been taught, as are Catholics in America, that, yes, you would go to heaven but, no, you would not get there if you killed yourself, he replied that he had been taught that but he did not believe this part of the teaching. He felt there was nothing one would not be forgiven if one repented. The last thing he had done before turning on the gas was to say a prayer in which he asked forgiveness for what he was about to do; with that, he felt confident that his admission to an afterlife was assured. His attitudes in these matters turned out to be quite typical of Danish patients.

And in fact the best and most perceptive prototypes of such reunion-in-death fantasies, apart from the dreams of individual patients, are to be found in that singular Danish literature, the fairy tales of Hans Christian Andersen. There is "The Little Match Girl" who, while freezing to death in the cold, lights her matches and sees the image of her grandmother, who is the only person who ever loved her and with whom she is reunited after her death. There is "The Steadfast Tin Soldier" who can only be united with the ballerina doll in the fire that destroys both of them. The Andersen stories are a mine of these fantasies of death, dying, and afterlife. Suicide itself is treated almost directly in "The Old Street Lamp." The lamp fears decomposition, and it is relieved of this fear when it obtains the power to kill itself, so to speak, by turning to rust in one day. (Suicidal patients often feel a sense of mastery over all sorts of anxieties, including fears of death: their idea is that they can end their lives at will.) The lamp finally decides not to use this power, that even though a new existence might be better, it will not seek it, since there are others (the watchman and his wife) who care about it and whom it must consider.

Fantasies of rebirth are often associated with reunion after death. "The Ugly Duckling" appeals to the idea that, while in the present life one may be unloved and unwanted, in some future existence one's whole state can be quite different, the duckling is "reborn" as a swan. While there is no dying in the story, the psychological idea of rebirth is there.

By and large, the love-death theme—the idea that without love there will be death, but that perhaps in death the desire for love will be gratified—runs through the Andersen stories. The boy who is in bondage to "The Snow Queen" is emotionally frozen: he has a "heart like ice" and can obtain pleasure in reason only. It is only by the strength of the love and faith of little Gerda that he can be returned to normal.

One should point out that these are by no means the universal themes of all fairy tales. Only consider that in the Andersen tales competition and performance are not important. Neither giants nor dragons have to be killed in order for the hero to succeed in whatever he is up to.

To be sure, death is as taboo a subject in Denmark as in the United States, if not more so. Parents are uncomfortable when their children bring it up. The Danes find funerals painful and wish them over as soon as possible, and they are often uncomfortable around a bereaved person. They expect a short period of grieving and then the subject is to be dropped. And such discomfort is in keeping with their anxiety about separation, loss, or abandonment by a source of dependency gratification. Several Danish psychiatrists, psychologists, and sociologists have expressed the idea that a longer period of grieving would probably be salutary, a sort of safety valve.

Suicide itself is less taboo than it is in the United States and is probably much less so than in Catholic countries. Patients who make suicide attempts and fail express less shame at having made the attempt than do such patients in the United States. The Danish patient is more apt to express shame at not having successfully completed the act than he is over having made the attempt. While the wife or husband of the suicidal patient may feel some shame, the attitude of those around the patient is generally one of sympathy or pity. A Danish clergyman has admitted to me that the early church teaching that suicide is immoral has little effect, even in religious families, when suicide actually occurs or is attempted. Then, too, there is bound to be a weakening of such a taboo when so many Danes know personally friends and relatives who have killed themselves or made suicide attempts. Suicide does not have to become institutionalized, as it is in Japan, for it to be a known and almost acceptable expression of unhappiness.

I have dwelt on differences between the Danish and American characters. But it is certainly true that, in studying suicide in the United States, one may observe any one of the character traits that I have described. American patients of English extraction or Puritan heritage will exhibit great control over the expression of aggression—but people of this background also discourage feelings of excessive dependency. Patients of southern or eastern European background often use the arousal of guilt to express hostility or to obtain obedience to their wishes; but, just as characteristically, they don't suppress aggression as do the Danes. It is the combination of traits we have examined that would seem to make the Danes liable to suicide rather than to other forms of discharge of aggression and frustration.

The study of suicide in Denmark (or elsewhere) throws light on the particular anxieties and preoccupations of the people in that country. Yet one pattern often associated with suicide elsewhere is important in illuminating Danish character by the very fact of its rarity among the Danes.

And in speaking of it, we shall return to the question of socialism raised at the beginning.

The pattern I refer to is organized around performance and competitiveness—and it seems to have little bearing on Danish suicide. If only because of Denmark's proximity to Germany, and because part of her land area had once been controlled by Germany, I looked for the frequently described Germanic hyperconsciousness about performance. In this pattern, the individual has rather fixed, high, and rigid expectations of himself, and a great deal of aggression is tied up with the achievement of these expectations. Failure of achievement in such a culture can be a direct cause for committing suicide. And in such cultures the failure to achieve love will not be interpreted, as in the Danish culture, as an emotional deprivation but more importantly as a poor performance in which the individual gives himself, so to speak, a low mark on love. I have noted that competitiveness and performance do not figure significantly in the Hans Christian Andersen fairy tales. But the conquest of giants and dragons is crucial and decisive in the folklore of Germanic cultures and the winning of the heroine at the end may be only incidental. In the light of all we have said about Danish family life, upbringing, and attitudes, it is probably not surprising that this performance pattern does not have the life-and-death meaning in Denmark that it appears to have in Germany, Switzerland, and in Japan as well.

Although he finds his fair share of competition in school, the Danish child is not particularly encouraged toward competitiveness by his family, and in general it is understood among both children and adults that one should not stand out too much in any direction, an attitude by no means unknown among Americans, but which is more intense among the Danes. Anyone who violates this rule against conspicuous high performance, whether it be the child at school or the adult at work, is subject to a good deal of envy and dislike.

What is the importance, then, of Danish socialism in fostering the national attitudes toward competition and dependency? Certainly most of these attitudes appear to antedate the social and economic changes of the last few decades in Denmark. All that can be said, I think, is that Danish socialism may give expression to and reinforce these qualities and attitudes in the national character, and these qualities and attitudes, in turn, undoubtedly shape the particular form that social change has taken. Government concern for the individual gives a kind of permission for the overt expression of the longing to be taken care of. Even the tone of the letters to the newspapers in Denmark indicates a feeling of passively endured injustice, particularly under personal economic difficulty, and reflects a lesser feeling of responsibility for one's personal destiny than we are accustomed to.

The numerous social-welfare agencies give opportunity to those wishing to care for the dependent needs of others, and there is a greater concern than in the United States on the part of those administering the help—whether it be medical care or financial aid—with the welfare of everyone; and there is a virtually unanimous tendency to feel personally responsible for all suffering. In discussing this at a seminar in Copenhagen, one doctor gave me as an illustration—with the aptness of which all agreed—that the entire country can experience a wave of guilt in reading a newspaper account of a man who died in his room and whose body went undiscovered for several days. It is assumed that he was lonely, uncared-for, and probably without friends; virtually everyone may feel personally responsible.

But this is all a far cry from equating socialism and suicide. The earlier-mentioned presence in Norway of equally developed social-welfare measures together with a particularly low suicide rate demonstrates the falsity of the equation.

Let us look more closely at the Danish socialistic system. With its lack of natural resources, it is difficult to visualize Denmark as wealthy today under any economic system. Were she to lean toward more capitalistic practices, there would be no great amount of wealth for her to "capitalize." It is also hard to imagine Denmark surviving in the competitive international economy without a greater degree of internal economic cooperation and planning than we seem to find necessary.

Both the lack of wealth within the country and the high taxes required for Danish social-welfare activities limit the accumulation of wealth by individual men. The very fact of this limitation may make for less competition. Individual initiative will accomplish less for someone trying to change his economic situation than it may, for example, in the United States or in Denmark's wealthier neighbor, Sweden. Thus, though in one sense economic life seems more difficult, in another sense Denmark appears to have escaped some of the pressure of the continuing chase for wealth and goods that is seen in so much of the rest of the Western world. Living in Copenhagen, one can actually feel in a relatively short time the more relaxed pace of life there in comparison with the pace in cities like New York or Stockholm.

We do not know for certain how a particular people hit upon a particular set of institutions and attitudes with which to regulate their lives, bring up their children, and earn their bread—out of the several alternatives that may be available. We do know that once they choose a particular way it will have profound *further* effects upon character attitudes and institutions. Yet psychosocial studies are not developed highly enough to allow us to pass judgment as to better or worse ways of doing things or to make very definitive suggestions about doing them differently, either in our own country or elsewhere. For the present, we must gather more knowledge as to the ways in which different social institutions and customs produce individual characters and attitudes. It seems to me that the relatively greater homogeneity of the people in each of the Scandinavian countries would make the study of the differences among those countries and between them and ourselves a particularly fruitful source of information. Further, the Scandinavian countries are pioneering in several social and economic measures in which the rest of the world is interested; some of their ideas and plans have been and will be followed by other countries. If we can learn something from the inevitable difficulties they are bound to encounter in going first, we can only be grateful and trust that they will not begrudge the fact that our paths have been made easier.

TARGET: TOMORROW

AN EDUCATIONAL AND VOCATIONAL GUIDE FOR TEENAGERS

BY RUTH STRANG

A guide written specifically for teenagers—from their point of view—which answers the really vital questions they are asking:

—Should I stay in school?
—What are my skills?
—Should I go to college?
—Where can I get help?

TARGET: TOMORROW shows teenagers exactly how to make those important decisions which will decide their future careers and lives.

LAUREL-LEAF LIBRARY   50c

*Two of
William Saroyan's
major works*

THE HUMAN COMEDY
60c

Set during World War II in Ithaca, California, this shows 14-year-old Homer Macauley's growing up to an understanding of the world and an acceptance of his brother's death. With Don Freeman's original illustrations.

MY NAME IS ARAM
60c

The world of boyhood is seen through the eyes of trusting and dauntless Aram. Among his adventures are "Locomotive 38, Ojibway," "The Pomegranate Trees," and "The Summer of the Beautiful White Horse." With Don Freeman's original illustrations.

If you cannot obtain copies of these titles at your local bookstore, just send the price (plus 10c per copy for handling and postage) to Dell Books, Box 2291, Grand Central Post Office, New York, N.Y. 10017. No postage or handling charge is required on any order of five or more books.

An astonishing new book
by a dazzling young writer

Stop-Time

by Frank Conroy

Frank Conroy is a sensitive young writer who has written a new kind of book for a new kind of world. STOP-TIME is a distinguished and unique autobiography with the intimate unprotected candor of a novel. It is the story of growing up in an America of autos, cities, broken families, sexual anarchy and rootless discontent. It is one of the extraordinary books of our decade.

"A documentary of chilling perception, a book whose honesty and evocation of youth is a triumph. STOP-TIME, free of rancor, rich with the half-mad, lonely characters who people our times, is one of the finest books about growing up I have ever read"
—*New York Times Book Review*

"Intensely readable . . . no one who starts it will fail to finish it . . . unquestionably a significant work of contemporary art . . . an important new American writer"

—*Commonweal*

A DELL BOOK 95c

A forthcoming major motion picture

If you cannot obtain copies of this title at your local bookseller, just send the price (plus 10c per copy for handling and postage) to Dell Books, Box 2291, Grand Central Post Office, New York, N.Y. 10017. No postage or handling charge is required on any order of five or more books.

There is one—and only one—
authorized biography of the Beatles.
This nationwide bestseller is it!

The Beatles

by Hunter Davies

Not too many years ago, Ringo, Paul, John, and George were middle-class English schoolboys. Today, they're the Beatles. Millionaires. Celebrities. And outrageously controversial.

Here is their complete and unexpurgated story, written by a man who traveled with the famous group for sixteen months. It is the story of four very intelligent, very talented, and very human young men caught in the act of symbolizing our era. Even people who have managed to resist their charm will find THE BEATLES a fascinating book.   Illustrated.

A DELL BOOK 95¢

If you cannot obtain copies of this title at your local bookseller, just send the price (plus 10c per copy for handling and postage) to Dell Books, Box 2291, Grand Central Post Office, New York, N.Y. 10017. No postage or handling charge is required on any order of five or more books.